Ecological Environment Design Under The Circular Economy Mode

Peng Jing

Bamboo & Pine Press

Publisher: Bamboo & Pine Press

       Zhu & Song Press, LLC

       Gaithersburg, MD

Editor：Julie Zhu

Editor's email：editor@zhuandsongpress.com

Designer: Bamboo & Pine Media

Publisher Website：www.zhuandsongpress.com

Printed and bound in USA, UK

ISBN-13:978-1-950797-40-0

ISBN-10:1-950797-40-6

Library of Congress Control Number:2019950945

About Author

Peng Jing was born in Wuhan, Hubei province of China. Currently, she is an associate professor of Art and media institute of China University of Geosciences (Wuhan). She specializes in Environment Design, and is a supervisor of master study.

Peng Jing is also an experienced teacher and researcher in environment design and public art design.

Preface

In 21st century, the contradiction between resources environment and economic and social development has become an important bottleneck for China's comprehensive construction of a well-off society and the realization of sustainable development. As a result, China's economic and development relations have entered an important period of strategic transformation. Taking the scientific concept of development as the guide, building a harmonious society as the goal, building an ecological civilization and resource-saving and environment-friendly society as the path, transforming the economic growth mode, saving energy and reducing emissions into other major actions, for the environment and development Strategic transformation builds a clear roadmap. It is precisely in this new situation and new stage of China's economic and social development that China's circular economy development has basically completed the first leap from concept to national decision-making from the turn of the century to 2005. Since 2006, it has quickly entered the stage of comprehensive pilot demonstration; with the "Circular Economy Promotion Law" as a symbol, it began to enter the overall promotion stage in 2009. Comprehensive pilot demonstration and overall promotion mean the second leap in the development of China's circular economy. China's economic policy is paying more and more attention to the development of recycling and the protection of the ecological environment.

As a result, the relationship between China's economy and development has entered an important period of strategic transformation. Taking the scientific concept of development as the guide, building a harmonious society as the goal, building an ecological civilization and resource-saving and environment-friendly society as the path, transforming the economic growth mode, saving energy and reducing emissions into other major actions, for the environment and development Strategic transformation builds a clear roadmap.

In this new situation and new stage of China's economic and social development, China's circular economy development has basically completed the first leap from concept to national decision-making from the turn of the century to 2005. Since 2006, it has quickly entered the stage of comprehensive pilot demonstration; with the "Circular Economy Promotion Law" as a symbol, it began to enter the overall promotion stage in 2009. Comprehensive pilot demonstration and overall promotion mean the second leap in the development of China's circular economy. China's economic policy is paying more and more attention to the development of recycling and the protection of the ecological environment.

Content

Part 1   Analysis on the Concept of Ecological Environment Design

Chapter 1 The theoretical basis of ecological environment design

1.1 The initial formation of the ecological design concept

"The concept of ecology was first proposed by the German biologist Hecker in 1869 and the discipline of ecology was founded in 1886. Ecology comes from the Greek "oikos" and "logy". The oikos means residences, hidden houses, families, etc., the logy means scientific research. He said, "We can understand ecology as the whole science of the relationship between organisms and the world around us and further interact with all living conditions. Therefore, later generations regard ecology as the science of exploring the relationship between living things and their living environment

Since the advent of human beings, human beings have accumulated experience and cognition between themselves and the environment in the process of survival. Early ecology was the study of the relationship between other organisms and the environment. With the development of the discipline, ecology has gradually placed people at the center of research, and the relationship between man and nature has become the core of ecological concern. Human ecology has truly become an independent branch. The representative of the Chicago School of America (Parker) first proposed it. "Human ecology is a discipline that studies the relationship between people and their surroundings and their laws. It studies the relationship between contemporary population, resources, environment and development, and studies the exchange of energy, matter and information between various elements in the human ecosystem. Relationship." From the development of the ecological discipline, it can be known that people's understanding of living conditions and awareness of the environment have been greatly improved. However, after the modernization of mankind, a series of intricate survival and environmental problems have emerged around the world, and it has become a topic of common concern around the world. The plundering of nature by mankind has caused a serious imbalance in the ecological environment. The environment has begun to declare war on mankind, and new contradictions and new problems have gradually emerged, putting humanity in deep dilemma. In 1972, the United Nations convened the "Human Environment Conference" in Stockholm. At the meeting, the slogan "Only one earth" was put forward. The "Human Environment Declaration" produced a major change in human environmental awareness and strongly promoted humanity. The development of ecology. Therefore, it can be said that the ecological environment problem is a great reflection on modern society and industrial civilization. It is precisely because of the rapid development of social modernization, which is based on the unreasonable unlawful exploitation of natural resources and the natural environment. On the base of destruction, the crisis of the ecological environment has arisen

1.2 Basic principles of ecology

According to modern ecology, ecosystems are a combination of living systems and environmental systems in specific spaces. However, in the ecosystem, a complex large ecosystem contains countless small ecosystems, all of which have a common pattern. Some of the rules that ecology provides us have a positive effect on our understanding of the Earth's ecosystem law. For example, the ecological law of China's ecologist Ma Shijun proposes the five laws of ecology, mutual restraint and interdependence, mutual compensation, mutual compensation and mutual Coordinated symbiosis law, regeneration law of material cycle transformation, co-evolution law of mutual adaptation and selection, and balance law of material input and output. Here, the author summarizes the following three principles on the methodology of ecology: the overall law, the law of material recycling and energy flow, and the law of environmental carrying capacity to propose the objective basis of the ecological environment of the environment. The law of ecology is the foundation. The research of the subject provides an important methodology

Overall rule

Materialist dialectics believes that nothing in the world exists in isolation. Each element interacts, restricts and interacts with each other. The whole nature is a unified whole that is universally connected. The connection between materialist dialectics requires adherence to ecological laws. The basic principle of ecological thought is holism. It sees the world as a "human-society-nature" complex ecosystem that includes people, animals, plants, microbes, and various environmental factors. Although each system contains different organizational levels, it cannot be separated to make it exist in isolation. The various elements of the ecosystem are interrelated and interdependent. The ecological world view believes that all species and everything in nature, as well as these species, things, and our human object activities are all integrated, all intrinsically linked, and it consists of dynamic, systematic, and overall The non-linear interactions form a complex network of relationships that make the world an inseparable organic whole. In this whole, due to the complementarity of their interactions, the whole is larger than the sum of the parts. Modern ecology compares the ecosystem to a network. On this huge network, each branch has several lines that are connected to other branches, so that the overall effect can be better resisted from the outside; on the contrary, if it is If a branch is artificially cut, then the whole system will be destroyed by the increase of cockroaches

Material recycling and energy flow rules

"The concept of ecosystems was first proposed by British ecologist A.G.Tansler in Introduction to Plant Ecology (1935). Ecosystems are all living organisms (biome) that live together in a given space and their environment. A unified whole formed by the continuous process of material circulation and energy flow. The various parts of such an ecosystem, biotic and abiotic, biological community and habitat constitute an interaction, the material continually circulates, and energy flows continuously. Ecosystem. In terms of the living environment of the whole organism, the food chain movement and the biological cycle are composed of the inorganic environment, the producer (green plant), the consumer (animal) and the decomposer (microorganism). Establish a coordinated ecological balance"

Energy flow and material circulation are the two basic processes of the ecosystem, and they are closely linked. The long-term survival and continuous development of ecosystems lies in the flow of energy and the recycling of matter. It guarantees the normal operation of the ecosystem through endless transfer, transformation and regeneration between biological and inorganic environments, organisms and organisms through certain energy, matter and information. The material cycle is the material basis for the development of ecosystems. Each material is interpreted as a process that is absorbed, multi-utilized by producers and consumers, and decomposed, released, and re-accepted

Energy flow is the driving force and source of the ecosystem to maintain normal operation. Without the flow of energy, there is no life. The energy flow in the ecosystem is carried out through food chain channels with various organisms as carriers. The food chain is a nutrient structure in the ecosystem, consisting of 4 to 5 links, such as grass-insect-bird-snake-eagle. There is a direct and indirect mutual predation relationship between organisms and living things. This relationship between feeding and being fed forms an intricate food network. The flow of matter is cyclical, and all kinds of substances can be returned to the environment in a form that can be utilized by plants. The energy flow of the ecosystem is one-way, it is neither cyclic nor reversible, and eventually dissipates in the form of heat. If the function of energy flow is destroyed, it is difficult for the ecosystem to sustain the existence and reproduction of life, and it itself will collapse due to the destruction of its stability

The basic processes of the two ecosystems of material recycling and energy flow make the system a complete functional unit between various nutrient levels and various components. Material recycling and energy flow occur simultaneously, and they are interdependent and inseparable. The material flow is the carrier of the energy flow, and the energy promotes the movement of the material. The two links the ecosystem into an organic unity and together constitute the driving force for the succession and development of the ecosystem. The earth's resources are limited, and the multiple utilization and recycling of raw materials, products and wastes are the basic countermeasures for the long-term survival and continuous development of ecosystems

Limited law of environmental carrying capacity

"The environmental carrying capacity, in a certain period or state, is the closed value of the human activities that a certain environment can withstand. A certain state or condition here refers to a realistic or proposed environmental structure. There will be no major changes that are obviously not conducive to human survival; the so-called sustainable means that it does not affect the normal function of the environmental system." The indoor environment design consumes a considerable amount of material resources, but the material resources on the earth are Limitedly, when people adapt their mining intensity to its own renewal or within the limits and capacity that the ecosystem can withstand, it can gradually return to its original ecological equilibrium; when external disturbances exceed its limits, Then its self-regulating function will no longer work, and finally the ecosystem will decline and even collapse, leading to an ecological crisis. That is to say, although the ecosystem has certain self-regulation ability, this adjustment will only work within a certain scope and certain conditions. Otherwise, the overall ecological balance will be destroyed. Limited environmental carrying capacity is the content of limited environmental resources and limited ecological threshold. The various production activities carried out by human beings have the effect of promoting and limiting the duality of environmental carrying capacity. Human active activities can be protected by a full respect for the laws of nature, so that they form a good virtuous circle, and in certain areas, can enhance the carrying capacity of their ecological environment to a certain extent, and can also destroy environmental factors. Break the regularity of the environmental system and reduce the environmental carrying capacity, leading to a vicious circle. Because human beings are the only physical entities that can actively influence and change the environmental carrying capacity

The continuous development of science and technology has promoted the increase of material wealth in human society. The continuous increase of material wealth has improved people's living conditions. However, this kind of prosperity has increasingly aggravated the contradiction between human beings and the environment, and the environmental carrying capacity has been under unprecedented pressure. The development and progress of the indoor industry should be based on the global ecological environment and the progress of the ecological environment is false and retrogressive. Similarly, the application of interior environmental design to decorative materials must also be limited to the extent that environmental carrying capacity can withstand. As the United Nations Declaration on the Human Environment clearly states, the current historical phase requires humans to be more cautious in considering the consequences for the environment when planning their actions. Environmental problems are largely the result of human misconduct, but the human condition can be improved with tangible efforts. For the long-term interests of mankind, we must use our scientific knowledge to coordinate with nature on the principle of ecological environment capacity and environmental carrying capacity, and strive to improve the environment and build a beautiful home

The basic principles related to ecosystems in ecology will constitute the theoretical basis for our study of indoor environmental ecological design. However, these basic principles are only the original ecological principles. How to integrate them into the interior design ideas and how to make them A series of problems, such as deep implementation into the indoor industry, require us to think and explore further.

1.3 Traditional ecological knowledge and ecological ethics

Throughout the history of the development of human society, every step of history has always run through the picture of the interdependence and struggle between man and nature. Social progress and economic development are based on the development and utilization of natural resources. The earth has improved people's material living conditions, but this improvement is at the cost of destroying the ecological balance, seriously endangering the long-term interests of mankind, and the contradiction between man and nature is becoming more and more acute. In today's world, increasingly serious environmental pollution, desertification of land, energy shortages, endangered species, greenhouse gases, soil erosion, and natural disasters occur frequently. In the face of this series of serious natural alienation, we must profoundly reflect on our behavioral activities and give necessary moral constraints to behaviors that are contrary to ecological ethics. History is a mirror, reorganizing the basic points of traditional ecological thoughts, providing ethical and ethical resources for the proper handling of the relationship between man and nature, and greatly benefiting the construction of socialist ecological civilization

The natural ontology of "Heaven and Man are one" in traditional Chinese culture believes that man and everything are the coexistence of one another. This is the core of ancient Chinese environmental protection thoughts and one of the most positive aspects of modernization. Laozi said: "There is a mixture of things, born innate, I don't know the name, the word of the strong word. So the road is big. There are four big in the field, and people live in it. The land of law, the law of heaven, the law of heaven, the law of nature." Laozi's point of view is that heaven, earth, and people are all derived from the Tao. People follow the heavens and the earth, the heavens and the earth follow the Tao, and the Tao is nature. People are united. Zhuangzi inherited the thoughts of Laozi and put forward the idea that "the heavens and the earth are the same as me, and everything is born with me." The Confucian doctrine also contains rich ecological ethics. Confucius made "Yi Chuan", which is based on the idea of   "Heaven and Man". Confucius puts people as the spirit of all things and heaven and earth. It constitutes the three major elements of the universe and tries to establish a system of worlds. Whether it is Taoism or Confucianism, although they differ in their expressions, their basic ideas are the same. The shining point is the wisdom of harmony between man and nature. Traditional ecological ethics has many implications for how to deal with the relationship between man and nature and how to optimize the ecological environment:

1. Establishing the idea that human beings and nature coexist. Nature is an organic whole, and human beings are part of it. They are interdependent and mutually constrained. 2. We must follow the laws of nature and maintain the harmony between man and nature. The world is universally connected, things are moving forward, and human beings depend on nature for survival. While using nature, they should be based on respect for the laws of nature. 3, should continue to enhance the sense of responsibility. Mankind must undertake the mission of protecting the ecological environment, establish an ecological ethics, vigorously advocate the construction of ecological civilization, strive to extend moral care to the natural realm, step out of the narrow "anthropocentrism", and strive to achieve a win-win situation in dealing with the relationship between the them.

1.4 The aesthetic connotation of ecological design

From the perspective of ecology, aesthetics originated in the 1980s. Before and after 1994, Chinese scholars put forward the topic of ecological aesthetics, and then published a monograph on related ecological aesthetics, which marked the entry of ecological aesthetics in China. A more standardized and in-depth discussion. Ecology is a discipline of natural science, and aesthetics is a philosophical discipline that studies the relationship between humans and aesthetic objects. However, these two disciplines are grafted into a new type of ethical aesthetics, which are based on the ecological aesthetic relationship between man and nature, between man and environment. Ecological aesthetics, in a broad sense, includes the ecological aesthetic relationship between man and nature, society and man, and is a contemporary ontological aesthetic that conforms to ecological laws

Aesthetics, a kind of cognitive and spiritual state of human culture based on human social activities, is the expansion and extension of human life activities into the spiritual realm. Modern design aesthetics emphasizes the opposition between aesthetic subject and aesthetic object, and advocates that beauty is the practice of human essential power. It regards nature as the alien power of human beings, attaches importance to the conquest and transformation of man to nature, and regards man as the absolute of nature. The master, therefore advocates the support of design with machine-style aesthetics, functional aesthetics, and technical aesthetics. This functionally supreme, technologically supreme design idea is increasingly losing influence under the double impact of postmodernism and ecologism. The massive outbreak of ecological crises and ecological movements has changed human perceptions of their relationship with the world. The new discovery of bioethics and life worship will inevitably lead to the birth of new aesthetics. New aesthetics will emerge from new beliefs rather than from new technologies. This belief emphasizes that we are in harmony with nature and subordinate to nature, and we are part of nature. Under the influence of this belief, ecological aesthetics came into being. Ecological aesthetics is a new type of ethical aesthetics that is grafted between ecology and aesthetics. Here, human beings and nature are no longer in a binary opposition. The aesthetic subject and the aesthetic object are a two-way fusion relationship. The two are united in the symbiotic movement of mutual symbiosis and mutual infiltration. The ecological beauty and harmonious beauty become the highest. The aesthetic category and the best aesthetic conception. Ecological aesthetics is to introduce the principles and methods of ecology into design aesthetics. It is the embodiment and practice of ecological aesthetics in the field of design. It emphasizes the interdependence of design and nature and environment with aesthetic principles such as ecological, synergistic and organic. To make natural humanization and naturalization of people, and achieve high-level interaction in the framework and system of ecological aesthetics. Its greatest contribution is to update the concept of design. It requires the design community to rethink the design and realize the ecological shift from concepts, methods and technologies, such as reducing production costs and reducing the cost of materials, labor and special equipment. Under the multiple backgrounds that many scholars emphasize that human beings are part of nature and subordinate to nature, ecological aesthetics came into being. Ecological aesthetics is an aesthetic understanding formed by the ecological concept as the value orientation. It is manifested in that the aesthetic subject human and the aesthetic object are no longer in opposition to each other. It transcends the aesthetic subject's love for his own life and transcends the servant. Nature is the narrow value orientation I use to make people and nature harmoniously blend

Beauty is a value existence. Aesthetic value is a kind of value attribute that objective things have meet satisfy people's aesthetic needs. Ecological beauty is an aesthetic existence that can satisfy people's aesthetic needs. In the human's environmental experience of good ecology, it evokes the aesthetic subject's feelings towards nature, empathizes the principles of ecological aesthetics, and focuses on the ecological effects produced by the relationship between man and nature, with his own subjective aesthetics. The paradigm shapes the ecological environment. The aesthetics of eco-design is to introduce the principles and methods of ecology into the design aesthetics. It is the practice and concreteness of the field of eco-aesthetic design. It emphasizes the coordination and mutual unity of design and nature and environment. Ecological aesthetic consciousness is not only a recognition of the value of one's own life, but also a discovery of external natural beauty, but a sense of commonality and joy to the relationship between human beings and natural life

The scope of ecological beauty is very wide. It is not only manifested in the relationship between man and nature, but also in the state of social life. From the perspective of indoor environmental ecological aesthetics, including the pleasantness of the environment, the indoor environment can give people a physiological Psychological comfort; and the cleanliness of the living environment; in addition, the sense of order in the indoor environment space, the rationalization of the layout and so on

Chapter 2 The method of ecological environment design Analyzes

The ecological environment design method is a new environmental design method theory based on the comprehensive reflection of the traditional environmental design methods and the ecological values as the starting point. Practice reflects the times and local characteristics with guiding ideology, specific methods, creative skills, and implementation steps which emphasizes **people-centered and pursues the coordinated development of people and nature.**

2.1 Guiding ideology of ecological environment design

The development of the city has not been completely synchronized with the value of human beings, but has lagged slightly. When people are tempered from the harsh urban environment, they find that we are not only facing urban problems, but our guiding ideology. We must be based on the common development of human, biological and abiotic inside of continue in the original mode.

Ecological values

The problem of urban ecological environment is first manifested in the destruction of the harmonious relationship between man and nature, because its value orientation is anthropocentrism. "Anthropocentrism" insists that people have the highest value and basically do not recognize the intrinsic value of other organisms. With the advancement of science and technology and the development of social productive forces, human beings have fully demonstrated the interests of those who meet their own needs for survival and development in the process of conquering nature, transforming nature, and destroying nature.

Everything exists for their own purposes, and human beings are not absolutely important philosophies. To fundamentally solve environmental problems, human beings must use another way to understand the world's ecological values.

The ecological values are all anthropocentrism centered on human interests and with economic growth as a single indicator. It is recognized that only by rational social control over the direction and behavioral consequences of human ability can we ensure the enhancement of human creativity. The weakening of human destructive power minimizes the negative effects of the relationship between man and nature. The world is the glorious gift of nature.

Ecological values are a new type of relationship between man and nature. They regard the earth as the only homeland on which human beings live. They respect the nature and maintain the natural environment instead of possessing and conquering nature, and expanding human rights to nature. At the same time of interest, human beings are required to bear corresponding responsibilities and obligations to nature. The correct ecological values require people to pay attention to and understand the evolution process of natural ecology. At the higher level of man and nature - the "human-natural" system is the center to realize the overall harmonious development and common evolution of the system.

Ecological ethics

The ethical and moral relationship between human and nature has gradually been recognized by relevant scholars and gradually reached a consensus. Ethics is the normative consciousness that human beings maintain the existence of the community and limit their own behavior. This old ethical concept reflects people-oriented thinking and aims at the equality and efficiency of human society. Old ethics is selfish. Some thoughts are not misunderstood or biased. Therefore, it is necessary to seek a global ethics that extends the scope of moral objects from human to other members of the ecosystem, but also from each creature. Species extend to ecosystems and the entire natural world.

The construction of ecological ethics marks the progress and perfection of human morality. It is a new perspective and new thinking of human beings dealing with environmental and ecological issues in the new era, and it is a new realm of human morality. The ecological ethics pays special attention to the concept of equality of human beings and the concept of equality between man and nature. He advocates equality of living, equality of interests and development equality between people and people, that is, the development of some people cannot be at the expense of the interests of another group of people. The ecological ethics is based on the principle of respecting and protecting the ecological environment, and taking human sustainable development as the starting point. The ecological ethics emphasizes its own normative consciousness, emphasizing the interdependence, mutual promotion, and coexistence of people and the natural environment. It is required that human beings use their own subjective actions to enhance the self-organized evolution of nature, rationally develop nature, regulate human production methods and lifestyles within the limits of the ecosystem, and advocate the love of nature, respect for nature, and protection of nature. On the basis of maintaining ecological balance, we actively and actively transform and utilize nature.

2.2 Basic principles of ecological environment art design

The study of environmental design in eco-city planning mainly studies how to refine several aspects of planning principles into specific design methods, and transforms the concept of "ecology" into operational design of spatial layout and material construction. Eco-environment design must be based on the balanced integration of human and nature, centered on the dynamic harmony and coordinated development of human and nature, and the human, biological and abiotic environments gradually form a harmonious and balanced system through long-term interaction. To this end, the design of the ecological environment should follow the design principles and viewpoints of the following aspects.

Principle of human nature

In environmental design, we realize that people are the theme in the environment, and the core value of environmental design is to create appropriate heights of spiritual life and optimize the quality of living environment based on satisfying people's basic material living conditions. That is, people-oriented, people-oriented design.

Through effective planning and design, people can satisfy the physiological and psychological needs in the environmental space, satisfying the requirements of use, comfortable and beautiful, pleasant environment, and finally produce certain economic, social and ecological benefits. The principle of human nature does not exclude the combination with nature. Human nature and nature often conflict with each other, but in the end it should be integrated. That is to achieve the highest realm of "Heaven and Man" and "Heaven and Earth", to achieve symbiosis and share common beauty.

The principle of integrity

The term "environment" itself emphasizes the issue as viewed from a holistic perspective. The principle of holism requires that both the biosphere and the technological circle within the human living space be considered as an integral part of the human ecosystem. Local interests must be subject to the overall interests, and temporary interests must be subject to long-term, sustained interests. In the design of the environment, from the principle of integrity, the environment is regarded as a whole, a system larger than its parts. Arrange and coordinate the various elements of environmental design (including natural, biological and cultural), and study the structural and functional relationships between environmental elements in order to make the spatial and temporal structure of the overall human ecosystem, through human design and management, Energy, logistics and information are at their best.

Local principles

The environment design should first consider the geographical location of the design. Any village or dwelling that we admire is the creative design based on the long-term observation of nature and the experience of real life. Therefore, environmental art design reflects the material and spiritual life characteristics of the time and the local, and imprints the imprint of history. Modern environmental art emphasizes that we must understand local characteristics, including geology, hydrology, sunshine, wind direction, climate, meteorology, landscape and other natural geographical environments, but also understand economic, political, historical, cultural and other factors and how to properly design in the design reflect. Respect traditional culture and local knowledge and consider their implications for design. However, the needs of modern people may not be the same as the needs of people in the region in history, and as the ecological environment deteriorates, we cannot deliberately imitate and stick to the traditional forms. The design of ecological environment should still be based on the natural process of the region. Based on the geographic and social factors, social factors, cultural factors and the input and output laws of material energy, a new design process that integrates all these factors.

Ecological principle

Humans consciously shape matter, energy and processes to satisfy their higher pursuit of living environment, but excessive disorderly development and uncontrolled abuse lead to the destruction of nature. There are many natural resources on the earth that are not regenerable. To realize the survival and continuation of human beings, we must make effective use of non-renewable resources. This is the ecological principle to be grasped in the design. Combined with the "4R" design, according to the Reduce, Reuse, Recycle and Renewable principles, the material, energy consumption, resource utilization and waste reduction are reduced throughout the operation of the natural system. To reduce the pollution of the environment and make the artificial environment change from pure consumption to recyclable.

Scientific and artistic integration

Emphasis on science and artistry is another important principle of environmental design work. Environmental art is a green art and science, creating art and science that is harmonious and lasting. The improvement of environmental quality depends on the dual satisfaction of science and art. The advancement of social life and science and technology, the evolution of people's values and aesthetic tastes, the environmental art design must pay full attention to and actively use the new achievements and new achievements of contemporary science and technology, including new materials, structures and construction techniques, as well as creating good sounds. Facilities and equipment used in light, thermal environments.

When carrying out specific engineering design, we will inevitably encounter environmental problems of different types and different functions. We will focus on both scientific and artistic aspects, but it is by no means split or opposite. Only the two are indispensable. The close combination can make the design work have lasting vitality.

Chapter 3 Analysis of the status quo and problems of ecological environment design

3.1 The development of "ecological architecture concept"

From the perspective of ecological research, ecological architecture is an important sub-discipline of ecology. In the 1960s, American Italian architect Paola Solaris merged the concepts of Ecology and Architecture into "Agrology" and proposed a new concept of "sexual architecture." In 1962, the American biologist Rachel Carson's "Silent Spring" revealed for the first time the terrible consequences of the destruction of the ecological environment. This work on the green movement It has played a very important role in promoting the official birth of the discipline of ecological architecture ("Design and Nature" (1969) by the famous American landscape architect Kehahag. In summary, the international study of ecological architecture There are two main categories.

First category: theoretical aspects. His representative works include: biologist J. Todd in "From Eco-Cities to Living Machines: Principles of Ecological Design" (1969); Schumacher Published "Small is Beautiful" (1974), he opposes the use of high-energy technologies and promotes the appropriate technology for renewable energy; Will's "Green Building: A Future for Sustainable Development" And Design (1991); The National Parks Press, "Guidelines for Sustainable Development Design" (1993) lists the architectural design rules for sustainable development; Yang Jingwen's "Design combines nature: the ecological basis of architectural design (1995); Sim Ryan and S. Stuart Cowan co-authored ((Ecological Design)) (1996), known as architecture, landscape, urbanology, and technology. A revolutionary attempt: Edwards' Sustainable Buildings (1999) and Green Buildings (2002). These theoretical studies have combed the policies, systems and technologies of countries in the sustainable development of architectural space, and many viewpoints are instructive.

Second category: practical and technical aspects. Ogoya's Design and Climate: A Bioclimatic Study of Architectural Regionalism (1963) emphasizes the natural comfort of the human body through natural rather than mechanical means. His "bioclimatic design approach" takes a comprehensive view of the impact of all climatic factors on architectural design, as well as the corresponding indoor thermal environment and thermal comfort issues. In 1976, the pioneer of the ecological building movement. Schneider founded the Institute for Building and Ecology in West Germany, emphasizing the use of natural building materials and using natural ventilation, wind and heating to ensure the interface environment of the building, advocating an architectural art that is conducive to ecological benefits. . K. Daniels's "Ecological Building Technology" (1994), he believes that the conflict between buildings and nature is solved by simple methods, while architects, engineers and owners are encouraged to focus on ecological design. In 1994, Simvanderryn held a conference in the city of Bigsur on the participation of academic leaders in eco-design. The conference created the

"International Ecology Association" proposal to combine the scattered research results to guide the younger generation and publish The THEBIGSUR Declaration calling for the "ecological revolution"; K. Daniels further perfected the theoretical system of ecological technology in "Low Technology, High Technology, Light Technology: Architecture in the Information Age" (1998). Yang Jingwen's "Bioclimate Skyscraper" (1997) puts forward the concept of ecological technology according to local conditions, and believes that architects should comprehensively analyze the factors such as orientation, location, facade treatment, greening and shading by regional bioclimatic characteristics. In 1999, the 20th International Construction Association Conference was held in Beijing to adopt the "Beijing Charter", which comprehensively expounded the major principles and key issues of the coordinated development of society, economy and environment related to "21st Century Architecture" and proposed the establishment of a generalized building. Scientific thinking. Among them, it is necessary to face up to the ecological dilemma and strengthen the idea of   ecological awareness. F. Ingeberg's "Thomas Hull: Architecture + Technology" (2001) proposes systematic development of architecture and technology based on Herzog's innovative ecological architecture, in order to be based on their respective regions. Features Building different buildings will give the building system the flexibility to adapt to different usage requirements. G. Baird's "Architectural Performance of Environmental Control" (2001) explores the interactive model of ecological design through a large number of examples, and proposes important viewpoints of architectural technology integration and local performance. In 2002, Berlin's World Architects Conference on the theme of "Resources and Architecture" reflected the architect's deep understanding and attention to resources and clearly assigned professional responsibilities at the conference.

The ecological architectural concept is an extension of the ecological concept in the direction of the architectural field, which reflects the reduction of the damage to the natural and social aspects of the architectural design. In summary, the ecological building includes the following main aspects: ecological building requires minimizing the consumption of non-renewable energy, energy needs to be recycled; use natural lighting, heating, ventilation as much as possible; buildings must comply with the local climate Comprehensive conditions such as resources and culture are tailored to local conditions.

3.2 Development of ecological building technology at home and abroad

Throughout the examples of existing ecological buildings, the ecological expression in the context of architecture is reflected in many aspects, including functional lighting, natural ventilation, thermal insulation, shading strategy, glare avoidance, energy and environmental protection, etc. The way is divided into natural light source utilization, underground water storage recycling, solar photovoltaic system, photoelectric glass window, photoelectric sun visor, photoelectric roof system, solar power wall, automatic opening and closing ventilation window, double curtain wall, curved Top, modern science and technology and the progress of building materials provide a certain technical guarantee for ecological buildings. At present, these are the characteristics of ecological architecture, and some of the equipment not only gives the building ecological function, but also gives the building a special decorative effect. Photoelectric glass is the integration of optoelectronic technology into glass. It breaks through the single enveloping function of traditional glass curtain wall and converts the sunlight that shields the surface of the building into its electric energy. At the same time, this composite material does not occupy much of the building area, and its unique decorative effect gives the building a distinctive modern sense of technology and the color of the times. This section starts with three examples of the application of ecological building technology at home and abroad, expounds the design method of its ecological architecture, which will help expand the interior design and take the ecological road, in order to learn from the ecological indoor design practice.

Example 1: 2008 Olympic Games Laoshan Bicycle Hall

The roof of the Beijing Laoshan Bicycle Museum is a round curved roof with steel structure, and its natural lighting mainly works through the roof skylight. The glass sunroof uses intelligent dimming technology and can be adjusted differently depending on the weather. On a sunny day, the light can be evenly illuminated by adjusting the angle of a small hundred pages in the cavity of the roof panel; in rainy days, the amount of light entering can be increased by opening a small hundred pages. In normal times, you only need to deal with daily sports training, and you don't have to turn on the lights in the venue. The windows in the pavilion are automatically controlled by the system. When a fire hazard occurs, these windows will automatically open to eliminate smoke from the room. A sound-insulating membrane is installed in the air compartment between the two panels to reduce the impact of rain. The small hundred pages of the window are covered with a reflective coating that is illuminated at night with the diffuse light of its reflective luminaires, eliminating the glare that interferes with the athlete.

Laoshan Bicycle Pavilion effectively integrates the ecological functions of roofs and windows, and truly

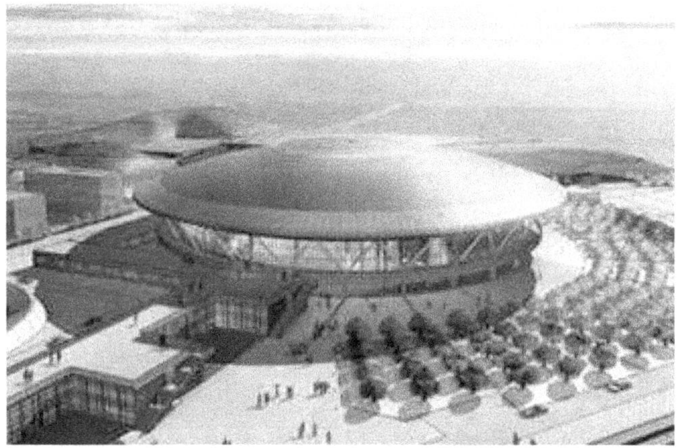

handles the contradictory climate of lighting and shading, heat preservation and ventilation in northern buildings, and at the same time artistically compensates for the defects of solar panels' own sound insulation and heat insulation.

Example 2: Brundtland Exhibition and Convention Center in Toftlund, Southern Denmark

The Brundtland Exhibition and Convention Centre in Toftlund, southern Denmark, is a 2,000-square-meter office building and an exhibition building. It has an advanced daylighting system that includes blinds on the exterior walls, light windows in the central attic, and reflective ceilings. The conference center is also equipped with a PV photovoltaic panel array. The photovoltaic panel is combined with the roof glass. It not only has the function of generating electricity, but also functions as a sunshade member to avoid indoor overheating caused by sunlight exposure. And the sunlight can create vivid and interesting light and shadow through the photoelectric panel. It will change rapidly with the seasons, the weather and the time of day, which will add unlimited vitality and fun to the ordinary atrium space.

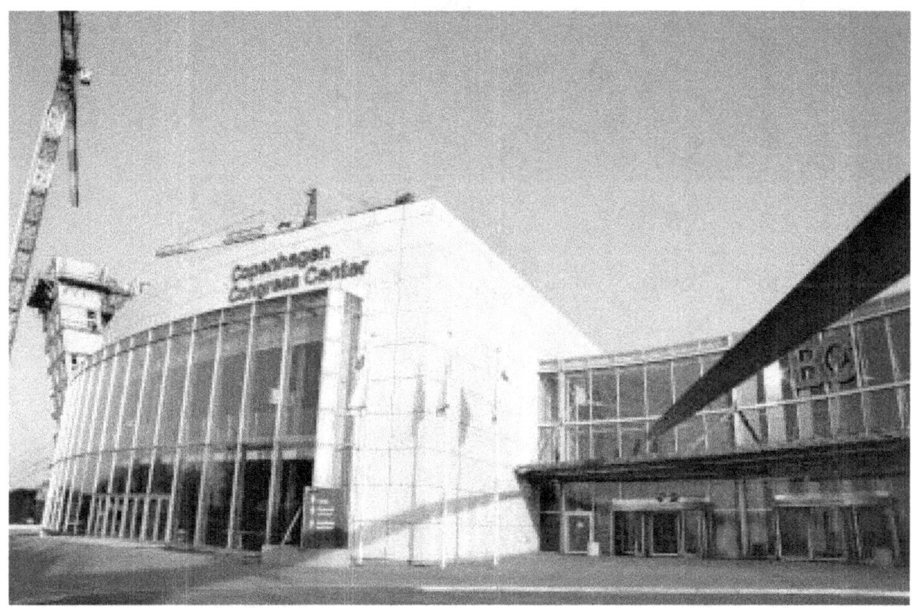

Example 3: Linz Design Center

The Linz Design Center is a classic example of the Thomas Herzog Eco Building. In the design of this large-span building space, Herzog used a lot of low-energy, recyclable steel, glass and other materials to ensure high light output in the exhibition hall, but the architect needs to achieve the guarantee. Ensure high standard lighting quality in the display area, but not increase energy consumption. In order to solve this problem, the solar grid system was developed by Herzog and optical expert Battenbach. A plastic grille for translucent roofing is placed on the roof panel through complex refraction and reflection. Only the diffuse light from the north enters the building, and the direct light from the south is shielded, thus avoiding overheating in the summer. The grille is only 16mm thick and is coated with a thin, pure aluminum reflective coating that is mounted between the roof double glazing. The geometric division of the grid is determined by a computer program designed to take into account several factors: the elevation and azimuth of the sun in different seasons; the obstruction of the building and the orientation of the building and the slope of the roof.

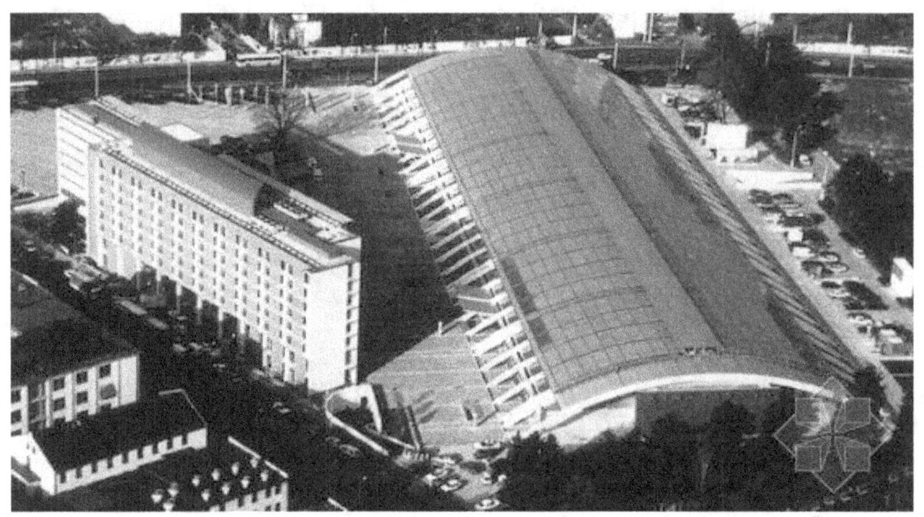

Part 2   Analysis of the basic theory of circular economy

In the process of promoting the development of circular economy in China, there have been three main problems: Why should we develop a circular economy? What is a circular economy? How to develop a circular economy? In the early stage of the development of circular economy, the question of "why" is the primary issue, that is, to solve the problem of whether the development of circular economy and the development of circular economy are beneficial to all sectors of society, especially policy makers. After the 2004 Central Economic Work Conference, especially the State Council issued the "Several Opinions on Accelerating the Development of Circular Economy" in July 2005, the "why" problem was basically solved at least at the national level. The question of "what is" runs through the whole process of the development of circular economy. Although it is a problem that needs to be continuously enriched and improved, the newly promulgated "Circular Economy Promotion Law" gives a clear and scientific meaning about the current circular economy. Definition. At the same time, the theoretical community has done a lot of research work on the connotation and theoretical basis of circular economy, and published a large number of articles and monographs.

In comparison, the "how" problem is the main problem facing the current development of circular economy, especially after the promulgation and implementation of the Circular Economy Promotion Law, this issue is particularly important. It mainly involves two aspects: First, what kind of policies need to be formulated to promote the development of circular economy; Second, in practice, how to organize economic and social related activities according to the principle of circular economy, that is, the development model of circular economy. The policy and model issues are interdependent, the establishment of the policy-driven model, and the model puts forward the requirements for policy formation; they depend on the connotation and development stage of the circular economy.

Chapter 1 Exploring the development of circular economy

The development of circular economy in China has experienced three stages of concept advocacy, national decision-making and pilot demonstration, and has begun to enter the stage of comprehensive promotion.

1.1 Idea Advocacy Stage (End of 20th Century - 2002)

At the end of the 20th century, according to the relevant practices of Germany and Japan, Chinese scholars began to introduce the concept of circular economy (Min Yimei, 1997; Zhu Dajian, 1998). At that time, China had basically emerged from the era of "short economy" and was in the period of economic strategy adjustment that began to attach great importance to the transformation of economic growth mode. The environmental management strategy was also in an important transition period from the end of governance to the source and process control, and the promotion of cleaner production. Work is more active. Therefore, the circular economy concept first attracted the strong interest and high attention of the Chinese environmental protection department. The former State Environmental Protection Administration played a substantial role in advocating the concept of circular economy in three aspects. First, it organized experts and scholars to study the theory and practice of circular economy; second, organized and guided enterprises to carry out clean production activities, and started in 1999. Demonstration work on the construction of eco-industrial parks, discussing the specific practices and experiences of circular economy-related practices; third, proposing to the central government to develop a circular economy, which is crucial for incorporating the circular economy into the agenda of national decision-making. In October 2002, Comrade Jiang Zemin pointed out at the 2nd General Assembly of the Global Environment Facility: "Only by the path of circular economy based on the most effective use of resources and environmental protection, sustainable development can be realized." This is China. The top government leaders first mentioned the concept of circular economy.

1.2 National decision-making stage (2003-2005)

Since 2003, the term "circular economy" has frequently appeared in relevant speeches by Chinese President Hu Jintao and Premier Wen Jiabao, and the development of circular economy has officially entered the decision-making agenda of the central government. By 2004, the Central Economic Work Conference clearly stated for the first time that the development of circular economy should be a long-term strategic task for economic development. In 2005, the Chinese government formally decided to incorporate the development of circular economy into the national economic and social development plan of the "Eleventh Five-Year Plan"; in July of the same year, the State Council issued "Several Opinions on Accelerating the Development of Circular Economy" (hereinafter referred to as "Several Opinions" "), marking the national will of China to develop a circular economy.

At this stage, while the former State Environmental Protection Administration continued to publicize and popularize the concept and knowledge of circular economy, an important task was to establish several regional circular economy pilots and more than ten ecological activities in Guiyang, Liaoning and Jiangsu provinces. The pilot of the industrial park will accumulate experience for the comprehensive promotion of circular economy practice. In the academic world, there has been a boom in circular economy research in China. A large number of articles, papers and seminars have heatedly discussed the hot issues of the meaning, connotation, international experience and theoretical basis of the circular economy, but the circular economy practice model and policy issues are only Initially involved, or limited to the introduction of the situation in Germany, Japan and other countries.

In China, the concept of circular economy can quickly become a national development strategy from a foreign-influenced concept in just a few years. It has its urgent practical needs and profound political foundation. Whether it is academic or 'political, whether domestic or international, it has become an indisputable fact that China's resources, especially mineral resources and fossil energy shortages, and serious environmental pollution and ecological degradation have become a problem. In the 21st century, this issue is particularly prominent. It has become a "bottleneck" constraint that restricts China's modernization drive and is a political issue for China. Therefore, alleviating the contradiction between economic growth and resources and environment is the realistic demand for China to develop a circular economy. At a higher level, the new Chinese government leadership collective put forward a people-oriented, comprehensive, coordinated and sustainable scientific development concept in 2003. The scientific concept of development is rich in content.

Among them, taking a new road to industrialization, improving the quality of development, conserving resources, protecting the environment, and promoting harmony between man and nature are important aspects. Therefore, in response to the severe resource and environment situation, the Chinese government put forward the strategic goal of building a resource-saving and environment-friendly society in 2005. In December 2005, the State Council issued the "Decision on Implementing the Scientific Outlook on Development and Strengthening Environmental Protection." At the Sixth National Environmental Protection Conference held in June 2006, Premier Wen Jiabao put forward the requirements for realizing the "three transformations" in handling the strategic relationship between environmental protection and economic development and measures to protect the environment. At the Fifth Plenary Session of the 16th CPC Central Committee held in 2006, the Chinese government will build a socialist harmonious society as the goal of development, emphasizing the harmony between man and nature. At the Fifth Session of the Tenth National People's Congress held in 2007, the Chinese government adjusted the guiding principle of economic development from "fast and good" to "good and fast" for the first time, indicating that the goal of determining economic growth is to use resources and energy. Based on efficiency and pollution reduction. Subsequently, the "17th National Congress of the Communist Party of China" held in 2007 put forward a new concept and strategy for building ecological civilization, and the development of circular economy as an important part of ecological civilization construction. So far, China has clearly entered the period of strategic transformation of environment and development. Moreover, the "17th National Congress" is guided by the scientific concept of development and has established a clear road map for this strategic transformation. This is the political and policy foundation for the circular economy to receive high attention and be rapidly promoted in China.

1.3 Pilot demonstration phase (2006-)

Marked by the "Several Opinions" and the "Outline of the Eleventh Five-Year Plan for National Economic and Social Development", China's circular economy development has entered a comprehensive pilot demonstration stage, and the Ministry of National Environmental Protection and other relevant ministries and commissions have been identified. Coordinated management system. In October 2005, the National Development and Reform Commission and the former State Environmental Protection Administration and other six ministries and commissions jointly issued a pilot work program for circular economy, and organized pilot projects for circular economy in key industries, key areas, industrial parks and provinces. Key industries include steel, non-ferrous metals, coal, electricity, chemicals, building materials, light industry, 7 high energy consumption, high pollution industries. The focus area refers to the field of waste recycling and recycling. Industrial parks include different types of industrial and agricultural parks. The provincial and municipal pilots refer to the selection of different types of provinces and cities to carry out regional circular economy pilots. The first batch of pilot units launched in 2005 included 10 provinces and municipalities, 13 regenerative industrial parks or enterprises, and 42 enterprises. The second batch of pilot units launched in 2007 has added 17 provinces and cities, 16 regenerative industrial parks or enterprises, 37 enterprises, 4 agricultural villages or towns or enterprises, and 19 industrial parks. In addition, the Ministry of Environmental Protection, the Ministry of Commerce and the Ministry of Science and Technology jointly launched 25 pilot projects for the construction of ecological industries.

1.4 Comprehensive advancement phase (2009-)

Since 2009, China's circular economy has entered a comprehensive promotion stage, mainly in two aspects: First, in general, the number and scope of circular economy pilots are rapidly increasing and expanding, covering 27 provinces and cities and many industries. , showing a comprehensive practice situation; Second, from January 1, 2009, the "Circular Economy Promotion Law" officially began to implement. Regardless of the administrative area covered or the economic and social fields involved, the implementation of the law undoubtedly means the full spread of circular economy practice.

Chapter 2 Analysis of the Connotation and Practice Forms of Circular Economy

2.1 Cognitive characteristics of China's circular economy

Due to the different stages of social and economic development, the environment and sustainable development issues are different, and the direct objectives pursued are different. China and Germany, Japan and other countries have more distinct China in terms of understanding and practice of circular economy. The characteristics have formed a richer connotation at the beginning.

After developed countries gradually solved industrial pollution and some life-type pollution, a large amount of waste caused by post-industrial or consumption-type social structure has gradually become an important issue for its environmental protection and sustainable development. The post-industrial society also means that advanced and clean production technologies and management are basically in place in the production field, and the end technologies and facilities for pollution control are relatively mature. In this context, the reduction, reuse and recycling of waste ("3R") has become the starting point and core content of its circular economy and related concepts and practices.

It is worth noting that although the waste problem is the direct cause of the circular economy-related practices in Germany and Japan, in fact, renewable energy, climate change and other resource and energy sustainable use and environmental protection issues are also important factors in promoting the development of circular economy.

Germany's circular economy originated from the "junk economy" in the consumer sector, and subsequently extended to the reduction, reuse and recycling activities in the production and consumption sectors. At present, it is exploring the development of regional circular economy with material flow management as the core. Due to the extreme restrictions of natural resources and land, Japan's "circular society" also originated from industrial and domestic waste issues. Compared with Germany, Japan has proposed more laws, policies and industries in establishing a recycling society. The complete system and higher goals are aimed at changing the traditional model of "mass production, mass consumption, and mass abandonment" in social and economic development. Although other developed countries do not have the term "circular economy", the "3R" principle has always been the core in terms of resource utilization and waste disposal. In the field of production, clean production, ecological industries (gardens), "industrial symbiosis", "zero emissions", "minimum waste" are the common practices or efforts of many countries.

In comparison, there are two aspects that determine the unique understanding and practice of China's circular economy.

China is still in the mid-stage of industrialization characterized by heavy chemicals. On the one hand, from the perspective of the entire development process, the process of compression industrialization and urbanization has made China at a lower stage of development, and at the same time encountered a complex ecological environment problem consisting of various problems, especially the environmental pollution problem. This determines that an important purpose of China's development of circular economy is to slow down the intensity of industrial pollution from the source and process of economic development. On the other hand, in the 21st century, China's mineral resources and fossil energy are difficult to continue to support its rapid and sustained economic growth. Among them, there are both shortages of absolute resources and reasons for inefficient use. Improving the efficiency of resource and energy use and reducing the total amount of resources and energy consumption have become another direct goal of China's development of circular economy. Therefore, in addition to the waste problem in the consumer sector, the implementation of clean production and the construction of eco-industrial parks in the production field has become the first concern of China's development of circular economy from the very beginning. Of course, judging from the ultimate goal pursued and the advanced nature of the technological economy and eco-efficiency of the developed countries in the production field, there is no essential difference in the connotation of circular economy between China and developed countries, but the focus of practice is different. Moreover, From the trend of the development of circular economy in Germany and Japan, there is a clear convergence.

The connotation of China's circular economy

There are many domestic sayings about the connotation of China's circular economy. However, the definition of the circular economy is basically a more comprehensive, concise and authoritative definition. The circular economy refers to production, circulation and consumption. The general term for the reduction, reuse, and resource utilization activities carried out in the process." According to this definition and other domestic statements, the essence of China's circular economy practice can be understood from five aspects or with five key elements.

The goal of developing a circular economy

Obviously, the goal of China's development of circular economy is to alleviate the sharp contradiction between economic growth and resource environment, improve the efficiency of resource and energy use, reduce the intensity of pollution emissions, and build a resource-saving and environment-friendly society.

The extension of circular economy activities

The essence of circular economy is a new "economic activity or economic development model". The "circulation" is a description of the characteristics of this new economic model from the traditional economic model. Therefore, the extension of circular economy activities includes production, exchange, circulation and consumption, with emphasis on production and consumption.

From the perspective of industrial division, some activities in the field of exchange and circulation can be classified into the consumption field, and some can be classified into production areas, such as the service industry.

Therefore, from the perspective and extension of China's circular economy, it is in line with the concept and practice of establishing sustainable consumption and production models that the international community is carrying out.

A sign that is different from the traditional economic development model

As a new economic development model, from the perspective of effect, the most direct sign that the development model of circular economy is different from the traditional economic development model is the "high resource energy input, low economic output, high pollution emission" of the traditional economic development model. (ie "two highs and one low") changed to "two lows and one high" (low resource and energy input, high economic output, low pollution emissions). Of course, conventional technological advancement and institutional innovation may also make this effect of economic development. Therefore, the circular economy must have fundamental differences.

Different from the fundamental characteristics of the traditional economic development model

From the perspective of ecological economics, the problem of resource shortage and environmental pollution is essentially a failure of the material exchange relationship between the socio-economic system and the ecological environment system. That is to say, the demand for resources and energy in the socio-economic system exceeds the supply capacity of the ecosystem, and there is a shortage; the waste generated exceeds the self-purification capacity of the ecosystem, and pollution problems arise. Therefore, the theoretical essence of circular economy is: regulate the mode of material flow and flow in economic activities, and equalize resources and capital, labor, technology and system as the endogenous variables that affect economic development. This is also the difference between circular economy and Economic theory manages the core characteristics of economic activities. Intuitively speaking, it is the material circulation mode of transforming the linear resource flow mode of "resource-product-waste" of traditional economy into "resource-product-renewable resource".

Principles, methods and core standards for achieving circular economy

To regulate the flow and flow of material in the traditional economic model, the principle is "reduction, reuse, resource and harmlessness", and the method is material flow management. According to German and Japanese experience and existing theoretical results, material flow analysis and management is the core means and method for regulating the flow and flux of material flow in social and economic activities.

In a circular economy, the purpose of changing the way things flow is to reduce "flow" and adapt it to the resource supply and self-cleaning "capacity" of the ecosystem. The "flow rate" is given to the time, the amount of input and other parameters, and is converted into efficiency. Efficiency is a common measure of economic growth performance. Traditional efficiency indicators are the productivity of labor productivity or other capital factor inputs. The "flow" that the circular economy pays attention to is the material, the resource energy and the waste, so its efficiency should be the resource energy productivity and the pollutant emission intensity. This is the internationally popular concept of eco-efficiency, a "node" indicator that connects resources, the economy, and the environment. High ecological efficiency necessarily means low resource and energy input, high economic output and low pollution

Development status of China's circular economy policy

Since 2005, China's process of formulating a circular economy policy has been greatly accelerated. In general, China's circular economy policy system is being continuously established and improved along two paths, and a unique framework system has been initially formed. The first is to form a circular economy special legal system and policy with the "Circular Economy Promotion Law" as the leader; the second is to incorporate the circular economy principle into relevant laws, regulations and policies, or called the circular economy related laws and policies.

From the current situation, the policy framework specifically for the development of circular economy includes seven categories:

a) comprehensive category, including the "Opinions on Accelerating the Development of Circular Economy" issued by the State Council in July 2005; in October 2005, the National Development and Reform Commission and the former State Environmental Protection Administration and other six ministries and commissions jointly issued a circular economy pilot program; The Circular Economy Promotion Law, adopted in August 2008 and implemented in January 2009.

b) the Clean Production Promotion Law and its supporting policies that were implemented in 2003 and are being revised and improved.

c) the management and preferential policies for the comprehensive utilization of waste resources that have been implemented for many years and are being continuously revised and improved.

d) the evaluation criteria. In September 2006, the former State Environmental Protection Administration issued standards for the vein industry, industry and comprehensive eco-industrial parks to evaluate and standardize the construction of eco-industrial parks. In June 2007, the National Development and Reform Commission, the former State Environmental Protection Administration and the National Bureau of Statistics jointly issued the "Circular Economy Indicator System", including comprehensive categories and industrial parks.

e) about policies related to the construction of eco-industrial parks. On the basis of several years of piloting, in 2007, the former State Environmental Protection Administration, the Ministry of Commerce, and the Ministry of Science and Technology jointly issued documents requiring the existing economic development zones and high-tech development zones to transform and construct eco-industrial parks in accordance with the principles of circular economy.

f) green consumption. In October 2006, the Ministry of Finance and the former State Environmental Protection Administration jointly issued the "Opinions on the Implementation of Government Procurement of Environmental Labeling Products", requiring state organs, institutions and organizations at all levels to use fiscal funds for procurement. For products marked, products that are harmful to the environment and human health may not be purchased. This is an important sign that China has begun to establish public green procurement.

g) the investment policy of the circular economy pilot. Since the first batch of pilot projects for circular economy started, the National Development and Reform Commission has provided a certain amount of special funds for the pilot projects.

In addition to the above seven types of policies specifically for the development of circular economy, the laws and policies related to circular economy play a simple or fundamental role in the development of circular economy. It mainly includes three categories: one is general resource energy and environmental policy, especially the energy conservation and emission reduction policy: the second is the resource energy and environmental policy that explicitly incorporates the principles and requirements of circular economy, such as the newly revised Energy Conservation Law and The Law on the Prevention and Control of Environmental Pollution by Solid Wastes; the third is the price and taxation policies of resources and energy. For example, the fuel tax, as well as the reform of policies such as consumption tax on products such as large-displacement cars, wooden disposable chopsticks, and solid wood flooring, and product export tax rebates play an important and fundamental role in promoting the development of circular economy.

2.2 The main practice form of China's circular economy

At present, China's circular economy practice activities are mainly carried out at the three levels of enterprises, industrial parks and society, involving all aspects of resource extraction, production, circulation and consumption.

The circular economy at the enterprise level generally uses the clean production method to realize the recycling of raw materials and the cascade utilization of energy within the enterprise, improve the efficiency of resource utilization and reduce or not discharge pollution. Corporate circular economy activities are sometimes referred to as building "small loops."

The eco-industrial park includes new construction and ecological transformation of various types of parks. The core content of the eco-industrial park is twofold: one is to build an ecological industrial chain between the enterprises in the park (raw material-waste-raw material chain or energy cascade utilization chain); The second is to build a park infrastructure system that efficiently shares public resources such as energy and water. The circular economy activities carried out in industrial parks are sometimes referred to as the "middle cycle". In the field of ecological agriculture, China has a long history and successful models, such as a hybrid system for breeding and breeding, and various models with biogas as a link.

At the social level, China's exploration of circular economy practice is mainly concentrated in two aspects: First, the establishment of recycling, recycling and resource recycling of various waste industries, equivalent to Japan's "venous industry"; Second, in the field of consumption, advocate Resource energy conservation, rational consumption and green consumption, implementation of government green procurement, energy conservation and environmental labeling product certification, and creation of a green society. The circular economy activities carried out in the whole society are sometimes referred to as the "big loop".

Part 3   Research on the Development Model of Circular Economy

The circular economy development model refers to the application of the concept of circular economy, the specific practice and practice of transforming the existing economic development model, that is, applying the concept and principle of circular economy, and transforming the industrial organization of existing production and consumption activities.

At present, in China, the circular economy is still in the development stage, and theoretical research and practical models of circular economy are being explored. Therefore, this chapter will focus on the development model of circular economy, draw on international experience, refer to the specific practices and practices of developed countries, and at the same time summarize and refine the pilot and practice of circular economy actively carried out in various parts of China to form a suitable country for China. A characteristic circular economy development model.

Chapter 1 Research on the Strategic Model of the Development of Circular Economy Model

1.1 Overview of China's Circular Economy Development

An Overview of the Regional Strategic Model of China's Circular Economy Development

According to the current pilot practice of China's circular economy, from the perspective of regional economic development stage, technical and economic conditions and recent development goals, China's current circular economy development has emerged three regional strategic models, which refer to different regions. Under different economic development levels, technical and economic conditions, resource and environmental conditions, the development of circular economy as a strategic choice and transformation of different types, its specific practice models have their own characteristics, and also have different needs in related policies.

Jiangsu Sunan, Shanghai, Shandong and other places are the most developed areas in China. From the perspective of development, the development of circular economy and the industrial upgrading and economic transformation in the eastern region are synchronized and coordinated, and the technical and economic bases and institutional conditions are relatively good. It can be said that the development of circular economy in this region is a spontaneous strategic transformation model. For the development of circular economy in this kind of region, as long as the country's legislation and policies are in place and institutional arrangements are in place, the circular economy can basically develop smoothly based on local resources.

The practice of circular economy in Liaoning Province is a strategic transformation mode of resource-based regions with a certain technical and economic background in the context of revitalizing the old industrial bases in Northeast China. The revitalization strategy of the old industrial bases in Northeast China has brought significant development opportunities for the development of circular economy in Liaoning Province. The development of circular economy has also become an important strategic measure for the revitalization of the old industrial base in Liaoning Province. The development of circular economy in Liaoning not only has special needs in its own development process, but also has important demonstration significance for the sustainable development of the revitalization of the old industrial base in the northeast and even the resource-based regions in the west. For this type, the state needs to provide external funds, technology and policy support. The relevant support should be integrated into the country's series of tilting policies for the revitalization of the old industrial bases in Northeast China, and the two should be integrated into one. It is not appropriate to engage in two sets of support policies. In contrast, Guiyang's pilot demonstration is an attempt to develop a circular economy in the western region. It is a typical leap-forward strategic transformation, that is, advanced development strategies and roads are selected before industrial upgrading and economic transformation. The technical and economic difficulties it faces are naturally much larger than those in the east. It is relatively easy to advance on the spot and in part. The comprehensive advancement will face many challenges. The state should give strong external support. While integrating capital, technology and special policy support into the preferential policies for the development of the western region, it also needs special support for the development of the local circular economy.

The above three regional strategic models have different economic and technical resources and environmental conditions, and therefore have different characteristics in specific practices and practical modes.'

Eastern spontaneous strategic transformation model

The development model of circular economy in Jiangsu Province

Jiangsu Province is located in a developed area in eastern China, and the development of circular economy has a good technical and economic foundation. In combination with the construction of the ecological province, Jiangsu Province has established the circular economy, recycling agriculture, recycling service industry and recycling social planning based on the economic and social development and resource environment of the province. On this basis, the circular economy of Jiangsu Province has been formulated. Development planning, and actively carry out pilot projects of circular economy throughout the province to explore the development model of circular economy.

Main contents of the Jiangsu model

1) Recycling industry. Industry is an important part of the economic structure, and industrialization is the main driving force of economic development. Therefore, the recycling industry is the main body of the development of circular economy in Jiangsu Province. The construction of recycling industry in Jiangsu Province is mainly reflected in the industrial ecological structure reorganization around the recycling industry model. According to the symbiotic structure of producers, consumers and decomposers in the ecosystem and the principle of food nutrition chain network, the input and output materials energy of industrial systems. The flow elements form an ecological industrial system around the organization of the product and its production process. Focus on promoting the research and development of green products, comprehensively launching

clean production of enterprises, accelerating the ecological adjustment of industrial structure, and vigorously developing eco-industrial parks, regional recycling-type industrial comprehensive demonstration zones and recycling-type industrial infrastructure construction.

First, the development of green products. Focus on promoting green material products, energy-saving and water-saving products such as energy-saving products, non-toxic, harmless or degradable environmentally-friendly products, recycling and dismantling products that are beneficial for recycling, recycling, recycling, and functional replacement. Research and development of products. Improve the ratio of environmental labeling products, promote the ecological transformation of industrial structure, and enhance the international competitiveness of products.

Second, comprehensively deepen the clean production of enterprises. Intensify the implementation of clean production in enterprises according to law, and vigorously reduce the resource and energy consumption and pollution in the industrial production process, focusing on large and medium-sized enterprises such as metallurgy, chemical industry, textile and papermaking, and vigorously carry out water conservation and energy conservation as the basic content. Clean production, promote the continuous deepening and continuous improvement of clean production, and lay a solid foundation for the construction of recycling industry.

Third, vigorously promote the industrial ecological transformation. On the basis of deep processing of products and optimization and upgrading of green product structure, we will actively promote the ecological adjustment of industrial structure, vigorously reduce the structural resource consumption and pollution production of industrial systems, and promote the evolution of Jiangsu industry towards eco-industrial systems. In combination with the industrial structure of Jiangsu Province, it will focus on promoting the ecological transformation of high-pollution and high-energy-consuming industries, including chemical, printing and dyeing, papermaking, machinery and equipment, promoting clean industrial technology, accelerating wind energy and solar energy, and regenerating under the premise of improving resource utilization. Development and utilization of energy. Promote the organic combination of informationization and ecologicalization, vigorously develop the information industry, strengthen information and humanized management, and increase high-tech support for energy utilization.

Fourth, actively promote the development of eco-industrial parks. Promote the economic integration development of Jiangsu, especially the industrial parks with high density of distribution along the Yangtze River, market-oriented, overall planning and management, strengthen the control of land resources, and implement the comprehensive control requirements of the economic and resource environment of enterprises entering the park.
Combined with the integration of industrial parks and the construction of featured parks, the park will actively bring into play the industrial agglomeration and industrial ecological effects of the park, fully utilize the laws of industrial ecology, and promote the construction of eco-industrial parks. Through the construction of centralized pollution control and centralized heating system, the park will realize the sharing and large-scale operation of the infrastructure, promote the construction of waste exchange system and energy cascade

utilization system within the park and between the parks, and develop the coordination of information and logistics network management across the park. Institutions accelerate the evolution of industrial parks to eco-industrial parks.

Fifth, co-ordinate the organization of a comprehensive demonstration of regional recycling industrial networks. Based on the urbanization process and relying on the city, we will integrate the multi-level recycling industry construction of enterprises, parks, industries and infrastructure into the process of urban development and construction, and build a regional recycling industrial network. Strengthen the regional division of labor and cooperation between industrial clusters, actively cultivate and support the waste recycling industry, and bring into play the absorption functions of wastes such as cement, steel and energy industries, and promote regional cooperation and rational allocation of industries. Support the construction of the maintenance and replacement of the CCP's technical equipment and the construction of the leasing service industry, and promote the overall optimization and upgrading of the ecological system along the Yangtze River.

Sixth, strengthen the construction of recycling industrial infrastructure and establish a waste recycling classification and dismantling base. We will establish a base for the recycling and harmless treatment of household appliances and electronic waste, focusing on the construction of household appliances such as washing machines, refrigerators, televisions and air conditioners, and promoting the construction and demonstration of recycling systems for electronic products such as used household appliances. Focusing on the waste recycling industry in key areas such as Taicang, we will collect and recycle the recycling and recycling of waste tires, waste plastics, scrap steel, scrap copper, waste paper and waste household appliances, attracting foreign and private capital to participate in industrial waste reduction and waste exchange. The whole process of waste recycling, waste treatment and disposal.

Recycling agriculture
Recycling agriculture is a concentrated expression of sustainable development ideas and circular economy concepts in agricultural development. The development of circular agriculture in Jiangsu Province integrates the comprehensive utilization of agricultural clean production and agricultural waste, adopts the basic laws of ecosystem operation and economic activities, and its core is to use the principle of food chain to optimize the production of agricultural products to the entire industrial chain. Structure, the use of natural resources and environmental capacity in an environmentally friendly way to achieve an ecological turn in agricultural economic activities.

The development of circular agriculture in Jiangsu Province requires that the economic activities of agricultural related industries be organized into a closed-loop process of "natural resources-products-waste-renewable resources". Material inputs and energy can be most rationally utilized in this continuous cycle. Therefore, the harmful effects of agricultural industrial chain activities on the natural environment are minimized.

Recycling service industry

In the production and service activities, in accordance with the requirements of the circular economy, follow the principles of reduction, reuse, recycling, reduce material consumption, avoid and reduce waste, fundamentally reduce resource depletion and environmental pollution, will circular economy The concepts and methods are implemented in various industry sectors within the service industry to carry out activities such as creating green restaurants and green catering businesses. Due to the unique characteristics of "circulation and service" in the service industry, it plays a role in connecting other industries and social life, and can effectively connect and promote the development of recycling industries, agriculture and recycling society.

Recycling society

The circular society is the embodiment of the circular economy concept in social life. It requires the integration of green consumption and life patterns into social life, and gradually forms a circular lifestyle and consumption pattern. Use recyclable products or green products as much as possible in daily life to reduce the generation of waste during consumption, establish a waste sorting treatment and utilization system, realize the recycling and harmlessness of urban waste, and recycle useful waste as much as possible. Materials are recycled to form a resource-saving society.

The innovative features of the Jiangsu model

Under the guidance of the overall circular economy plan, Jiangsu Province launched a pilot program of circular economy, and identified 108 pilot units of circular economy, involving different industries in agriculture, industry, and service industries, as well as enterprises, parks, and social consumption sectors. The goal of "recycling, recycling, recycling" actively promotes the circulation of resources within the enterprise, between different enterprises and different industries, and has achieved obvious economic, environmental and social benefits. With a relatively strong technical and economic advantages and a deeper understanding of the circular economy, Jiangsu Province, especially the southern Jiangsu circular economy practice, has demonstrated the characteristics of advanced, rich content and diverse models, and its specific model of circular economy development and its innovative characteristics in four ways.

Emphasis on social cooperation and inter-industry linkages, rather than simply and blindly constructing various closed loops. The principle of ecological economics tells us that matter can be repeated, reused and circulated, but it is impossible to close the cycle at different system levels; the flow of energy is unidirectional and non-cyclic, and is decreasing. The practice of circular economy cannot realize the complete closed-circuit recycling of materials in enterprises, parks and even regional levels, but more attention should be paid to the material connection and recycling between enterprises, industries, production and consumption fields or systems. This not only conforms to the laws of the ecological economic system, but also makes full use of the social division of labor to improve technical and economic benefits.

Zhangjiagang Shagang Group has established a recycling model for waste resources outside the "two heads". The social recycling system provides 2.5 million tons of scrap steel to Shagang Group each year; Shagang Group sells a large number of blast furnace slag and steel slag to related companies as raw materials.

In August 2004, Epson Company of Suzhou High-tech Zone basically achieved the goal of "zero emission". However, this zero-emission is not a closed-end zero-emission within the company created by Japanese companies in the 1990s, but is associated with related waste utilization and safe disposal companies to achieve open zero emissions that ultimately do not pollute the environment.

Zhangjiagang and Changshu will establish a cycle of resources between industry and industry as the focus of their circular economy practice. While building an agro-ecological chain, Zhangliangang Nanfeng Town Yonglian Village actively explores the grafting of enterprises and agricultural chains. For example, the waste heat from the production of village-run steel mills can be used to save energy costs of more than 200,000 yuan per year in the wintering greenhouse heating and edible mushroom processing and cooking process in aquaculture. Changshu City connects soybean planting, soybean oil processing industry, bio-organic fertilizer and general planting industry through soybean protein extraction protein fiber technology.

In addition, the southern part of the country has placed an important position in the resource recycling industry. Suzhou High-tech Zone is constructing a recycling system for waste resources, including an environmental service center, a solid waste disposal center, and an electronic waste dismantling and recycling center. Taicang City has initially established an industrial park for recycling and recycling of used resources. At present, many foreign resource recycling enterprises are stationed in Suzhou and Taicang. With the development and expansion of the waste resource recycling industry system, it is expected to establish a bridge for resource recycling between enterprises, production and consumption.

Strategic model for the development of circular economy

Zhangjiagang Shagang Group practices circular economy with significant benefits

In recent years, Zhangjiagang Shagang Group actively applied the "3R" principle of circular economy to organize and implement the production and environmental protection activities of enterprises, and achieved remarkable economic and environmental benefits. In order to strengthen related management work, the Group has formulated the "Environmental Protection Management System" and the "Clean Production Management System", and established an environmental management team to establish institutional and institutional guarantees.

The circular economy practice of Shagang Group focuses on two aspects:
First, the introduction of advanced production and environmental protection technology and equipment, the implementation of cleaner production, in the source and process of "reduction", reducing energy consumption and pollution intensity. The steelmaking power consumption of Shagang Group decreased from 471.26kW·h/t in 1995 to 283.53kW·h/t in 2003; the comprehensive fuel consumption of rolled steel decreased from 45.19kg/t to 26.31kg/t in recent years, and the annual reduction rate reached 5.88. %; the dust collection rate of steelmaking tail gas reaches an average of 12.5kg/t; the desulfurization rate of tail gas is above 90%.

Technological progress has not only effectively reduced the production energy consumption of Shagang Group, but also reduced pollution emissions. At the same time, it has also reduced the production cost of Shagang Group. The cost of steelmaking has dropped by 80-100 yuan/ton compared with 1995, and the discharge of sewage charges has dropped significantly.

Second, the implementation of "reuse and recycling" at the end, the establishment of "two-head" outside the open waste recycling system, Shagang Group absorbs nearly 2.5 million tons of various types of scrap recovered from the social recycling system for steelmaking production process; A large number of blast furnace slag and steel slag are sold to enterprises in need after initial processing or deep processing. Shagang Group built a production wastewater and waste gas recovery and recycling system in 1995, recycling them in all aspects of production. The reuse rate of industrial water has reached 95.24%, which is higher than the 94% standard set by the National Economic and Trade Commission for resource conservation and environmental protection major demonstration projects for metallurgical enterprises. At present, Shagang Group's steelmaking consumption of fresh water is 3.69 tons, and the annual water conservation fee is 30.547 million yuan. In 2003, Shagang Group comprehensively utilized the industrial "three wastes" economic benefits of 122.43 million yuan, reduced organic pollutants more than 4,500 tons, implemented "green investment" and "node investment" to build an industrial ecological chain.

In the southern part of the country, many industrial parks with advanced production technology and high environmental management level have been built, such as Zhangjiagang's Yangzijiang Chemical Industrial Park, Changshu Economic Development Zone, Suzhou High-tech Zone, and Suzhou Industrial Park. How to link enterprises with no logistics demand relationship in the park is an important issue in the construction of ecological industry. To this end, Zhangjiagang, Changshu and Suzhou have implemented "green investment" and "node investment" plans.

"Green investment" and "node investment" refer to the selection of investment projects based on the existing industrial structure and industrial park positioning, according to the concept of circular economy. Screening can not only stay in the advanced nature of technology and the superiority of environmental protection. On the basis of this, it is also necessary to examine whether it is in the "node" position in the existing industrial chain, connect existing industries and construct a unique ecological industrial system; at the same time, such projects often have industrial agglomeration effects. To guide the composition and flow of international and domestic industrial capital. After applying this investment concept, Jiangsu Yangzijiang Chemical Industrial Park successfully attracted a number of international chemical flagship projects and leading enterprises to settle in, which led to a large number of "downstream" enterprises rushing to the industrial park. As a result, the industry chain of "lip and tooth dependent" is gradually forming, including four major industries of chemical industry, grain and oil, electromechanical and textile.

Suzhou Epson Company Zero Emissions Mode
Suzhou Epson's zero-emission model complements the construction of the comprehensive utilization system of resources in Suzhou High-tech Zone. Suzhou Epson Company was established in February 1996 and is a

high-tech enterprise in Jiangsu Province. Its main products are liquid crystal displays and crystal vibrators. The principle of "symbiosis with nature" is based on "contributing to the realization of a sustainable society and striving to become a pioneer in environmental protection that people agree with everywhere" as a basic foothold and actively promotes cleaner production. In 1999, it obtained ISO14000 certification. The "zero emission" activities of waste recycling in the company are very distinctive.

In order to build a recycling-oriented enterprise, since 2002, the company has carried out "zero emission" activities of waste recycling. Through publicity and education, the waste is thoroughly classified in the plant area, and industrial waste is realized by various technical means. 100% reuse of the material; the domestic waste of landfill treatment is reduced, from the original 160g per person per day, controlled to 50g per person per day, the domestic garbage is reduced by more than 60%, and the annual cost can be saved 80 Ten thousand yuan, in January 2004 passed the Japan Seiko Epson Group "zero emission level I" certification.

Following the principle of circular economy, Suzhou Epson Company has carried out green procurement and green product activities in product design, process flow and raw material substitution, and formed a product-based metabolic eco-industry. Since the beginning of its establishment, the company has consistently carried out energy-saving activities. Factories, equipment, and energy consumption are considered as a whole, focusing on the reform of production processes and equipment, and improving management by constantly trying various energy-saving methods.

Since 2001, the accumulated energy-saving crude oil has reached 3,300 m3, the energy consumption per million yuan has been reduced by 75%, and the water consumption per 10,000 yuan of GDP has dropped to 10 tons. By the end of 2003, the company's green procurement rate of production materials has exceeded 90%. While reducing the environmental load, it also greatly increased productivity.

The zero emission model implemented by Suzhou Epson Company is not the absolute zero discharge of waste, but the comprehensive utilization and safe disposal of waste on the basis of reduction. The final waste is safely disposed of by the socialized environmental service center and solid waste disposal center that are built in the high-tech zone. The reform of the urban-rural integration system creates opportunities for the development of circular economy.

The overall level of the economy in southern Jiangsu is relatively high, and the gap between urban and rural areas is shrinking. Due to the continuous development of the township economy, the destruction of land resources in rural areas has become increasingly serious, and rural infrastructure is seriously inadequate. In order to further coordinate the coordinated development of urban and rural areas, the reform of the urban-rural integration system in southern Jiangsu is very strong. The main content of the reform is to withdraw towns and villages, strengthen land use management, increase infrastructure construction, and improve rural living conditions. Zhangjiagang plans to withdraw the original 20 towns and towns into 8 towns. Changshu City plans to plan more than 10,000 villages in the city into 52 concentrated residential areas for rural residents in 12 years. The withdrawal has brought a series of opportunities and changes to rural ecological environmental protection and regional circular economy development. First, the expansion of villages and towns is conducive to unified planning and construction and environmental supervision and management. All towns in Zhangjiagang and Changshu are planning or constructing sewage and garbage centralized treatment facilities. Second, many villages are gradually relocating villagers to a unified planning and infrastructure-owned community, which not only improves the living conditions of farmers, but also provides possibilities for rural living environment pollution control. Third, after the withdrawal, it is conducive to centralized land management and intensive management. All enterprises must enter the planned park, which not only solves the problem of disorderly occupation and destruction of land resources, but also creates a centralized management of rural industrial pollution and the development of ecological agriculture. condition. Fourth, after the withdrawal, the level of infrastructure construction has been improved. The promotion of rural renewable energy such as solar energy and biogas in southern Jiangsu has accelerated the strategic model of economic development. Fifth, the climax of the creation of a beautiful township in the whole country or Jiangsu Province was promoted in southern Jiangsu, which led to the integration of urban and rural areas in the entire southern Jiangsu region and promoted the coordinated development of urban and rural areas. At present, two towns in Changshu have won the title of National Township and Township, and three towns have been awarded the title of Jiangsu Province.

The reform of urban and rural integration is an important institutional innovation for the overall planning of urban and rural development, creating a unified practice stage for the development of ecological cities and the development of regional circular economy to the countryside. Jiangxiang Village in Changshu City and Tangqiao Town in Zhangjiagang City and Yonglian Village in Nanfeng Town have achieved great success in this respect.

Green node investment practice of Jiangsu Yangzijiang International Chemical Park

Jiangsu Yangzijiang International Chemical Industry Park was established in May 2001 and is managed by Zhangjiagang Free Trade Zone. It enjoys the preferential policies of the Free Trade Zone. The park is mainly centered on the chemical industry. At the beginning of 2003, Zhangjiagang City was listed as a pilot city for circular economy in Jiangsu Province. Zhangjiagang City decided to transform the park into an ecological industrial park. The key tasks and means of transformation are how to connect existing enterprises and industries through green investment and node investment. stand up. At present, the Suzhou fine chemical industry chain and grain and oil processing industry chain in the park have begun to take shape.

The state fine chemical industry is a company that moved from Suzhou to the chemical park. The original pollution was serious. After entering the Yangtze River Chemical Park, the company reduced pollution emissions through technological process transformation and environmental management. On the other hand, the park management committee introduced investment projects that can absorb the products and by-products of Suzhou Fine Chemicals through green node investment. To gradually form two eco-industrial chains with Jiangsu Fine Chemicals as the core: Introduce a US company (node   enterprise) to produce methyl chloride and chloroform from the products of Suzhou Fine Chemicals, hydrogen, chlorine and hydrogen chloride; Methyl chloride is used as raw material, and another American Dow Corning Company (node company) is introduced to produce silicone, further producing sealant, silicone rubber, textile auxiliaries and pharmaceutical intermediates. At the same time, chloroform is sent to Changshu Chlorine Industrial Park. Raw material for the production of refrigerant. Introduced a company (node　　company), which produces high-purity hydrogen from the hydrogen of Suzhou Fine Chemicals, and supplies Falsun Company in Jiangyin City. At the same time, using high-purity hydrogen as raw material, Mitsui Chemicals (node　　company) was introduced to produce PTA and other products; PTA was used as raw material to introduce PET project, and the product was supplied to Xinxin Chemical Fiber Co., Ltd.

The grain and oil chain is mainly represented by the East China Sea grain and oil. The existing Donghai Grain and Oil, Tongqing Food, Fuji Oil and other enterprises, the development direction is mainly grain and oil processing. After years of operation, Donghai Grain and Oil has made great efforts in reducing waste, maximizing raw material utilization and recycling of production waste, and has achieved good economic and social benefits. It has become a pilot unit of circular economy in Jiangsu Province.

The innovation of green investment and node investment concept has brought about great changes to the industrial structure of Yangzijiang International Chemical Park. With the introduction of the node project, isolated enterprises are gradually linked into the ecological industrial chain and develop towards a complex and orderly regional eco-industrial network structure. The circular economy industrial chain generated by "green investment" finally makes the chemical park become An "ecological industrial park".

In addition, the more famous one is the main practice of urban and rural integration construction in Changshu. In the construction of urban and rural integration, Changshu proposed the construction idea of "taking planning as the leader, building the concentrated residential areas of rural residents as the incentive for government support, and focusing on improving rural production and life". It is planned to use the whole city for 12 years. More than 10,000 natural villages have built 52 rural peasant concentrated residential areas, forming a new rural community with good living conditions, complete facilities and beautiful environment. In the planning and construction process, public facilities such as centralized sewage treatment, garbage collection and centralized disposal, community management and medical education will be completed, the living environment will be beautiful, and the greening rate will reach 30%.

In order to strengthen the construction of environmental infrastructure in the town, Changshu City issued the "Notice on Accelerating the Construction of Sewage Treatment Plants and Pipe Network Supporting Projects in the Towns". The municipal finance subsidies 2 million to 3 million yuan per year for the towns that started the construction of domestic sewage treatment plants. At present, five towns have built domestic sewage treatment plants and supporting pipe networks; three new environmentally-friendly thermal power projects using circulating fluidized bed for power and dust removal have been built, and regional networked heating is implemented to reduce air pollution caused by small boilers.

In the construction of concentrated residential areas for farmers, according to the standard of 2,300 to 3,500 households in each residential area, a new rural community with complete supporting facilities and beautiful environment will be built. Changshu plans to reduce the land occupation per household by 667m2 through urban-rural integration. Below 400m2, the land can be reclaimed to nearly 6,700hm2. On this basis, the promotion of the use of clean energy such as biogas and solar energy has been completed, and three straw gasification stations have been built. Many new houses have been installed with solar energy equipment, which has improved living conditions and reduced environmental pollution.

In the prevention and control of industrial pollution in rural areas, we must first strictly control the point source and implement the concentration of enterprises in industrial parks. At the same time, relying on the environmental infrastructure of the industrial park, we will implement centralized pollution control and centralized heating, improve the level of pollution control, carry out upgrades and meet the standards, and implement the first-level emission standards for the chemical, printing and dyeing industries to promote clean production within the enterprise.

The development model of circular economy in Shandong Province

The development of circular economy in Shandong Province is closely combined with the construction of ecological provinces. In the Outline of Ecological Environment Construction and Protection Planning of Shandong Province, it is clearly stated that the construction of ecological demonstration zones in Shandong should be carried out from point to point, from small to large, and gradually develop. To realize the construction goals of the ecological province, after continuous exploration and summarization of the level and mode of the circular economy, a circular economy development model with "point, line and surface" with Shandong characteristics was initially established.

"Point, line, surface" circular economy development model

First, in the enterprise, establish a small loop on the point. Promote clean production, ISO14000 environmental management system certification, in accordance with the concept of eco-efficiency and clean production requirements, using ecological design and modern technology, the unit consumption and pollutant emissions of the unit products are limited to the scope of the advanced standards. Realize the comprehensive utilization and recycling of resources within the enterprise. In terms of cleaner production: Shandong Province has gradually advanced from the eastern to the western, from the developed areas to the underdeveloped areas, from heavily polluting industries to other industries. More than 200 companies have implemented cleaner production, and more than 50 companies and more than 200 products have received environmental labels.

Through the implementation of cleaner production, the company reduced emissions by 10.0%, and the emission reduction rate of 10,000 yuan was 9.36%: the sulfur dioxide emission reduction rate was 16.9%, the emission reduction rate of 10,000 yuan output was 34.2%, and the emission reduction rate was 17.9%. The emission reduction rate of 10,000 yuan is 15.1%; the wastewater reduction rate is 27.5%, the emission reduction rate of 10,000 yuan is 22.5%; the COD emission reduction rate is 29.3%, and the emission reduction rate of 10,000 yuan is 23.2%; The rate is 15.2%, the emission reduction rate of 10,000 yuan is 14.4%; the annual economic benefit rate of enterprises is 5%.

ISO14000 Environmental Management Certification: A total of 180 enterprises and 8 development zones (tourist areas) in Shandong Province have passed national certification. Three of the development zones have been approved as "ISO14000 National Demonstration Zones", accounting for one-third of the total number of demonstration zones in the country. Since 2003, the energy consumption and water consumption of more than 1,000 enterprises in the province have decreased by 12.4% and 31% respectively.

Second, in the industry, establish a middle cycle on the line. Develop and implement guiding standards by industry to optimize industry and product structure adjustment. Using the principles of ecological economy, according to the inter-industry linkage, through the integration of materials, energy and information, the eco-industrial industrial chain will be extended and expanded to form an ecological park composed of one or more industries, and the various entities in the park will be promoted to form complementary interactions and symbiosis. A common organic industrial chain network, transforming the mode of economic growth and taking a new road to industrialization.

Shandong is a large industrial province, and water pollution mainly comes from papermaking, brewing, starch and other industries. Shandong Province first grasped the papermaking industry, which consumes more water, has heavy pollution, and has difficulty in pollution control. It has taken the lead in releasing and implementing the "Pulp and Emission Standards for Paper Industry". In 1998, there were 326 papermaking enterprises in Shandong Province, with an annual output of 2.791 million tons, profits and taxes of 1.298 billion yuan, and COD emissions of 651,000 tons, accounting for 66.1% of industrial COD. Shandong Province has actively developed the circular economy and improved the quality of regional economic operations by adopting measures such as clean production audit, environmental system certification, deadline treatment, shutdown and elimination, and standard guidance. By 2003, there were 214 papermaking enterprises in Shandong Province, with an annual output of 8,321,100 tons, profits and taxes of 5.283 billion yuan, and COD emissions of 176,000 tons, accounting for 46.8% of industrial COD. In 2003, compared with 1998, the number of enterprises decreased by 43.4%, but the output and profits and taxes increased by 198.1% and 307% respectively, and COD emissions were reduced by 73.0%. Shandong Quanlin Paper Group has passed the treatment of papermaking wastewater for more than ten years. At present, the water consumption per ton of pulp is reduced from 160m3 to 60m3; the extraction rate of black liquor is increased to 90%; the acid lignin produces organic fertilizer; the middle water is biochemical After treatment, the oxidation pond is further treated to reduce the COD emission concentration to below 150mg/L, which is close to the requirements of the third period of the local discharge standard of the papermaking industry in Shandong Province; the treated wastewater is partially reused, and part of it is used for giant reed and triple the body white poplar is watered to achieve a benign cycle of forestry-paper integration and water resources.

Since 2003, Shandong Province has gradually extended the guiding industry standards to textile printing and dyeing, petrochemical, brewing, starch, chlorination, metallurgy, electronics, machinery manufacturing, chemical, pharmaceutical and other industries, and obtained economic benefits of more than 500 million yuan, COD. The average reduction rate of emissions is over 40%, the average reduction rate of wastewater discharge is 40%~60%, and the industrial dust recovery rate is 95%.

Through years of efforts, Shandong Lubei Enterprise Group Corporation has formed three green industrial chains of ammonium phosphate-sulfuric acid-cement co-production, seawater-water multi-purpose, and salinity-heat cogeneration. The water recycling rate of the ammonium phosphate-sulfuric acid-cement industry chain reached 91.3%, the utilization rate of solid waste of the main equipment reached 100%, the utilization rate of solid waste of enterprises reached 95%, the disposal rate reached 100%, and the wastewater reuse rate reached 100%. The main pollutants such as sulfur dioxide, soot and dust all meet the national emission standards: the emission of pollutants per 10,000 yuan of output value is 0.045 tons, reaching the leading level in the domestic industry. It was called "China Lubei Eco-Industry Model" by the Ministry of Environmental Protection and awarded the title of "National Eco-industrial Demonstration Park" and "National Environmental Friendly Enterprise". The Ministry of Science and Technology named Lubei Enterprise Group as "Lubei Marine Technology Industry Base".

Third, in the social area, the establishment of a large cycle. Guided by the concept of circular economy, we will carry out series creation activities as the carrier, build a recycling-oriented society, establish an eco-industrial system among various industries and industries, advocate ecological civilization, create an environmentally-friendly industrial cluster, and gradually build a recycling-type Society, the realization of social science development.

Over the years, Shandong Province has actively carried out pilot projects at the regional social level based on pilots on points and lines. Based on the situation, it has carefully prepared circular economy plans, steadily and steadily promoted circular links at the social level, and selected Yantai Development Zone and Rizhao City in advance. For the pilot, significant results have been achieved. Yantai Development Zone was listed as a national-level eco-industrial demonstration park by the state, and Rizhao City was approved as the National Sustainable Development Experimental Zone, the National Ecological Demonstration Zone Construction Pilot City and the National Circular Economy Pilot City. At present, these two pilots are progressing in depth and breadth according to the circular economy plan.

While pursuing clean production, ISO14000 environmental management certification and guiding standards, Shandong Province adheres to the concept of circular economy and regards the series of "creation" activities carried out by the state as an effective carrier for establishing a "face" on the big cycle, cultivating and establishing A group of models that promote the coordinated development of the environment and economic society have promoted regional harmonious development.

Third, the "eight creations" activities promote the development of circular economy
On the basis of practice, Shandong Province explored the development model of "point, line and surface", and through the "eight creations" activities, the circular economy was closely integrated with the existing work, and the circular economy development model was infiltrated into daily work measures. Making creation activities become the catcher and carrier of the circular economy development model has greatly promoted the development of circular economy.

First, creating an ecological demonstration zone. Shandong Province has established 12 national ecological demonstration zones, and has built 6 national nature reserves, 3 scenic spots and 26 forest parks. The province's natural reserves accounted for 1.8% of the province's land area from 1998 to 6.1% in 2003; forest coverage increased by 1 percentage point per year.

Second, creating an environmentally friendly model city. Ten cities in Shandong Province have won the honorary title of National Environmental Protection Model City. Weihai City has taken the lead in creating a national environmental protection model city group and won the UN's 2003 UN Habitat Award. It is actively creating a national eco-city. Qingdao actively established the first sub-provincial environmental protection model city group in the country; Shandong Peninsula City is working together to create a peninsula environmental protection model city group; Linyi City has stepped up to create the first environmental protection model city in the national revolutionary old district.

Third, creating a beautiful township. Shandong Province has carried out the work of creating beautiful towns and towns within the province. At present, there are 7 state-level environmentally-friendly towns and towns and 3 provincial-level environmentally-friendly towns and towns.

Fourth, creating green communities, green schools, and ecological residential communities. There are 9 state-level green schools and 50 provincial-level green communities in Shandong Province. The provincial government has approved Qingdao Olympic International Garden and Taishan Panlong Mountain Resort as pilot projects for the construction of provincial-level ecological residential communities.

Fifth, creating an ecological industrial park. Strictly implement the national macro-control policies and build eco-industrial demonstration parks with high standards. At present, 13 provincial industrial demonstration parks have been established.

Sixth, creating an environmentally friendly company. Shandong Province has launched the "National Environmentally Friendly Enterprise" activity in the province. Lubei Chemical Group and Qingdao Port Co., Ltd. were rated as the first batch of environmentally friendly enterprises in the country by the Ministry of Environmental Protection, and commended 43 provincial-level environmentally friendly enterprises.

Seventh, creating a pilot unit for circular economy. The Ministry of Environmental Protection approved the establishment of a national-level circular economy demonstration city and an eco-industrial demonstration park in Rizhao City and Yantai Development Zone. The province has announced 45 provincial-level circular economy pilot enterprises and two circular economy pilot counties. Eight is to create an ecological city (county, district). Shandong Province has identified 20 cities (counties and districts) as pilots for ecological demonstration counties.

The pilot project of "point, line and surface" circular economy system explored and intensively carried out by Shandong Province emphasizes that the small cycle on "point" is based on the promotion of cleaner production by enterprises, and achieves a win-win situation between economic development and environmental protection; The circulation in the industry is based on clean production audit, do a good job in ISO14000 environmental management system certification, gradually establish a local pollutant emission guidance standard system, promote the industry to actively optimize the industrial structure, transform the economic growth mode, and take a new industrialization road; The big cycle on the "face" is supported by "points and lines", with the social area as the unit, guided by the circular economy plan, with the series as the carrier and the establishment of the recycling society as the goal, promoting the harmonious development of man and nature. "Points, lines, and faces" is an organic whole that is progressive, interrelated, and symbiotic.

The technical economy and institutional basis of the development model of circular economy in the eastern region

Other eastern regions have also carried out pilot practices of circular economy which are similar to those in Jiangsu Province and Shandong Province. For example, Zhejiang Province has formulated a resource-saving economic action plan to build a strategic position for building advanced manufacturing bases and ecological provinces, saving resources and developing. Circular economy, improve resource utilization efficiency, ease the constraints of development factors, and promote the transformation of industrial economic growth mode from high consumption and high emission to resource conservation and ecological environment. Summarizing the model of circular economy development in the eastern region, it can be found that it has some common characteristics, which are inseparable from the technical and economic conditions and related institutional foundations in the eastern region, including the resource and environmental situation, the stage of economic development, the level of environmental management, and the technical ability. The degree of market development and institutional reforms have formed a spontaneous strategic transformation model for the development of circular economy in the eastern region. This development model is based on a certain technical economy and institutional development. Here, Jiangsu Province is taken as an example to analyze the technical economy and institutional basis of the model.

Resource and environmental situation, economic development stage and environmental management level promote circular economy

On the issue of resource and environmental bottleneck constraints, Jiangsu seems to be more severe than the rest of the country. 80% of Jiangsu's energy supply is supplied outside the province. The current power shortage is 8 million kW·h, and there is a serious shortage of industrial raw materials. The industry is basically an industrial system of "two heads out". Jiangsu Province, which accounts for 1% of the country's land area, feeds 1/6 of the country's population and produces 1/10 of the national economy. The contradiction between supply and demand of natural resources, energy, land and water resources is very prominent. At the same time, the characteristics of the heavy chemical industry are very obvious. The proportion of the secondary industry in the economic structure is 60%. The resource-intensive and polluting industries such as steel, cement, building materials, petrochemicals and printing and dyeing account for a large share of the secondary industry. Since 2000, there have been only 172 steel construction projects with a total investment of 69.3 billion yuan; 26 cement construction projects with an investment of 5.4 billion yuan. The economic aggregate and structural problems have overwhelmed Jiangsu's resource environment. According to the national pollution total control target, Jiangsu Province is already saturated in the total discharge of major pollutants such as water and gas, and the environmental capacity, especially the water environment capacity resources, is almost exhausted. The exhaustion of total quotas and environmental capacity has already had a serious constraint on the sustainable development of Jiangsu's economy. Therefore, Jiangsu faces greater pressure to change its economic growth mode and improve its ecological efficiency, with stronger demand and more urgent tasks.

From the perspective of economic development level and industrialization characteristics, the timing of Jiangsu's industrial upgrading and transformation, especially in southern Jiangsu, has arrived. Even without the concept of circular economy, upgrading and transformation characterized by reducing resources and energy consumption, improving economic efficiency, and reducing pollution emissions are also It will happen. The per capita GDP of the southern part of Jiangsu is currently about 5,000 US dollars. If it is converted according to the international concept of actual purchasing power, it is equivalent to 15,000 US dollars, which has reached the income level of the middle or even the upper country. Such a level of economic development means not only the affluence of the people, but also the inevitability of higher technological and economic capabilities and industrial upgrading and transformation of enterprises and the entire economic system. In comparison, Sunan is currently in the post-industrialization stage. The experience of developed countries shows that coordinating the ecological efficiency of factors such as resource consumption, economic output and pollution emissions is the core goal pursued by post-industrial society. This judgment is consistent with the conclusion made by the famous economist Wu Jing-lian on his economic transformation after his investigation in southern Jiangsu. The "green investment" and "node investment" that are currently practiced in southern Jiangsu are practical cases. Before the implementation of the circular economy, Zhangjiagang began to raise the threshold for attracting investment. The concept of investment promotion has been upgraded from the beginning of the development process to the current "pick and pick", and the "grab project" has been selected. ". The introduction of the project adheres to the principle of "three no-management". Projects with low scientific and technological content and heavy environmental pollution will not be carried out. Projects with large resource consumption and poor economic returns will not be implemented, and projects that do not conform to the national industrial policy will not be implemented. Since 2000, more than 350 industrial projects have been rejected and dissuaded.

Advanced environmental management and high environmental status provide a good political and social stage for the environmental protection department to advocate circular economy. In comparison, the advanced environmental management work in Jiangsu Province, especially in southern Jiangsu, is an indisputable fact. The higher environmental status is manifested in two aspects: First, the people's needs have entered a higher stage, the ecological environment needs to become an important part of life, the people support environmental protection; second, the government's work content and focus change with the needs of ordinary people. With continuous adjustment, the environmental protection department has become an important member of the government's comprehensive decision-making. There has been a major shift in the past when the Environmental Protection Director sought the mayor and the mayor now looks for the Environmental Protection Director. In the decision-making process, Zhangjiagang and Changshu have established an expert consultation system. Major issues do not listen to expert opinions and do not make decisions; establish a joint meeting system for major departments, and do not listen to opinions from environmental protection departments for major development issues; establish publicity and hearing systems, and major issues are not Listening to the opinions of the masses does not make decisions, so that environmental protection, economic construction, and social development are simultaneously considered, deployed, and promoted simultaneously.

It can be seen that the resource and environmental situation, the stage of economic development and the level of environmental management have made the circular economy "in time" in Jiangsu, especially in southern Jiangsu. The concept of circular economy conforms to the needs of local economic upgrading and transformation, and provides a timely practice mode for local Grasp the hand.

Market promotion and technical support are the foundation. Government guidance, corporate practice, and public participation are principles and mechanisms

First, the circular economy is an economy supported by advanced production technologies and key connectivity technologies, and is an economy supported by knowledge and information. Therefore, the circular economy must be a high-end economic model based on technological progress and innovation support systems, and requires a technical support system with high technical content and high added value. These technologies can be summarized as: technologies to improve the efficiency of natural resource use, alternative technologies for non-renewable resources, technologies for the development and utilization of renewable energy: key technologies for eco-industry; and economically viable resource recycling technologies, including products and services. Various types of reduction, reuse and recycling technologies; information service platform technology. It is the high-tech that extracts protein fiber from soy protein. Changshu Jianghe Tianrong Fiber Co., Ltd. can connect soybean planting, soybean oil processing, fiber extraction, textile, bio-organic fertilizer and general planting. The technical level of Sunan enterprises is generally high, especially the production technology of a large proportion of foreign-funded enterprises and domestic large enterprises is basically synchronized with the international level. For example, Shagang Group, a private enterprise of Zhangjiagang, has introduced the international advanced technology and equipment in the same period twice, making its comprehensive technical and economic strength at the forefront of the country.

Second, the circular economy must be a market economy. This means that the market mechanism is the basic enterprise of circular economy operation is the main body of circular economy practice. From the perspective of the Sunan model, the market mechanism plays two important roles in the circular economy. First, the circular economy must conform to the laws of the market, and it must be profitable for the enterprise to make money. Only in this way can circular economy practice continue and enterprises be proactive. The reason why the South Jiangsu region has achieved significant benefits in the pilot economy of the enterprise level is that the market mechanism is playing a role. It is also the reason of the market mechanism that the current pilot project in Sunan is top-down in launching the organization. In the specific practice, it is bottom-up. The role of government departments such as environmental protection is service and technical guidance. Second, with a good market mechanism and environment, advanced production technologies and key link technologies will follow, and the two complement each other. Therefore, the green investment that is generally implemented in southern Jiangsu will work. For example, the birthplace of high-tech extraction of protein fiber from soy protein is Henan, but it eventually landed in Changshu City, where the market environment is an important reason.

The characteristics of the above-mentioned technologies and market mechanisms determine the basic positioning of the government in promoting circular economy work, and create, cultivate and standardize the market environment for the development of circular economy, that is, government guidance. To fulfill this function orientation, we must first establish an institutional system for the development of circular economy, including laws and regulations, economic incentive policies and standards systems; secondly, provide technical and information services.

The circular economy is a new thing. It is a leap-forward strategy for China to promote the transformation of economic development mode in the middle stage of industrialization. This determines the government's guidance, but also must have a powerful initiative, a strong organizational leadership system and a scientific and unified plan. . Therefore, China's circular economy management mechanism must be top-down in launching, and bottom-up in specific operations. At the same time, public participation is not only to create a good social atmosphere for the development of circular economy, but also the public has direct responsibilities and obligations in many areas of circular economy development such as green consumption, resource conservation and waste recycling.

In summary, at the project level of the circular economy in southern Jiangsu, market promotion and advanced technology support are the basic forces; in the macro management mechanism, a mechanism of government guidance, enterprise practice, and public participation is formed, but in the mechanism There are many areas that need improvement and improvement.

Strict environmental law enforcement promotes the development of circular economy

For enterprises, if there is no certain expectation of interest, they will not actively implement the circular economy. At this time, from the perspective of pollution control and environmental control, through strict law enforcement, enterprises can be driven from passive to active. The experience of Jiangsu Taicang Xintai Alcohol Co., Ltd. is the best interpretation of this mechanism.

For enterprises, if there is no certain expectation of interest, they will not actively implement the circular economy. At this time, from the perspective of pollution control and environmental control, through strict law enforcement, enterprises can be driven from passive to active. The experience of Jiangsu Taicang Xintai Alcohol Co., Ltd. is the best interpretation of this mechanism.

Xintai Alcohol Co., Ltd. is a manufacturer that produces cassava as raw material. The high concentration of organic wastewater generated in the alcohol production process causes serious pollution to local water bodies, and its COD emissions account for 70% of Taicang City. In the Taihu Lake Pollution Control Zero Action, the company was listed as a key deadline for governance, and the company faced two choices: either to completely control pollution or to be shut down. With the strong support and help of Taicang Environmental Protection Bureau, the company carried out technical research on alcohol wastewater treatment and invested 20.6 million yuan to establish a sewage treatment facility. In March 1999, Xintai Company's wastewater was fully discharged to the standard. At the same time, the 10,000 m3 of biogas generated in the sewage treatment process was returned to the production boiler, which produced good economic benefits. After technological transformation, the amount of biogas generated in sewage treatment facilities increased to 12 million tons in 2003, and the economic benefit was 4 million yuan. After deducting the operating cost of pollution control facilities of 3 million yuan, the net profit was 1 million yuan. Through pollution control and energy substitution, the company can discharge 4,500 tons of COD57261, BOD3400U suspended solids, 216 tons of sulfur dioxide and 360 tons of soot per year. At present, the company has formed two recycling systems: alcohol waste liquid-sewage treatment system-sludge recovery biogas, biogas instead of coal, reducing waste water and exhaust emissions; separation sludge-organic compound fertilizer or separation sludge-mixed with coal The boiler burns. With the help of the environmental protection department, Xintai plans to develop a recycling chain for wastewater reuse, that is, to treat sewage-deepening treatment-boiler water, reduce the amount of fresh water, and reduce the total amount of COD, BOD and suspended solids.

Of course, in this process, you must use big sticks and carrots. It must be strictly enforced, and it must be supported and motivated by technology and funds. In this way, the best results can be achieved and a partnership between the government and the enterprise can be formed.

The main practice of Changshu Municipal Government in promoting the development of circular economy

Changshu has developed economy, dense population and relatively shortage of resources. Economic development and population growth have brought great pressure on the resources and environment. At present, the environmental capacity is basically saturated, and the bottleneck effect of resources and environment on regional economic development has become increasingly prominent. In order to fundamentally solve the contradiction between regional social and economic development and resources and environment, Changshu City proposed the strategic concept of building an ecological city and developing a circular economy in 2002, vigorously promoted the development of regional circular economy, achieved achievements and accumulated experience.

The main practices of Changshu City in promoting circular economy are as follows:

First, strengthen organization and leadership, and give full play to the guiding role of the government. Changshu has set up a "Changshu City Eco-city Construction and Development Circular Economy Leading Group" with the mayor as the team leader, responsible for the unified organization and coordination of the city's eco-city and circular economy construction.

Second, the government strictly controls the construction projects at the source, and implements the "first-level responsibility system", "environmental first approval authority system" and environmental protection "one-vote veto" system. Implementing green investment and preferential investment, the chemical projects with an investment of less than 10 million yuan and the printing and dyeing projects with an investment of less than 100 million yuan will not be approved; all new industrial projects must enter the industrial park; Changshu Economic Development Zone stipulates foreign investment projects. Projects with an average investment intensity of less than $300,000 and a registered capital of less than RMB 1.5 million for domestic investment shall not be approved.

Third, strengthen the promotion of ecological city construction and the development of circular economy. In Changshu's main media, we opened up a circular economy column, publicized the knowledge and ideas of circular economy, and reported on the typical demonstration and key projects of circular economy with high density. We led the leading cadres, enterprises and the public to participate in the construction of ecological city and circular economy, and established "Ecological Changshu". The quarterly publication, compiled the "Changshu Citizen Environmental Protection Handbook", and launched activities such as green communities, green enterprises, and green schools to comprehensively promote the development of circular economy and ecological city.

Fourth, the government formulates policies and measures to promote the development of circular economy in accordance with the principle of "point-to-face, typical approach, overall planning, and step-by-step implementation". Specific measures include: the government allocates funds to reward the typical circular economy, promotes the circular economy in a point-to-face manner; promotes the clean production audit and ISO14001 environmental management system within the enterprise, builds the enterprise ecological culture, and promotes the development of the internal circular economy; based on science and technology and the market, Construct ecological industrial chain and promote the development of ecological industry. Among them, Changshu soybean protein fiber ecological industrial chain is a prominent representative; financial funds support, attract private capital, accelerate the construction of township environmental infrastructure, improve the concentration of industrial and domestic pollution centralized disposal, reduce environmental pollution load The subsidy policy encourages the comprehensive utilization of manure in the aquaculture industry, promotes the development of ecological agriculture with the concept of circular economy, accelerates the integration of urban and rural areas, combines pollution control with points and surfaces, and builds beautiful towns and towns to achieve coordinated urban and rural development.

Revitalization of the Northeast Old Industrial Base and the Development Mode of Circular Economy in Liaoning Province

Liaoning Province is a pilot province for the pilot construction of circular economy in the country. Through the development of circular economy, the transformation of old industrial bases and the economic transformation of resource-exhausted cities, the transformation of economic growth mode from extensive to intensive, and the reconstruction of old industrial bases. The mode of economic development.

1. The relationship between the development of circular economy and the strategy of revitalizing the old industrial bases in Northeast China

After the founding of New China, the state concentrated on investing in a strategic industry and backbone enterprises with considerable scale in energy, raw materials and equipment manufacturing in the Northeast. The old industrial base in Liaoning has formed an independent and complete industrial system and national economic system for China, and has made historic and significant contributions to reform, opening up and modernization. With the continuous deepening of reform and opening up and the continuous reduction of the stock of resources, the deep structural, institutional and resource environment accumulated by the old industrial base has become increasingly prominent, and many difficulties and obstacles are faced in further development. In the "structural" problem, the resource-based industry and economic structure is an important aspect. "High consumption, low efficiency, high emissions" is a prominent feature of the economic growth mode under this structure. The consequence is that resources are getting less and less, many resources are almost exhausted, and pollution is getting heavier. Although governments at all levels have made great efforts in recent years, there is still no way to fundamentally change the serious pollution.

Therefore, structural adjustment, industrial upgrading, taking a new road to industrialization, and transforming the mode of economic growth are important strategic measures for revitalizing old industrial bases. This has been well reflected in the "Revitalization Plan of the Old Industrial Base" in Liaoning Province. However, how to implement this revitalization strategy, in addition to the transformation of mechanisms, institutional innovation, and the support of major projects, is important to the renewal of ideas and the transformation of development strategies. The circular economy provides a new economic development concept and development model for realizing this transformation, which is suitable for the actual situation in Liaoning.

Many problems arising from the old industrial bases are the special difficulties and challenges facing Liaoning. However, the revitalization of the old industrial base is an opportunity for Liaoning to develop a circular economy and reproduce its historical glory. Liaoning Province combines the revitalization of old industrial bases, and has carried out circular economy construction work in a planned, step-by-step, large-scale and all-round way, in the transformation of old industrial enterprises, economic transformation in resource-exhausted areas, adjustment and transformation of old industrial areas, and economic development zones. The integration and improvement, the recycling of waste resources and other aspects have achieved initial results, and the development momentum is good, which has important demonstration significance for the development of circular economy and the new industrialization road.

2. The "3+1" mode of developing circular economy in Liaoning Province

Liaoning Province has formulated a pilot program for the development of circular economy, launched a pilot program of circular economy, and explored a practical "3+1" development model for circular economy in

Liaoning Province. This development model is similar to the "point, line, and surface" model of Shandong Province and has certain reference and demonstration effects for other parts of the country.

The so-called "3+1" mode, "3" refers to three cycles, and "1" refers to one industry.

The first is a small cycle, combined with technological transformation, the implementation of cleaner production and the creation of "zero emission" enterprises, and achieved significant economic and environmental benefits. More than 350 enterprises in the province have completed clean production audits, and implemented more than 6,000 clean production audit programs. The annual economic benefits are 1.2 billion yuan, water saving is 150 million tons, energy saving is 150 million kW·h, and annual wastewater reduction is 1.6. 100 million tons, COD 14,000 tons, sulfur dioxide 14,000 tons, smoke dust 25,000 tons. Combined with the total discharge of wastewater and the concentration of pollutants in the "two-way control", efforts were made to carry out the "zero emission" work of rolling steel, beneficiation coal washing wastewater and power plant ash water to improve water reuse. At present, more than 50 enterprises such as Iron and Coal Group and Beipiao Power Plant have basically realized zero discharge of wastewater. In the construction of a circular economy demonstration enterprise in a number of large-scale joint enterprises such as Anshan Iron and Steel. Anshan Iron and Steel has built more than 40 comprehensive utilization projects such as steel slag development, converter gas recovery and water reuse. The water recycling rate has reached 91.7%, achieving the "zero emission" of metallurgical slag, blast furnace gas, converter gas and coke oven gas. Since December 2003, the three 100-ton converters of the No. 2 Steelmaking Plant of Anshan Iron and Steel Co., Ltd. have realized "negative energy steelmaking", which basically formed the prototype of the development of circular economy.

Secondly, the middle cycle, combined with the economic transformation of resource-exhausted areas, the integration of economic development zones and the adjustment and transformation of old industrial areas, the construction of ecological industrial parks, and improve the quality of regional economic operations. The three pilot projects of Fushun Mining Group, Dalian Development Zone and Shenyang Tiexi New District were organized to carry out the construction of eco-industrial parks. Fushun Mining Group takes the "one mine, four plants and one gas" conversion project as the backbone, and relies on key technological innovation and system integration to build an ecological industrial park integrating coal mining, oil refining, power generation, building materials and development of coalbed methane; Dalian economic and technological development By re-integrating the energy flow, water flow, material flow, waste flow, information flow, etc. of the park enterprises, the district introduces key link projects, builds eco-industrial parks, realizes resource recycling, and improves the quality of park construction. 8 ecological linkage projects such as comprehensive utilization of waste and waste household appliances, recycling of industrial media (phosphorizing solution, cutting fluid), wood-plastic composites instead of wood, comprehensive utilization of fly ash and sewage resource utilization; industrial ecology of Shenyang Tiexi New District The concept of learning and circular economy has fully started the construction of eco-industrial parks. At present, 47 enterprises are involved in the formation of 9 industrial eco-industrial chains, forming five eco-industrial recycling networks, building industrial ecosystems, consumer ecosystems and supporting safeguard systems, and promoting Eco-industrial cycle and consumption ecological cycle. The Ministry of Environmental Protection has approved the construction of the National Eco-industrial Demonstration Park by Dalian Development Zone and Fushun Mining Group.

Once again, it is a big cycle. In accordance with the principle of "reduction, recycling, and harmlessness", we will vigorously carry out urban water reuse and waste separation and utilization, and improve the utilization rate of social renewable resources. In combination with the construction of urban sewage treatment plants, vigorously carry out urban water reuse. Among the 16 sewage treatment plants that have been built in the province, Dalian Malan River Wastewater Treatment Plant and Anshan Western First Wastewater Treatment Plant have been used for water reuse. The daily return consumption is 810,000 tons, which is mainly used for industrial, urban river landscape and greening water. Focusing on Shenyang and Dalian, we will actively build water reuse projects in residential quarters, schools, hospitals, hotels, large enterprises, government agencies, etc. The province has built more than 80 projects and reused 25,000 tons of water. Since 2007, Shenyang City has built 50 water reuse projects every year, achieving an annual increase of 20,000 t/d of recycled water. Shenyang City has established a solid waste information exchange platform, which has initially realized the exchange and utilization of available waste between enterprises, industries and regions. The creation of a "green community" campaign with the theme of waste sorting has been launched throughout the province.

"1" refers to the resource recycling industry and the recycling of waste resources, focusing on fly ash and coal gangue, recycling resources and cultivating new economic growth points. The province has successively built a batch of fly ash and coal gangue comprehensive utilization projects such as Iron and Coal Group Hollow Brick Factory and Chaoyang Hua-long Group. In 2003, the comprehensive utilization of fly ash and coal gangue in the province reached 5.03 million tons and 4.05 million tons respectively, which was 2 million tons and 1.5 million tons respectively increased compared with 2000.

Strategic significance of developing circular economy to realize leap-forward development in the western region

1. Overview of the development model of circular economy in the western region

Guiyang is located in the southwestern part of China. Compared with other parts of the western region and other parts of China, there are unfavorable factors such as inconvenient transportation conditions, lack of funds and technology, lack of human resources, and ecological fragility. Due to the economic level restrictions, the consumption level is low, the radiation belt is not enough, and the product market needs to be continuously cultivated.

In the past 20 years of reform and opening up, Guiyang's GDP has increased by 9.6 times, with an average annual growth rate of 10.4%. However, the input of major resources has increased by 3.3 times, with an average annual growth rate of 6.3%, much higher than the national average. The resource input of Guiyang has been showing a steady upward trend. The total resource input has increased from 4.43 million tons to

19.03 million tons, an increase of 3.3 times and an average annual growth rate of 6.3%. Although the total input per unit of GDP in the same period showed a downward trend, it fell by about 60% in 24 years (as of 2002), but the decline was limited. On the contrary, the per capita resource input in the 24 years (until 2002) increased from 1.89 tons/person to 5.63 tons/person, an increase of nearly 2 times. Judging from the relationship between GDP growth and total resource input growth, Guiyang's GDP growth still depends on the increase in total resource input, and the total amount of resources invested is large. Guiyang's economic development and resource consumption are far from being "decoupled".

From the perspective of the structure of resource use, non-renewable resources such as coal mines, phosphate rock and metal minerals (mainly aluminum mines) account for a considerable proportion. As an extensive resource-based city that relies heavily on local (non-renewable) resources, Guiyang is faced with a dual strategic choice of short-term resource extension and long-term resource dependence weakening. If we continue to maintain the existing economic development model and pollution control (BAU scenario), by 2020, while economic growth will triple, the required resource input and pollution emissions will reach three times the current level. The existing resource input and pollution emission levels have brought tremendous pressure on the ecological environment and caused the deterioration of the ecological environment. If we maintain a higher level of resource input and pollution emission levels in the next 20 years, it will inevitably bring greater disasters to the ecological environment, and will also prevent the economy from maintaining sustained and rapid growth.

Guiyang's economic development has shown a strong "high resource input, high pollution emissions" characteristics, and is an extensive resource-dependent development model. The high resource consumption and high pollution emissions brought about by this economic development model will inevitably bring about a wide range of irreversible regional environment and ecological disasters. Therefore, changing the development model and realizing the "decoupling" between economic development and material input is Guiyang. Major development strategy issues that must be addressed.

The western region like Guiyang is at the beginning of the medium-term industrialization process. At this stage, with the acceleration of industrialization and urbanization, the level of economic development continues to increase, and resources and environmental pressures are also increasing. The development model, the current resource constraints and environmental pressures will not be able to withstand the traditional development model characterized by large investment, large pollution, small output and high consumption. It can no longer take the path of economic growth at the expense of high resource investment and sacrifice of the environment. This requires a western region like Guiyang City to take advantage of the post-development and take the path of leaping development.

The development model of circular economy provides advanced ideas, methods and ways for the western region to achieve leap-forward development. Therefore, when exploring the development model of circular economy, Guiyang City fully considered the combination of circular economy and market economy, the combination of ecological city structure and function, the combination of sustainable development and the construction of a comprehensive well-off society, guided by economic laws and ecological laws. To achieve the unification of economic, social and environmental benefits and realize the leap-forward development of Guiyang City.

The mode of developing circular economy in Guiyang has important demonstration significance for other western regions. In the long-term domestic division of labor, the industrial structure in the western region is very unreasonable. One of its characteristics is that the energy and raw materials industries with high resource consumption and high pollution emissions account for a large proportion; second, the traditional industries account for a large proportion. Most of the traditional enterprises are backward in technology and outdated equipment, which can neither compete with advanced enterprises in the east and cause environmental pollution. In 2002, the GDP and industrial added value of the western region accounted for 18% and 15% of the national total, respectively, but its industrial waste gas and sulfur dioxide emissions accounted for 24% and 30% of the national total. The pollutants emitted by the western region will be 1 to 5 times higher than the eastern region. Therefore, in the western region, only by changing the economic growth mode at the expense of energy consumption and consumption, and vigorously developing a circular economy characterized by low energy consumption and recycling, valuable resources in the western region can be effectively protected and sustainable exploited. The economy of the western region can develop healthily. Therefore, the circular economy has important strategic significance for the leaping development of the western region.

The development of circular economy in the western region is a leap-forward strategic transformation due to the development stage and technical and economic conditions, that is, advanced development strategies and roads are selected before industrial upgrading and economic transformation. The technical and economic difficulties it faces are naturally much larger than those in the east. It is relatively easy to advance on the spot and in part. The comprehensive advancement will face many challenges. Therefore, in the development model of circular economy, the western region should combine the advantages of local resources to transform the existing industrial system, realize the optimization and upgrading of industrial systems as the core and priority areas, and build a circular economy development model.

In terms of policy needs, the development of circular economy in the western region requires more external support, such as economic policy support and funding needs. Therefore, the state should give strong external support; and integrate capital, technology and special policy support into the preferential policies for the development of the western region. At the same time, special support is needed for the development of the local circular economy.

2. The mode and practice of developing circular economy in Guiyang City

As a resource-based city, Guiyang City faces the triple pressure of resource depletion, low resource recycling rate and large amount of pollution discharge. It shows the characteristics of "high resource input and high pollution emission". The extensive resource-dependent model has been developed. It has brought a wide range of irreversible regional and ecological disasters to Guiyang. The construction of circular economy provides a feasible way and strategy for realizing the great leap of economic and social development, improving economic efficiency and improving the development potential of the city. The development of circular economy in Guiyang is closely integrated with the strategy of building an ecological city. In 2004, Guiyang City formulated a circular economy eco-city construction plan, which defined the development model and goals of the circular economy in Guiyang.

The construction of Guiyang's circular economy eco-city adheres to both production and consumption, and fully considers the overall impact of the city's overall activities on the ecological environment. The overall idea of   Guiyang's circular economy eco-city construction is to take benefit as the center, take the project as the carrier, take the reform as the breakthrough, and use the science and technology as the driving force to integrate the construction of the circular economy industrial system and the construction of the eco-city, and become a comprehensive well-off society in Guiyang. The implementation provides a leap-forward development model. The model of building a circular economy eco-city in Guiyang can be summarized as "two links, three core systems and eight recycling systems", including:

(1) Grab two key links. One is the transformation of the production link model; the other is the transformation of the consumption link model.

(2) Building three core systems. The first is the framework of the circular economy industrial system, involving three major industries; the second is the construction of urban infrastructure, focusing on water, energy and solid waste recycling systems; the third is the construction of ecological security systems, including Green building, human settlements and ecological protection systems.

(3) Promote the construction of the eight major recycling systems. The first is the phosphorus industry recycling system; the second is the aluminum industry cycle + ring system; the third is the Chinese herbal medicine industry cycle system; the fourth is the coal industry cycle system: the fifth is the ecological agriculture cycle system; It is the recycling system of architecture and urban infrastructure industry; the seventh is the tourism and circular economy service industry system; the eighth is the cyclical consumption system.

Under the guidance of circular economy planning, Guiyang City has enacted the Guiyang City Construction Circular Economy City Regulations in line with the actual needs of Guiyang. This is China's first local basic regulation on the development of circular economy. Legal means to promote the development model of circular economy and guide pollution prevention and sustainable production and consumption. Guiyang City has also launched a number of pilot projects for circular economy and has made certain progress. Among them, Shandong Yankuang Group has decided to cooperate with Kaiyang Phosphate Mining Group to invest 2.5 billion yuan to jointly participate in the development and construction of Kaiyang Phosphorus Coal Chemical (National) Eco-industrial Demonstration Base. More than 20 eco-industrial projects based on the concept of circular economy have been planned to have cooperative investment partners, and some projects have started construction.

3. Limitations of the development model of circular economy in pilot areas
At present, there are basically two situations in the demonstration model of circular economy experiment in various places: First, it has a more systematic model system. Liaoning proposed the "3+1" model, namely,

three cycles of enterprises, parks and regions and one comprehensive utilization of waste resources; the Jiangsu model includes recycling industry, recycling agriculture, recycling tertiary industry, recycling society; Guiyang and The pattern of Shandong has similarities with the Liaoning and Jiangsu models, but the degree of classification varies according to local characteristics. Second, there is no systematic model system, only to explore a certain aspect or type, such as cleaner production, eco-industrial parks, and ecological agriculture.

These models are practical models put forward by localities according to local conditions, and have played an important guiding role in the local demonstration of circular economy experiments. However, these models also have obvious traces of understanding of circular economy. There are some shortcomings, and it is still difficult to guide the whole country. The practice requires system improvement. For example, the "3+1" mode has two drawbacks: one is that the logical correspondence is not good. "3" refers to the characteristics of three levels of circular economy, namely "small cycle", "middle cycle" and "big cycle"; "1" suddenly emphasizes an industry. In addition, the expressions of the large, medium and small cycles are easily misunderstood, thinking that the development of circular economy is to construct a variety of loops, which is ambiguous about the essence of circular economy. Second, the connotation is narrow. From the textual expression, it seems that only the industrial system is emphasized, and other industries in the production field, such as ecological agriculture, are not clearly defined; at the same time, the content of the relevant consumer field is not clear or imperfect.

The "circular industry, recycling agriculture, recycling-type tertiary industry and recycling-type society" in the Jiangsu model is not popular enough, and it is separated from the concepts of "ecological industry and ecological agriculture" that have been widely accepted. In fact, the circular economy is not a passive water, no roots, but a concept and practice model at the meso level, which is based on inheriting the existing sustainable development theory and practice. It is an ecological economy. Clean production, ecological industry, ecological agriculture, new energy and energy technologies, green consumption, etc. All the theories and technologies that are conducive to the realization of "low consumption, high efficiency, low emissions" of social and economic activities. Therefore, there is no need to create new ideas that are different from the widely accepted eco-industrial and ecological agriculture. In addition, the "circular society" in the Jiangsu model mainly refers to the circular economy practice in the consumption field, especially the waste recycling industry, but the current name is easy to cause ambiguity, because the extension and connotation of the recycling society and the circular economy are currently There is still much controversy in the theoretical academic community.

In summary, at present, it is necessary to overcome the limitations of the practice process according to the specific practice of China's circular economy and the connotation of circular economy development, study the model and strategic focus of China's circular economy development, and select priority areas for the country, nationwide. Promote circular economy to provide decision support.

1.2 China's future circular economy development model and strategic focus

According to the definition of the circular economy and the essential characteristics of China's circular economy, the development model or strategic focus of China's circular economy can be summarized into two key areas and four key industrial systems.

The two key areas are that the focus of the circular economy is to capture the production and consumption sectors; the four key industrial systems are the eco-industrial system, the eco-agricultural system, the green service industry system, and the recycling and disposal of waste resources. Known as the "venous" industry). The construction of eco-industrial system, eco-agricultural system and green service industry system is an important part of national economic industry and the main body and important symbol of circular economy in production. The industrial system for recycling and harmless disposal of waste resources consists of three parts: industrial waste resource recycling industry, domestic waste resource recycling industry and final waste harmless disposal industry. It is not only one of the key points in the field of consumption, but also the link between production and consumption. It is the basic symbol of a recycling society. At present, the regional circular economy in practice (the so-called "big circle") should be an organic combination of two key areas and four industrial systems supported by regional economic and environmental-infrastructure systems. In other words, only when a region has established an eco-industrial, eco-agriculture and green service industry system, can its economic growth mode be fundamentally changed, and it is possible to form a sustainable production model that constitutes a cycle and symbiosis between different industrial systems. At the same time, only by establishing a developed industrial system for the recycling and disposal of waste resources, the "resource-product-renewable resources" cycle of the entire region can be rotated to form a sustainable consumption pattern and sustainable production. The mode is docked to form a "big loop" of the area. Of course, in theory, even if the "big cycle" of the region is not an absolute and closed cycle, there will inevitably be some exchange of material and energy with other systems, especially a small part of the existing technology economy. Unusable waste at the level, which needs to be treated harmlessly and eventually discharged to the environment, through the circular economy development model, so that the final discharge to the environment is minimal.

Drawing on international experience, according to the current practice model of circular economy development, it can be seen that the two key areas and the four cyclical economic development models of the four industrial systems are mutually infiltrated and mutually supportive, and cannot be independently dispersed to form their own systems and cycles. Organically integrated. Therefore, the circular economy model at the regional level is the combination of these two key areas and four industrial systems.

Production area

The development model of circular economy in the production field is to transform and reconstruct various industries involved in the national economy, and transform it into an ecological direction. The key points include the construction of an ecological industry system, an ecological agriculture system and a green service industry system, in which the existing Industrial systems and the construction of ecological industrial systems are the core content of the production field.

Simply, the eco-industrial system is an industrial system with high ecological efficiency, or low resource consumption, high economic efficiency, and low pollution emissions. Based on existing knowledge, technical means and practical experience, the establishment of an eco-industrial system can be achieved through three levels of practice.

(1) the "small cycle" with clean production as the core at the enterprise level. All enterprises within the eco-industrial system must first implement a cleaner production enterprise, which is the basic unit of the eco-industrial system.

(2) the "middle cycle" of the eco-industrial park. There are two types of eco-industrial parks in a broad sense: one is a physical park formed by clusters of enterprises, and the parks are connected by different cycles of resources and energy flows. Most of the parks that China is currently experimenting with are of this type. The other is that there are both enterprise groups and communities in the park, and there is not necessarily a natural material dependence between the groups. For the construction of this type of park, China needs innovative concepts and standards to grasp the infrastructure and public resources (such as water) and energy in the park can be shared, each enterprise achieves a continuous improvement of clean production and environmental management system, the overall ecological efficiency of the park The key content of the largest circular economy can be, and it is impossible to artificially connect the logistics and energy flow "circulation circle" without the customer's condition and the violation of market rules.

(3) the eco-industrial network. In theory, after a company implements cleaner production, it does not necessarily maximize the social reuse of all its waste within the enterprise. There must be a part that can be used by other companies in a cost-effective manner. Discharge to the environment. In reality, it is not possible to use all of the remaining useful waste from companies that have implemented cleaner production to build a material energy chain that connects all businesses. Therefore, it is necessary to digest this part of waste by establishing an industrial waste recycling industry. At the same time, the waste-free industry will be established to safely dispose of wastes that cannot be utilized under the existing technical and economic conditions, connect all enterprises, and form an ecological industrial network. Or called the virtual eco-industrial park.

In view of the current characteristics of China's industrial industry structure, when constructing an eco-industrial system, it is necessary to give priority to industries with high energy consumption and high pollution, focus on the applicable technologies for the development of circular economy, and explore the development model of the industry. These industries include metallurgy, coal, petroleum, petrochemical, chemical, building materials, paper, and food.

The development of circular economy in the field of agricultural production should strengthen the construction of ecological agriculture system, actively adjust the layout of agricultural production and product structure, vigorously promote environmentally friendly ecological agricultural products, comprehensively utilize straw, utilize and handle the disposal of livestock and poultry manure, and vigorously develop biogas projects to solve The rural energy problem promotes the multi-level utilization and virtuous circle of the material and energy of the Agro-ecosystem, and realizes the unification of economic, ecological and social benefits. The future development focus is to improve relevant laws and regulations and incentive policy systems. On the basis of existing models, in accordance with the theoretical requirements of circular economy and national development strategy requirements, the scale of ecological agriculture will be expanded and the level of various models will be upgraded.

Generally eco-industrial and eco-agriculture are the "sources" for the development of circular economy. They are highly dependent on the level of economic development and scientific and technological progress. In the short term, it is impossible to cost-effectively and comprehensively practice, but it can be promoted in a focused and orderly manner. In comparison, according to the experience of developed countries, the consumption field is a "booster" for the development of circular economy and an important strategic link.

Consumption field

Production and consumption are mutually causal. The experience of developed countries shows that the recycling and reuse of waste in the consumer sector can provide a large amount of renewable resources to the production field, reduce the pressure of end processing, lengthen the industrial chain and create new employment opportunities. The company can strengthen the reduction, reuse, recycling and harmlessness of resources through the extension system of production responsibility. In addition, from the perspective of technical and economic feasibility, the recycling of waste in the consumer sector is more likely to make breakthroughs in China.

In the field of consumption, there are four aspects to the circular economy that China can vigorously promote. First, environmental labeling, organic food and energy-saving product certification. The second is the construction of eco-efficient buildings and the creation of green communities. The third is to advocate public green consumption, use financial and taxation and other economic means to encourage public green consumption, such as tax incentives for the production and consumption of certified green products, and impose high punitive taxes on products that waste resources and harm the environment. Wait. The fourth is the government's green procurement. From the characteristics of the government's green procurement, the single entity, the government's obligation to play a leading role, and the experience of developed countries, the government's green procurement should be one of the important measures for China's recent circular economy.

Waste resource comprehensive utilization industry

The comprehensive utilization of waste resources is a key industry in the field of circular economy development, and belongs to the node industry, which has special significance. The core content of the circular economy in developed countries is the development of comprehensive utilization of waste resources, such as the construction of ecological parks in Japan. For China, the comprehensive utilization of waste resources is also an important part of the circular economy system.

The comprehensive utilization of waste resources has a long history in China, and has formed a certain scale, resulting in considerable economic, environmental and social benefits. According to statistics, among the main materials such as steel, copper, aluminum, lead and paper in China, the proportion of renewable resources as raw materials accounts for 20%, 25%, 16%, 18% and 50% respectively. According to calculations, compared with the waste mines produced in mining mines, 1 ton of renewable resources are recycled each year, which is equivalent to reducing the amount of domestic waste generated by 4 tons, saving valuable land resources occupied by landfill due to large amount of landfill, reducing the number of Environmental pollution. In addition to economic and environmental benefits, the comprehensive utilization of waste resources can also generate social benefits, create employment opportunities through emerging industries, and solve employment problems.

American remanufacturing can arrange employment of 1 million people by 2005. Research shows that for every 100 jobs created in the remanufacturing and recycling industries, the mining industry and the solid waste safety treatment industry will lose 13 jobs. Compared with the two, it can be seen that the employment created by the remanufacturing and recycling industries Opportunities are far greater than their reduced employment opportunities.

However, the overall situation of the industry in China is still small in scale, the recovery system is not perfect, the policies are not matched, the degree of industrialization is low, and the utilization level and added value are low. This situation has intensified during the transition of the market economy, especially in the recycling and reuse of domestic garbage. As China gradually enters a consumer society, issues such as packaging, home appliances and office electronics, automobiles and building materials have begun to emerge, and they are also areas where they can make a difference. Therefore, expanding China's waste resources recycling industry is an important starting point for promoting the development of China's circular economy.

Regional level circular economy development model
The circular economy development model at the regional level is an organic combination of the above two key areas and the circular economy practice of four industrial systems. At present, the development model of circular economy at the regional level is basically closely integrated with the construction of ecological city and ecological province. That is to say, in practice, the concept and method of circular economy are the guiding ideology, and the ecological city and ecological province are Building as a carrier to jointly promote the transformation of regional economic development mode and move towards sustainable development.

As a new economic development model, circular economy is a way of material flow and resources for production, circulation and consumption in social production and reproduction activities in accordance with the principles of "reduction, reuse, recycling and harmlessness". The regulation of energy efficiency and the establishment of an economic development model with high ecological efficiency and sustainability are concepts of an economic category.

An ecological province or city is a region with productive development, rich life and good ecological environment. It is a space concept with rich and specific connotations. It indicates that under certain development stages, a region has fully achieved its sustainable development goals.

For an example, eco-city, the development model and relationship of regional circular economy are analyzed. Circular economy is an important part of eco-city. The economic system in the region is composed of industrial system and consumption system, but not all. Eco-city also includes social system, ecological environment system and infrastructure system. Only a circular economy system with low resource energy consumption, high economic efficiency and low environmental load can not achieve all the goals of sustainable development or ecological city goals, and also needs a sound and efficient infrastructure system (or the principle of circular economy). Urban functional system), beautiful ecological landscape, high-quality population, and fair social system are supported. Similarly, cities with only a beautiful and beautiful ecological environment and a fair social system (such as ancient cities) are not ecological cities. Eco-cities also have developed economies, high-level quality of life and perfect social public service systems, especially To achieve coordinated development of the economy and the environment, to achieve this coordinated development, we must take the development path of circular economy. Otherwise, the economic system of "high consumption, low efficiency, high emissions" will restrict the healthy development of the city's ecological environment system, infrastructure system and social system, and the goal of eco-city cannot be achieved. Therefore, the development of circular economy is the core content of eco-city construction, and it is an important starting point: with the concept of circular economy and circular economy system, the city will operate in the most economical and efficient way, or build the ecology in the most economical and efficient way. city. Therefore, the development model of circular economy at the regional level focuses on transforming and reconstructing regional consumption systems and regional industrial systems, and transforming the main economic activities of the region into an ecological direction. Natural ecosystems are the basic material basis for regional survival and development. Urban functional systems (urban infrastructure construction) are also important supporting systems for maintaining the normal operation of urban areas, and can infiltrate circular economy concepts and methods into all aspects of urban functional systems. The social system is the object of urban service and the body of urban management and development. The ultimate goal of circular economy development is people-oriented and serving the social system. Among the above five systems, the economic system and the ecological environment system are the main bodies of the development of circular economy. The development of regional circular economy is the main line of solving the contradiction between economic growth and resource environment, and is the two-dimensional concept of "economics and environment". Of course, the circular economy can directly or indirectly generate some social benefits, such as employment problems, but it cannot solve the problems of social distribution, fairness and security. This is the core pillar of sustainable development and a social concern. This is also the cycle. The basic difference between the economic development model and the sustainable development model is that sustainable development is three-dimensional, and circular economy is two-dimensional. Therefore, the current development of China's regional circular economy should firmly grasp two areas and transform and improve the four industrial systems.

Chapter 2 Analysis on the Policy Support for the Development of Circular Economy Model

2.1 Evaluation of China's development of circular economy policy needs

overall evaluation

Generally after two stages of concept advocacy and state decision-making, China's circular economy basically solved the problem of why to develop a circular economy at the central and provincial governments and some enterprises, and partially answered what It is a problem of circular economy. After entering the comprehensive pilot demonstration stage in 2005, especially after the implementation of the Circular Economy Promotion Law, China has encountered problems in how to promote the development of circular economy. This issue has two implications: first, what kind of policies the government have to promote the practice of circular economy; second, how the government guides, or how the implementation entities of enterprises and other specific development of circular economy, that is, what practical methods and models are followed.

Regarding the policy issues of China's development of circular economy, Zhu Dajian combined the main body of policy role, the choice of policy means and the main links of circular economy, and proposed a policy system for developing circular economy including three mechanisms and three policy tools. The three mechanisms are modern government - state administrative mechanism, enterprise - market mechanism, non-governmental organization and public - social mechanism; three policy instruments are regulatory policy, market policy and participatory policy. The administrative mechanism embodies the government's top-down efforts; social mechanisms can promote NGOs' bottom-up efforts; and market mechanisms can motivate for-profit organizations to work horizontally.

According to the object and nature of the policy, Ren Yong and others believe that China's circular economy policy system should be based on Basic Policy, Core Policy, Fundamental Policy/policy for creation of enabling genvironment and publicity. Educational policy composition. The basic policy is the most fundamental and universally applicable guiding policy for promoting the development of circular economy, and it is the core policy, basic policy and education policy. The core policy is to directly promote the key practice areas of the circular economy (such as clean production, eco-industrial parks, and waste recycling). The core policies can be divided into laws and regulations and standards, economic incentives, and administrative supervision systems. The basic policy is a policy that creates a good institutional environment for the practice of circular economy key areas, such as national macroeconomic (industry) policies, basic economic systems such as national prices, taxation, finance and property rights, performance appraisal policies such as national economic accounting and cadre performance evaluation. .

Ren Yong and others further pointed out that China's current circular economy policy is focused on core policies, as existing policies involving clean production and waste recycling are generally weak, eco-industrial, ecological agriculture, green service industries and green consumption. There are structural vacancies in the aspects of the policy; when the conditions are ripe, laws and regulations similar to the Japanese Basic Law for the Construction of Recycling Society can be formulated as the basic policy of the circular economy. Before that, the "Several Opinions" issued in 2005 can play the role of basic policies. The reform of the basic policy is a long process that needs to be gradually improved.

Funded by the United Nations Environment Programme (UNEP), the Wuppertal Institute of Sustainable Consumption and Production (Wuppertal) and the Environmental and Economic Policy Research Center (PRCEE) of the State Environmental Protection Administration of China jointly launched in Guiyang, a pilot city for circular economy. According to a survey, there are four barriers to the development of the local circular economy: funding, technology, practical experience and knowledge, legislation and policy. In terms of policy, most respondents believe that management tools and economic instruments are important policy tools for promoting circular economy; information and education have not played a significant role so far; decision-making layers should use a variety of policy instruments, such as Management, economics, information, education and cooperation (Wuppertal et al., 2006). Taking into account the four stages of China's circular economy development stage, pilot content, new policy trends and the above-mentioned existing research results, China's current circular economy priority policy or urgent policy needs at the national level have two aspects: It is to play the role of the Circular Economy Promotion Law; the second is to formulate specific policies directly targeting the key areas of circular economy practice (pilot), especially economic incentive policies.

With regard to the development model of circular economy, China has initially explored the specific practices of developing circular economy at the micro level and industrial parks of enterprises; at the social level, it has also found important ways to establish waste recycling and chemical industries. In the regional subdivision, how to deal with the relationship between the micro level of the enterprise and the industrial park level based on the principle of circular economy, and establish a complete circular economy industrial system is still a new problem. It is both a method and a model, as well as a policy issue.

Policy is a decisive factor in the critical period when circular economy development is moving from concept advocacy and experimental demonstration to comprehensive advancement. There are two ways to establish and improve a circular economy policy system: one is to sort out and integrate existing policies that are conducive to the development of circular economy; the other is to formulate new policies. From the relationship between the two and the needs of actual work, combing and integration is the most urgent task and the foundation.

Analysis of Key Economic Policy Simulation Results for Promoting China's Circular Economy Development

1. Key economic policy simulation method for circular economy development

According to the above analysis, this study selects three types of key economic policies, uses static CGE model, carries out quantitative simulation and analysis: resource price policy simulation, mainly analyzes the impact of shortage of basic resource price increase on resource consumption and macroeconomic growth rate. Tax policy simulation mainly analyzes the effect of resource saving on the increase of resources and the impact on macroeconomic growth rate; the environmental tax policy simulation mainly analyzes the taxation of environmental use, such as increasing sulfur dioxide emission tax and carbon dioxide emissions. Environmental impacts of taxes, sewage discharge taxes, solid waste discharge taxes, and macroeconomic impacts.

This study mainly uses the CGE model to simulate the effect of policy effects. The study refers to the monograph of Davis et al. on CGE model and Zhang Zhongxiang's Chinese economic-energy-environment policy analysis CCE model. Combined with the characteristics of China's dual economy, a CGE model for China's environmental policy analysis is established. This model establishes a macroeconomic model based on microeconomic theory by setting the behavioral equations of economic entities in a time and using various equilibrium mechanisms to form a macroeconomic model based on microeconomic theory. The model consists of the following eight aspects.

First, it is the production function. We set: in the production of various products, there is no substitute between the capital labor and the comprehensive intermediate input. There is no substitute between the intermediate inputs: there is an alternative between coal input and petroleum processed products. We use a multi-level nested CES function and Leonieef function to describe the relationship between the output and input of each production department that contains which includes these content.

Second, it is the factor demand. The labor demand and the intermediate input demand of each production department are derived from the maximization of profit. About the capital demand, we assume that in any year, the existing capital stock of each department cannot flow between departments. Therefore, in the base year (2002), the capital stock of each production sector is both quantitative

The third is the price. In the basic version of the CGE model, the price of all products is determined by the competitive market; in the revised version, the prices of some products (coal, oil, petroleum processing, gas, electricity) are determined by the government. Whether it is a basic or modified version, the producer price of each item is unique and does not vary from user to user.

Fourth, it is income. Residents' income consists of wages, capital gains, and government transfers. The government's income mainly comes from the income tax on residents and enterprises, the tax on domestic products, and the tariff on imports.

Fifth, it is consumption. The model assumes that urban and rural residents consume a fixed proportion of their disposable income; the structure of consumer demand is determined by the maximization of utility under budget constraints; the utility function uses the Cobb-Douglas utility function. The total consumption demand of the government is treated as an exogenous variable: the government consumption structure is different from the household consumption structure, but the two are determined in the same way.

Sixth, it is savings and investment. The disposable income of each economic entity minus consumption is their net savings. The model assumes that the total investment (fixed asset investment plus inventory changes) is equal to the total stock of livestock (net savings plus depreciation). The ratio of fixed assets investment to total fixed assets investment in each department is equal to the ratio of the profit of each department to the total profit. The total amount and structure of inventory changes are treated as exogenous variables, taking the actual value of 2002

Seventh, it is international trade. Describe the import and export of various tradeable commodities. The CGE model accepts Armington's hypothesis: there is a difference between domestic and imported products and cannot be completely replaced. At the same time, the model assumes that the world average price of imports and exports is set externally, and China is in the position of price acceptor.

Eighth, it is the market settlement and macro balance. The general equilibrium requires the commodity market to be settled and the factor market to be settled. It is necessary to point out that the settlement of the labor market does not mean that the model is necessarily a sufficient employment model: our model treats the total labor as an exogenous variable, the model The difference between the import and export is related to the exchange rate; we use the exchange rate as an endogenous variable and the difference between the import and export as an exogenous variable (or vice versa, using the exchange rate as an exogenous variable and the difference between the import and export as an endogenous variable).

It needs point out that this CGE model is a large economic model, but it is still a basic model. According to different policy mechanisms, it is necessary to expand and improve this basic CGE model.

2. Simulation results of key economic policies for circular economy development
(1) Resource tax simulation results

The resource tax design of this study considers two kinds of resource taxes: comprehensive energy resource tax (including coal resource tax and petroleum resource tax) and comprehensive mineral resource tax. The method of collection is for the resource exploitation department and the resource extraction (production). tax. The model analyzes the impact of 10% and 20% of the energy and mineral resources tax on the macro economy and the production and consumption of coal, petroleum, metal minerals and non-metallic mineral resources. It can be seen from the analysis results that the resource tax can greatly reduce resource consumption and domestic resource consumption through the regulation of the market price mechanism, and has only a small negative impact on GDP. The comprehensive tax on coal and petroleum resources, which is 20% of the value of coal and oil, will reduce coal consumption by 6.4%; reduce domestic coal resource consumption by 8.9%; reduce domestic oil resource consumption by 10.2%, and reduce GDP by less than 0.1%. . A 20% comprehensive mineral resource tax will reduce the consumption of domestic metal resources by 11.75%; reduce the consumption of domestic non-metallic mineral resources by 8.13%; reduce the production of metal minerals by 11.75%; and reduce the output of non-metallic minerals by 8.13%. Therefore, resource tax is a good policy tool to achieve resource conservation.

(2) Improve resource price policy simulation results

In order to compare with the previous resource tax, this study proposed a resource price increase plan: coal price increased by 18.5%, oil and natural gas price increased by 6.6%, gas price increased by 5.8%, petroleum processed product price increased by 5.0%, and electricity price increased by 3.2%. This program is close to the impact of 20% of the coal and petroleum resources tax on the prices of these five products.

The analysis shows that the resource-saving effect of the appropriately designed price increase plan for coal and petroleum products is basically the same as the resource-saving effect generated by the corresponding resource tax. However, the impact of the two on social distribution is very different. The resource tax increases the government's income (1.25 billion yuan) and the income of other economic entities decreases. The price increase plan reduces the income of residents and the income of other economic entities increases. The burden of price increases is generally on the residents. Although there are differences in the impact of social distribution on both, it is important that both will effectively save resources and achieve the goal of improving the efficiency of resources. At the same time, increasing resource prices will also result in high service costs (including transportation, labor, etc.), which will also promote resource efficiency. Therefore, raising resource prices is a more effective economic tool.

(3) Sewage charges simulation results

In this study, the CGE model was used to study the impact of sulfur dioxide emission charges, wastewater discharge fees, and solid waste discharge fees on the economy.

The economic impact of sulfur dioxide emissions is mainly to change the pattern of income distribution: government revenues rise, and incomes of other economic entities decline. The sulfur dioxide emission fee has little effect on the sulfur emission through the price (the sulfur rate of 2,000 yuan per ton, so that the sulfur dioxide emission reduction in the industrial sector is not 0.4%). If the government uses the sulfur fee income to purchase and build sulfur dioxide treatment equipment, it can significantly improve the sulfur treatment capacity (the sulfur fee income obtained by the sulfur rate of 2,000 yuan per ton, if it is used for the purchase of sulfur dioxide treatment equipment, it can increase 35.5%. The sulfur treatment capacity can reduce 18.3% of sulfur dioxide emissions).

The economic impact of wastewater discharge fees is mainly to change the income distribution pattern: government revenues rise and other economic entities' incomes decline. Wastewater discharge fees have little effect on wastewater discharge through price. If the government uses the wastewater discharge fee income to purchase and construct wastewater treatment equipment, it can greatly improve the wastewater treatment capacity (the emission fee income obtained from the wastewater discharge rate of 3 yuan per ton. If it is used for the purchase and construction of wastewater treatment equipment, it can be increased. 50.3% of wastewater treatment capacity).

The main impacts of solid waste discharge fees on the macro economy are: a slight decline in GDP; a rise in government revenues; a decline in income from other economic entities; an increase in investment and a decline in consumption. The impact of solid waste discharge fees on the solid waste discharge of the entire industrial sector is not very large, and the impact on the solid waste discharge of the metal mining and dressing industry is large (the solid waste discharge rate of 50 yuan per ton, making the entire industrial sector Solid waste reduced by 2.2%, which reduced the solid waste of metal mining and mining industry by 4.2%.

The economic impact of sewage charges is mainly to change the pattern of income distribution: government income rises, other economic entities decline, and the impact on GDP is small. Sewage charges have little effect on waste emissions through price. Sewage charges only have a large or small impact on the output and prices of a few sectors, and have little impact on the output and prices of other (most) sectors. If the government uses the sewage charges to purchase and construct pollution control equipment, it can significantly improve the pollution control capacity.

2.2 China's policy composition to promote the development of circular economy

In recent years, the scope of China's circular economy development has been expanding, involving agriculture, industry and tertiary industries, resources, energy use, environmental protection and other fields, becoming a change to the traditional economic development model, requiring economic guarantees. At the same time of development, we will improve the efficiency of resource and energy use, reduce the level of environmental pollution, and take the road of harmonious development between man and nature. At this stage, the key areas of China's circular economy practice are concentrated in the comprehensive utilization of waste resources and related environmental protection industries, ecological industries, resource and energy development and utilization, ecological agriculture and environmentally friendly products.

Comprehensive utilization of waste resources and related environmental protection industrial policies

The comprehensive utilization of waste resources is a connected industry within the eco-industry and between production and consumption. It is an important industry in the circular economy system and a key area for the development of circular economy in developed countries. It is called "venous" industry in Japan. China's waste utilization comprehensive utilization industry has a long history of development and has gone through two stages. The first stage was from the early liberation to the 1970s. The private and corporate joint ventures and recycling people gradually developed into two systems under the public ownership system, which were managed by the materials department and the supply and marketing cooperatives. The second stage is after the reform and opening up, the state-owned recycling system has gradually declined, and private enterprises and unorganized "picking out the army" have prominence. Another important feature of this stage is that the environmental protection industry has gradually grown and developed, forming a larger industrial system that includes comprehensive utilization of waste resources or cross-cutting. Therefore, the relevant national policies include the recycling of general waste resources (also known as waste materials), as well as the recycling, utilization and safe disposal of industrial and domestic waste.

The state has always attached importance to the comprehensive utilization of waste resources and the development of environmental protection industries. Since the 1980s, the State Council, the National Development and Reform Commission (formerly the Planning Commission), the former State Economic and Trade Commission, the Ministry of Finance, the State Administration of Taxation, and the People's Bank of China have issued more than 20 policy documents. From the policy structure, it is divided into guiding policies and economic incentive policies.

Guiding policy

Strictly speaking, China does not have laws and regulations on comprehensive utilization of resources and environmental protection industries, and it is mostly an industrial guiding policy. However, environmental protection laws and regulations, especially the solid waste law and water pollution prevention and control law have played an important role in promoting the development of environmental protection industry.

(1) Provisions on the status and direction of industrial development. In 1985, the State Council approved the Interim Provisions of the State Economic and Trade Commission on Several Issues Concerning the Comprehensive Utilization of Resources, and called for active use of resources in all areas of society. And issued the "Resources Comprehensive Utilization Catalogue", including industrial "three wastes" recycling; industrial and mining enterprises waste heat, residual pressure and low calorific value fuel (gangue, stone coal, etc.) production of heat and electricity; with forest harvesting, material truncation And products produced by processing residues. In 1989, the State Council issued the "Decision on the Key Points of Current Industrial Policies", which listed environmental protection and energy utilization as national industrial priorities. According to the "Decision on the Current Industrial Policy Key Points", the Environmental Protection Committee of the State Council has formulated "Several Opinions on Environmental Protection Industry Development" and issued the "Development Catalogue of Environmental Protection Industry". In 1991, the State Council designated energy science and new energy, high-tech energy-saving technologies, ecological science and environmental protection technologies as high-tech. In 1992, the Environmental Protection Committee of the State Council put forward some measures to promote the development of the environmental protection industry, and issued it in the form of a notice.

By 1996, the State Council approved the Notice of the State Economic and Trade Commission and other departments on the further development of comprehensive utilization of resources. The notice is a deepening of the 1985 Interim Provisions on the Implementation of Several Issues Concerning the Comprehensive Utilization of Resources. From the perspective of adapting to the economic growth mode and implementing the sustainable development strategy, the resource utilization, waste comprehensive utilization and harmless treatment are proposed. Higher requirements. The "Resources Comprehensive Utilization Catalogue" revised in 1986 was supplemented, and the scope and field of comprehensive utilization of resources were expanded, and comprehensive requirements for solid waste, wastewater (liquid), and exhaust gas were put forward.

In the 21st century, in order to implement the scientific concept of development, accelerate the construction of a resource-saving society, promote the development of circular economy, solve the resource constraints and environmental pressures faced by building a well-off society in an all-round way, and ensure the sustained, rapid, coordinated and healthy development of the national economy. The "Notice on Resource Conservation Activities" was issued, which brought the comprehensive utilization of "three wastes" and related environmental protection industry technology to a higher strategic position. In the same year, the National Development and Reform Commission revised the Catalogue of Comprehensive Utilization of Resources.

(2) Requirements for industrial development mechanisms. After the 1980s, the management mechanism of China's waste materials industry has undergone major changes. This change is reflected in the main body of the industry. The early state-run recycling system has gradually declined. Private environmental protection enterprises and "picking the army" have gradually become the industry. On the other hand, with the change of investment entities, the management mechanism of the industry is also transferred from the government plan to the market mechanism. In 1992, the "Notice on Several Measures for Promoting the Development of Environmental Protection Industry" issued by the Environmental Protection Committee of the State Council clearly stated that "the production and development of environmentally friendly products and enterprises and institutions providing services shall be brought to the market, and supply and demand shall be combined, paid services, and equal competition. The survival of the fittest will put the environmental protection industry on the track of the socialist market economy." The "10th Five-Year Plan for Environmental Protection Industry Development" also requires, "Adhere to market-oriented, technology-led, efficiency-centered, and enterprise-oriented." Principles, strengthen policy guidance, rely on technological progress, cultivate standardized markets, strengthen supervision and management, gradually establish a macro-control system for environmental protection industries that is compatible with the socialist market economic system, and unify an open, competitive and orderly operation mechanism for environmental protection industry markets."

Garbage and sewage treatment are the last and most difficult area in the transformation of resources and environmental protection industry system and mechanism. To this end, since 2002, the National Development and Reform Commission, the Ministry of Construction, the State Environmental Protection Administration, the Ministry of Finance and other ministries and commissions have jointly issued several important general guidance on the issue of waste and sewage charges, industrialization and market-oriented development, especially for accelerating the environmental protection industry. The transformation of sewage and garbage disposal systems and mechanisms has played an important role in promoting social investment entities and introducing market operation mechanisms. In many cities, marketization has not only solved the shortage of funds for the construction of sewage and garbage treatment facilities, but also improved the quality and efficiency of treatment. At present, the country has integrated the sewage and garbage disposal market into the framework of the entire public utility system reform.

(3) Planning guidance. In order to implement the Outline of the Tenth Five-Year Plan for National Economic and Social Development, on the basis of researching and analyzing the status quo and development trend of the environmental protection industry, the State has formulated the "10th Five-Year Plan for Environmental

Protection Industry" and proposed the "10th Five-Year Plan" period. The annual growth rate of the environmental protection industry should reach 15%, independently research and develop environmentally-friendly technologies and products with international advanced level, and eliminate environmentally-friendly products with backward technology, forming 3 to 5 internationally-recognized environmental protection industry companies and enterprise groups, and improve Targets such as environmental protection service level of environmental protection industry; ten areas such as air pollution prevention and control, water pollution prevention and control, solid waste treatment and disposal, water-saving technology and equipment, comprehensive utilization of resources, and environmental services The field has also proposed the formulation and improvement of environmental protection industrial policies, relying on technological progress, strengthening supervision and management, cultivating and standardizing the environmental protection industry market, and exploring measures to establish an environmental protection industry development mechanism that meets the requirements of the socialist market economic system.

Economic incentive policy

In the 1990s, China issued some economic incentives for the comprehensive utilization of waste resources, involving tax incentives, handling charges, and credit support.

(1) Tax incentives

It is the focus of the industrial policy for the comprehensive utilization of waste resources, and has been continuously strengthened and continued in recent years. In terms of income tax, the Ministry of Finance and the State Administration of Taxation issued the "Notice on Certain Preferential Policies for Corporate Income Taxes" issued in 1994, which stipulates that enterprises that use waste water, waste gas, waste residue and other wastes as the main raw materials for production may be reduced within five years or Exemption of income tax, the scope of the preferential reference refers to the "Comprehensive Utilization of Resources" published in 1985; in addition, the high-tech enterprises in the high-tech industrial development zone approved by the State Council are subject to income tax at a rate of 15%, and newly-established high-tech enterprises. Since the year of production, the income tax has been exempted for two years.

In 1994, the State Administration of Taxation and the State Planning Commission also issued the "Notice on the Comprehensive Utilization of Fixed Assets Investment Regulating Tax Resources, the Notes on the Tax Rates of Storage Facilities" and the "Notice on the Taxation of Construction Taxes for Fixed Assets Investment Directions". The detailed provisions on the comprehensive utilization of resources, especially the zero-tax rate of investment in the sewage treatment plant, waste treatment plant and transfer station. The policy has now been abolished.

In terms of VAT preferential treatment, since 1995, the state has issued five notices. In 1995, the Ministry of Finance and the State Administration of Taxation issued the "Notice on the Return of Value-Added Tax on Waste Materials Recycling Enterprises", requiring that in 1995, the VAT taxpayers engaged in the management of waste materials shall be calculated according to the current regulations. After paying the value-added tax, the VAT will be refunded first, and returned to the enterprise according to 70% of the value-added tax. In 1997, the policy was consolidated and strengthened in the form of another notification.

In response to the issue of comprehensive use of product value-added tax, the Ministry of Finance and the State Administration of Taxation issued the "Notice on the Exemption of Value-Added Tax on the Comprehensive Utilization of Some Resources" in 1995, which incorporates not less than 30% of the coal produced by the enterprise. The building materials of the bottom slag of vermiculite, stone coal, fly ash and coal-fired boilers are exempted from VAT in 1995 for gold and silver produced by enterprises using waste liquid (slag). In 1996, another similar notice called for the continuation of the policy. By 1998, the "Notice on the Comprehensive Utilization of Some Resources and Other Product Value-added Tax Policies" made some adjustments to the policy, stipulating that the electricity produced by using stone coal should be levied at half of the VAT taxable amount, and the coal-fired power plant smoke The gas desulfurization by-products implement the VAT refund policy.

For the issue of value-added tax collection for sewage charges, the Ministry of Finance and the State Administration of Taxation issued the "Notice on the VAT Policy on Sewage Treatment" issued in 2001, which stipulates that the water supply fee (company) entrusted by the governments and competent authorities at all levels shall be charged with the water fee. Sewage treatment fee is exempt from VAT.

In addition, the comprehensive utilization of resources and the environmental protection industry can enjoy preferential tax policies on high-tech, enterprise technology research and development, and domestic equipment investment. In 1991, the state designated energy science and new energy, high-tech energy-saving technology, ecological science and environmental protection technology as high-tech. These enterprises in the high-tech development zones recognized by the state can enjoy certain policies of the National High-tech Industrial Development Zone. The preferential policies in the Provisional Regulations and the Provisions of the National High-tech Industrial Development Zone Tax Policy formulated by the State Administration of Taxation, such as export products produced by high-tech enterprises, exempt from export except for products restricted by the state or otherwise regulated. tariff.

(2) Credit support policy
Strictly speaking, China has not issued a credit support policy specifically for the comprehensive utilization of waste resources and related environmental industries. However, the Notice of the People's Bank of China issued in 1995 on the implementation of credit policies and issues related to strengthening environmental protection work (hereinafter referred to as the "Notice") has a certain positive role in promoting the environmental protection industry. The "Notice" requires that financial departments at all levels should not issue loans to projects and enterprises that are prohibited by the state and do not comply with environmental protection regulations, and recover loans that have already been issued; for industries that are strictly restricted by the state, they must pass the review of the environmental protection department, Institutions can provide loans to enterprises; enterprises that are environmentally friendly and polluting should be given active loan support to promote the development of environmental protection industries from multiple levels.

(3) Processing and disposal charging policy

After the 1990s, in the comprehensive utilization of waste resources in China, especially in the relevant environmental protection industry development policies, it is innovative to treat and treat urban domestic sewage and garbage. From 1999 to 2002, the relevant ministries and commissions jointly issued three notices on the collection of domestic sewage and garbage disposal fees. The significance of this policy is not only to open up a new channel for the city government to raise funds for sewage and garbage disposal, but also to create a new market, attract private capital to enter, and create a prerequisite for the expansion of the environmental protection industry; And the comprehensive utilization of garbage has played an important role in stimulating.

Eco-industrial policy

In China's current industrial policy system, industrial restructuring policies, eco-industrial park construction and cleaner production policies are important policy elements for promoting the industrialization of industrial systems. At present, from the composition and content of these policies, the eco-industrial park policy is basically absent, and it is the key link to establish and improve in the future; the industrial structure adjustment and clean production policy have made important progress in 2004, which can basically meet the current development of circular economy. It is required that the focus for the coming period will be to implement these policies in a practical manner.

Industrial structure adjustment policy

Starting from the "Ninth Five-Year Plan", China has placed industrial restructuring on the strategic height of transforming its economic growth mode and formulated many important policies. The core task of industrial restructuring is the upgrading of industrial structure. Around this task, China has accelerated the development of funds, technology-intensive industries and equipment industries, high-tech industries, and actively use new technologies to transform traditional industries, that is, through the upgrading of industrial technology to achieve strategic adjustment of industrial structure. In terms of encouraging the development of new industries and transforming backward industries, the former State Planning Commission and the former State Economic and Trade Commission successively issued the "Currently List of Industries, Products and Technologies Encouraged by the State (Revised in 2000)" and "Removing Outdated Production Capacity and Crafts". And the catalogue of products (first batch, second batch, third batch) has played an important guiding role in guiding investment and government investment management departments to manage investment projects. In 1999, the first batch of elimination catalogues eliminated 114 backward production capacity, processes and products in 10 industries that violated national laws and regulations, backward production methods, poor product quality, serious environmental pollution, and high raw materials and energy consumption. project. In particular, in accordance with the State Council's Decision on Several Issues Concerning Environmental Protection, 84,000 small enterprises that seriously waste resources and pollute the environment were shut down nationwide; a number of backward production capacities and equipment were eliminated, and a number of high materials consumption were restricted. Highly polluting industries have promoted technological transformation of traditional industries. The transformation of economic growth mode and structural adjustment have significantly improved the energy and energy efficiency of the industry and reduced the intensity of pollution emissions. From 1990 to 2000, China's GDP per 10,000 yuan of energy consumption decreased from 5.32t of standard coal to 2.77t of standard coal, with an average annual energy saving rate of nearly 5%, and energy efficiency increased from 25% in 1980 to about 34% today. According to statistics, from 1981 to 2000, the country saved a total of about 1 billion tons of standard coal, which played an important role in controlling air pollution. According to China's 1990 consumption of 0.58 tons of carbon dioxide per ton of standard coal, 0.023 tons of sulfur dioxide, this period is equivalent to reducing emissions of about 580 million tons of carbon dioxide, about 23 million tons of sulfur dioxide.

At present, the "Provisional Regulations on the Adjustment of Industrial Structure" (hereinafter referred to as the "Interim Provisions") newly formulated by the National Development and Reform Commission is seeking opinions from the society. According to the Interim Provisions, the objective of industrial restructuring is to promote the optimization and upgrading of industrial structure in accordance with the requirements of five overall plans, and gradually form an industrial structure with high-tech industries as the guide, basic industries and manufacturing as the support, and service industry to develop in an all-round way. To improve the overall international competitiveness of the industry. The principle of industrial structure adjustment is: adhere to the people-oriented and scientific development concept, promote the sustained, rapid, coordinated and healthy development of the national economy; adhere to the industrialization driven by informationization, promote informationization by industrialization, take high scientific and technological content, have good economic benefits, and consume resources. A new industrialization road with low environmental pollution and full human resources.

According to the "Interim Provisions", the direction and focus of industrial restructuring is: to select and focus on accelerating the development of high-tech industries such as information industry, new materials and biotechnology industries. To enhance the overall quality of the industry as the core, accelerate the upgrading of industrial technology and equipment. In order to accelerate the transformation of traditional industries as a breakthrough in the implementation of "informatization to drive industrialization", encourage the use of high-tech and advanced applicable technologies to transform and upgrade traditional industries such as machinery, automobiles, steel, petrochemical, nonferrous metals, coal, light industry, textiles and building materials. Promote the upgrading of traditional industrial technology. Adhere to the promotion of industrialization while achieving coordinated development of economy and population, resources and environment, transforming economic growth mode, relying on science and technology, reducing consumption, preventing pollution, improving resource utilization efficiency, and effectively protecting the ecological environment. Support the promotion of advanced technology equipment and products that use energy conservation, consumption reduction, water conservation and environmental protection, and force the elimination of backward production capacity, processes and products with high consumption, high pollution and poor quality.

Around the "Interim Provisions", a new "Guidance Catalogue for Industrial Structure Adjustment" (hereinafter referred to as "Catalogue") was formulated. The Catalogue is divided into encouragement, restriction, and elimination. The principle of inclusion in the encouraged catalogue is: the domestic technical foundation from research and development to industrialization is conducive to technological innovation and the formation of new economic growth points; there is a large market demand in the current and future period, and the development prospect is broad. It is conducive to improving the supply capacity of shortage goods, and is conducive to the development of domestic and foreign markets; having a high technical content is conducive to promoting enterprises to adopt new technologies, new technologies and industrial technology advancements, and to improve industrial competitiveness; in line with sustainable development strategies, it is conducive to Resource conservation and comprehensive utilization, improve the ecological environment; help to give play to China's comparative advantages, especially the energy, mineral resources and labor resources of the old industrial bases in the central and western regions, the Northeast, etc.; it is conducive to expanding employment and increasing employment. The principle of inclusion in the restricted catalogue is: the production capacity is seriously overcapacity, the new project has not improved the industrial structure; the technological technology is backward, and advanced and mature technologies and technologies have been replaced; it is not conducive to saving resources and protecting the ecological environment. The principles listed in the phase-out catalogue are: serious threats to production safety; serious environmental pollution; poor product quality; high consumption of raw materials and energy.

In terms of policy measures, the Interim Provisions also made substantive provisions. For encouraged investment projects: the self-use equipment imported within the total investment is exempt from customs duties except for the goods listed in the Catalogue of Imported Goods Not Exempted from Domestic Investment Projects and the Catalogue of Imported Goods Not Exempted from Foreign Investment Projects. Import value-added tax; for enterprises located in the western region, the operating income of the encouraged industrial projects accounted for more than 70% of the total income of the enterprise, before 2010, the enterprise income tax will be levied at a reduced rate of 15%. For restricted investment projects: the government investment departments at all levels must strictly follow the relevant investment management regulations; for unrestricted restricted investment projects, the government will not invest, banks and financial institutions will not lend, land management, cities The departments of planning, environmental protection, fire protection, customs, etc. shall not go through relevant formalities: those who violate the regulations for investment and financing construction shall be investigated for the responsibility of the relevant personnel. For projects that are eliminated, investment is prohibited: all regions, departments and related enterprises shall formulate plans, take effective measures, and resolutely eliminate them within a time limit; they shall not import, transfer, produce, sell, use or adopt eliminated production capacity, processes and products; For enterprises that fail to eliminate backward production capacity, processes and products on time, the relevant departments shall limit their production to stop production. If they are forensic products, the quality inspection departments shall cancel their production licenses, and the industrial and commercial administrative departments shall revoke their business licenses and relevant financial institutions. It is necessary to stop the loan; if the circumstances are serious, the legal responsibility of the directly responsible person in charge and other directly responsible personnel shall be investigated according to law.

In summary, the "Interim Provisions on the Adjustment of Industrial Structure" is in line with the requirements of comprehensively coordinating the sustainable scientific development concept and taking the road of new industrialization. It is an important policy innovation for China's industrial restructuring under the new situation of building a well-off society in an all-round way, and promotes industrial ecologicalization. There will be an important impetus and it should be promulgated as soon as possible.

Eco-industrial park construction policy

China's eco-industrial parks have not yet established supporting policies. The former State Environmental Protection Administration only issued regulations for the initiation and regulation of pilot projects: "Regulations on the Declaration, Naming and Management of the National Eco-industrial Demonstration Park (Trial)" and "Ecology" The Industrial Demonstration Park Planning Guide (Trial) is one of the important forms of eco-industrial parks as an ecological industry. The state should attach great importance to the establishment of relevant policies.

The specific directions are:

1. Upgrade the existing eco-industrial demonstration park to a national demonstration park, expand the number of demonstrations, and provide funds and tax incentives.

Although the current eco-industrial demonstration park is named after the National Eco-industrial Demonstration Park, it is still approved and named by the Ministry of Environmental Protection. Such a demonstration of the nature of the sector is difficult to support the corresponding national support policies. The local enthusiasm and ability alone affect the speed and quality of the development of the demonstration park. Therefore, it is very necessary to upgrade the eco-industrial demonstration park to a national demonstration park, which is approved by the State Council and entrusted by the Ministry of Environmental Protection and the competent economic authorities. Expand the number and coverage of demonstration parks by region and industry type. In the construction of the park, based on the market mechanism, the state provides support in terms of treasury bonds, credit and tax incentives, and at least enjoys the same policies as economic and technological development zones and high-tech industrial parks.

2. While encouraging the construction of new eco-industrial parks, the focus should be on transforming existing economic development zones, especially economic and technological development zones and high-tech industrial parks into eco-industrial parks.

The Economic and Technological Development Zone is a labor-intensive development zone established in a certain region in the early days of reform and opening up. It mainly focuses on the expansion of the "quantity" of economic development to solve the urgent need for economic development at that time. At present, there are 54 economic and technological development zones approved by the State Council, and a large number of local approvals. The high-tech industrial park is a technology-intensive development zone established in a certain area in order to improve the technological content of economic development, with a primary focus on the improvement of the "quality" of economic development. At present, there are 53 high-tech industrial parks approved by the State Council. After a long period of rapid development, China's national economic and technological development zones and high-tech industrial parks, as well as related parks established in some places, have developed into the leading domestic economic growth and technology diffusion, and are China's industrial technology and economy. The highest level. According to the general law of industrial upgrading and transformation, the next development direction of these parks is bound to be the industrial ecologicalization with the core of reducing resources and energy consumption, increasing economic output, and reducing pollution emissions. Therefore, under the background of taking a new road to industrialization, the state must seize the inevitable laws and opportunities of industrial upgrading and transformation of the park, and actively guide and establish the relevant national economic and technological development zones and high-tech industrial parks and some local governments. The park was gradually transformed into an ecological industrial park.

3. Formulate standards for eco-industrial parks and establish incentive systems.

To fully demonstrate and build an eco-industrial park, it is important to study and develop measurement standards, which are related to the direction and level of development of eco-industrial parks. Standards should adopt the concept of a generalized eco-industrial park in the world, not limited to the symbiotic relationship chain between matter and energy (such as the Kalundborg model). As long as all industries and communities in the park are symbiotic in terms of basic resources such as infrastructure, water and energy, and wastes are openly recycled, and the ecological efficiency of the individual and the park as a whole is the highest, it can be considered as an ecological industrial park. The principle of this standard formulation is of great significance to the ecological transformation of China's economic and technological development zones and high-tech industrial parks. If the narrow concept of constructing the industrial symbiotic chain is followed, the difficulty in transforming the existing park will be very great.

For the eco-industrial parks that meet the standards, the state and local governments should establish a matching reward system: honor and market image rewards, establish naming and regular verification systems; reduce environmental and related quality supervision and management procedures, establish a trust system; increase tax incentives and Amplitude, establish an economic incentive system; establish an information release system.

China's clean production policy includes three aspects: laws and regulations, technical guidance catalogues, standards and capacity building. In general, China's relevant policies are at the advanced level in the world, and can basically meet the requirements of clean production at the current stage of circular economy development strategy.

The "Clean Production Promotion Law" promulgated in 2002 and the "Interim Measures for Clean Production Audit" jointly issued by the National Development and Reform Commission and the State Environmental

Protection Administration in August 2004 (hereinafter referred to as the "Measures") are signs of an important breakthrough in China's cleaner production policy. In particular, the "Measures" have solved the two major problems of insufficient long-term economic incentives and enforcement without legal basis in China's cleaner production practice, which are manifested in three aspects.

（1）A combination of voluntary review and mandatory review.

The state encourages enterprises to voluntarily carry out clean production audits. Enterprises that discharge pollutants to meet national or local emission standards may voluntarily organize clean production audits and propose further resources conservation and reduction of pollutant emissions. However, for enterprises in two situations, mandatory audits can be implemented: first, pollutants that exceed national and local emission standards, or polluting enterprises whose total pollutant discharge exceeds the total emission control targets approved by the local people's government; Enterprises that produce toxic and hazardous materials or emit toxic and hazardous substances in production.

(2) Strict management measures are in place for mandatory audits.

First, a system for information dissemination and public supervision was established. For enterprises that should implement mandatory clearing and production audit according to regulations, the discharge of major pollutants shall be announced in the main media of the locality within one month after the publication of the list. The main contents of the announcement shall include: the name of the enterprise, the representative of the legal person, the address of the enterprise, the name of the pollutant discharged, the mode of discharge, the concentration and total amount of the discharge, the excess and the total amount. The administrative department of environmental protection at or below the provincial level shall verify the discharge of major pollutants announced by the enterprise in accordance with the management authority.

Second, the time limit for a clear implementation review is specified. Enterprises listed in the mandatory clean production audit list shall conduct clean production audits within two months after the list is published. For enterprises that implement mandatory clean production audits as required, the interval between two audits shall not exceed five years. Enterprises listed in the implementation of mandatory clean production audit list shall report the clean production audit report to the local environmental protection administrative department and the development and reform (economic and trade) administrative department within one year from the date of publication of the list. The centrally-owned enterprises shall submit the clean production audit report to the local administrative department for environmental protection and development reform (economic and trade), and copy the report to the Ministry of Environmental Protection and the National Development and Reform Commission.

Third, the illegal responsibility was determined. If an enterprise that is subject to mandatory inspection is not announced or does not require the publication of pollutant discharge, the environmental protection administrative department of the local people's government at or above the county level shall announce that it may impose a fine of less than 100,000 yuan. If an enterprise that uses toxic or hazardous materials for production or emits toxic or hazardous substances in production does not implement a clean production audit or audit but fails to report the results of the audit, the environmental protection administrative department of the local people's government at or above the county level shall order it to correct within a time limit.: If you refuse to make corrections, you can impose a fine of less than 100,000 yuan.

(3) Established supporting support policies.

The Measures stipulate that: First, enterprises that have implemented voluntary clean production audits and have achieved remarkable results after the implementation of cleaner production programs shall be commended by the provincial-level development reform (economic trade) and environmental protection administrative departments, and local Published in the main media. Second, the administrative departments of development and reform (economic and trade) at all levels should, when formulating and implementing national key investment plans and local investment plans, increase energy utilization, water conservation, and comprehensive utilization in the implementation plan of clean production. Clean production projects such as pollution prevention are listed as key areas, and investment support is increased. Third, sewage charges can be used to support companies in implementing cleaner production. For clean production projects that meet the requirements of the Regulations on the Administration of the Collection and Use of Sewage Charges, the financial departments and environmental protection departments at all levels shall give priority to the use of sewage charges. Fourth, the SME Development Fund should arrange appropriate amounts to support SMEs in implementing cleaner production as needed. Fifth, the cost of the company's clean production audit are allowed to be included in the company's operating costs or related expenses. Sixth, enterprises can establish an internal company's internal clean production commendation and reward system according to the actual situation, and give certain rewards to those who have achieved remarkable results in the clean production audit work.

In order to implement the Clean Production Promotion Law, the State Economic and Trade Commission issued the first batch of "Guidelines for the Clean Production Technology of National Key Industries" in 2000, covering five key industries of metallurgy, petrochemical, chemical, light industry and textile. Clean production technology, and specify the scope of application and investment benefit analysis methods of each technology. In 2003, the State Economic and Trade Commission and the State Environmental Protection Administration jointly announced the second batch of "National Key Industry Cleaner Production Technology Guidance Catalogue", covering 56 key industries of metallurgy, machinery, non-ferrous metals, petroleum and building materials, with a total of 56 clean production technologies. Compared with the first batch of catalogues, the second batch of catalogues adds information on the supply of clean production technologies. In the same year, China released and implemented the "Clean Production Standard Petroleum Refining Industry" (IU/T125-2003) and the "Clean Production Standard Coking Industry" (HJ/T126-2003), and prepared for other industries with serious pollution or waste of resources. (such as the steel industry, electroplating industry, cement industry, etc.) to develop clean production standards.

In addition, the construction of the China Cleaner Production Auditing Agency and the training of the audit team are carried out in parallel with the entire clean production work promotion process. In 2001, the State Environmental Protection Administration issued a special notice on the pilot work of the clean production audit institutions. The Clean Production Promotion Law and the Interim Measures for Clean Production Audit also make specific provisions for the construction of cleaning audit institutions and teams. According to statistics, China has carried out clean production audits in more than 20 industries and more than 400 enterprises in more than 20 provinces (autonomous regions and municipalities), and established 20 industrial or local cleaner production centers, with more than 10,000 participants. Different types of cleaner production training courses.

Resource and energy development and utilization policies

The development and utilization of resources and energy is an important part of the construction of circular economy. Resource and energy development efficiency, conversion efficiency, utilization efficiency and reuse are important indicators of the circular economy. China's per capita resources and energy share are low, insufficient protection for social and economic development, and low efficiency in resource and energy development and utilization are the main constraints to China's development of circular economy.

1. Natural resources development and utilization policy

The exploitation and utilization of natural resources is the basis for the operation of the national economy. In recent years, China has strengthened the management of resource development and utilization, and introduced a series of policies to improve the efficiency of resource utilization and conversion. The most important thing is to gradually improve the price mechanism of natural resources, promote the rational development and protection of resources, and save utilization. Natural resources involve a wide range of aspects, and here we focus on the policy situation of three important resources of water, land and minerals.

(1) Legislation: China attaches great importance to the development and management of resources, and has carried out special legislation on important resources, such as the Water Law of the People's Republic of China (1988), the Land Administration Law of the People's Republic of China (1986), The People's Republic of China Mineral Resources Law (1986), the People's Republic of China Coal Law (1996) and a number of supporting regulations. Based on these basic laws and regulations, various administrative departments have issued a series of specific policy measures.

Although the direction of national natural resource utilization management is similar, the focus of each resource area is still different. The policy of China's water resources and mineral resources development and utilization policy focuses on the formulation of resource utilization prices and corresponding reform measures, so that the use price of resources gradually becomes more reasonable. For example, the State Planning Commission, the Ministry of Finance, the Ministry of Construction, the Ministry of Water Resources, and the State Environmental Protection Administration promulgated the "Notice on Further Promoting the Reform of Urban Water Supply Price" issued in 2002 to establish a reasonable water supply price formation mechanism and improve various supporting facilities. Measures to increase the collection of sewage treatment fees, improve the collection standards for water resources fees, introduce market mechanisms and other aspects put forward specific requirements. In general, in the development and utilization of water resources and mineral resources, the government is more inclined to use the price mechanism to regulate the efficiency of resource development and utilization.

The focus of land use policy management is to maintain the dynamic balance of the total amount of cultivated land and control the unreasonable occupation of cultivated land by urban development and development zone construction. Land is a very special resource, and it is in a state of scarcity for a long time. Especially, urban land is an important resource that constrains the economic development of the city. Judging from the utilization of land resources in China, the unreasonable occupation of agricultural land by cities and development zones and the low efficiency of urban land use are still the main problems in the land use process. As a very scarce resource, the government ensures that the supply of land meets the needs of economic development, improves the efficiency of land use, and guides the development of low-efficiency (low-fertility) land, strengthening the management of land resources. Land approval, land use status review, and rational planning are the means.

(2) Economic policy: Economic policies related to resource development and utilization mainly include two aspects:
Resource pricing policy and tax and compensation policies. The resource pricing policies mainly include: "Measures for the Administration of Urban Water Supply Price" (1998), "Provisional Regulations on Urban Land Use Tax of the People's Republic of China" (1988), "Administrative Measures on the Use Fees and Prices of Exploration Rights and Mining Rights" (1999) The resource taxation and compensation policies mainly include: "Provisional Regulations on Resource Tax of the People's Republic of China" (1993), "Regulations on the Collection of Compensation for Mineral Resources Compensation" (1994), Land Acquisition Compensation and Resettlement for Large and Medium-sized Water Conservancy and Hydropower Project Construction Regulations (1991) and so on.

In order to better solve the problem of excessive dependence on resource consumption in the current economic development, the state actively adjusts the price relationship between resource products and final products, and promotes the comprehensive utilization of resources. For example, the "Measures for the Administration of Urban Water Supply Price" formulated in 1998, which regulates the price of urban water supply and the net profit margin of water supply enterprises, and also formulates management methods for sewage treatment prices and water supply pricing methods, which require The full use of the price reflects the full value of the resource.

In order to solve the current situation that many resource prices in China cannot fully reflect the true value of resources, some administrative departments have formulated resource taxes and compensation policies, which on the one hand effectively complement the resource price system, and on the other hand, promote resources. Efficient use. For example, the "Provisional Regulations on the Resource Tax of the People's Republic of China" promulgated in 1993 stipulates that units and individuals that open mining products or produce salt in China should pay resource taxes. The tax items and tax amounts of resource taxes are in accordance with the "Catalogue of Resource Taxes and Taxes". The relevant regulations of the Ministry of Finance are implemented. The "Regulations on the Collection of Compensation for Mineral Resources Compensation Fees" promulgated in 1994 requires that mineral resources should be paid in the territory of the People's Republic of China and other jurisdictions to pay mineral resources compensation fees in accordance with regulations, reflecting the value of resources.

2. Energy policy

Since the mid-1990s, energy conservation and energy efficiency have gradually become the mainstay of China's energy policy. In 1997, the Energy Conservation Law was promulgated, and energy efficiency standards for major industries and some products were released. Various energy conservation and consumption reduction activities were carried out. Five years of energy conservation planning was formulated and great achievements were made in improving energy efficiency. . During the "Ninth Five-Year Plan" period, China's energy consumption per 10,000 yuan of GDP (1990 price) dropped from 3.97 tons of standard coal in 1995 to 2.77 tons of standard coal in 2000, and accumulated savings and energy use reached 410 million tons of standard coal. According to the calculation of direct energy savings during the "Ninth Five-Year Plan" period, the energy value saved is about 66 billion yuan. The "10th Five-Year Plan for Energy Conservation and Comprehensive Utilization of Resources" also puts forward higher requirements for energy conservation and energy efficiency improvement, and technological innovation and generation of technologies such as saving and replacing petroleum technology, clean coal technology, and "three wastes" comprehensive utilization technology. Major demonstration projects such as oil demonstration projects, green lighting demonstration projects, and conservation-oriented clean enterprise demonstration projects have been the focus of development; proposed to strengthen the legal system, formulate and implement energy efficiency standards and certification marking systems, promote energy structure optimization, and improve energy The overall technical level of comprehensive utilization of resources and resources, research and formulation of incentive policies to meet the requirements of the market economy, and exploration of measures to promote energy conservation and comprehensive utilization of resources under the conditions of market economy.

Especially in the 21st century, under the grim situation of building a well-off society in an all-round way, facing the constraints of resources, energy and environmental bottlenecks, the situation of resource conservation and the efficiency of comprehensive utilization of resources have not been deepened. Only this year, the state has issued five related policies and laws: "Notice on the Implementation of Resource Conservation Activities by the General Office of the State Council", "Renewable Energy Law", "Medium and Long-term Energy Conservation Plan", "Energy Efficiency Label Management Measures" and "Government Energy Conservation" Product Purchase Notice. These policies fully reflect the requirements of the scientific development concept and the new industrialization road, and basically meet the needs of the current circular economy practice.

Energy conservation.

The Medium and Long-Term Plan for Energy Conservation (hereinafter referred to as the "Planning") has set a more ambitious energy saving goal:

Firstly，a macro energy-saving indicator: by 2010, the energy consumption per 10,000 yuan of GDP (1990 constant price, the same below) decreased from 2.681 standard coal in 2002 to 2.25 tons of standard coal, and the average annual energy saving rate in 2003-2010 was 2.2%. The energy-saving capacity formed is 400 million tons of standard coal; in 2020, the energy consumption per 10,000 yuan of GDP is reduced to 1.54 tons of standard coal. The average annual energy saving rate is 3% from 2003 to 2020, and the energy-saving capacity is 1.4 billion tons of standard coal. It is equivalent to 111% of the total new energy production planned for the same period of 1.26 billion tons of standard coal, equivalent to reducing sulfur dioxide emissions by 21 million tons.

Second, is the main product (workload) unit energy consumption index: in 2010, it reached or approached the international advanced level in the early 1990s. Among them, large and medium-sized enterprises reached the international advanced level in the early 21st century; in 2020, they reached or approached the international advanced level.

The Plan has identified three key energy conservation areas: key industries, including the power industry, the steel industry, the non-ferrous metals industry, the petrochemical industry, the chemical industry, the building materials industry, the coal industry; transportation, including road transportation, new motor vehicles, Urban transport, rail transport, air transport, water transport and agricultural fishery machinery; construction, commercial and civil, including buildings, household and office appliances, lighting fixtures. On this basis, the "Planning" has established 10 key projects: coal-fired industrial boiler renovation project, regional cogeneration project, waste heat and pressure utilization project, saving and replacing petroleum engineering, motor system energy-saving engineering, energy system optimization project, Building energy-saving projects, green lighting projects, government agencies energy-saving projects, energy-saving monitoring and technical service system construction projects. Through the implementation of these 10 key energy-saving projects, energy-saving 240 million tons of standard coal can be achieved, with significant economic and environmental benefits.

Although the "Planning" lists 10 safeguards, whether the energy conservation goals can be achieved will depend on whether the measures can be put in place and implemented effectively. This is the biggest challenge for China's future energy conservation.

(2) Renewable energy development. Renewable energy sources include non-fossil energy sources such as wind, solar, hydro, biomass, geothermal, and ocean energy. In order to promote China's renewable energy development and optimize energy structure, the Renewable Energy Law proposes five substantive measures:
First, formulate national and local renewable energy development and utilization targets, and develop national and local renewable energy development and utilization plans.
Secondly, in terms of industrial guidance and technical support: the state will formulate a catalogue of renewable energy industry development guidelines, national standards for renewable energy technologies and products; the state will include scientific and technological research and industrialization development of renewable energy development and utilization as technological development. Priority areas for the development of high-tech industries, incorporating national science and technology development plans and

high-tech industry development plans, and arranging funds to support scientific and technological research, application demonstration and industrialization of renewable energy development and utilization; incorporating renewable energy knowledge and technology General education, vocational education courses.

Moreover, in terms of promotion and application: the state encourages and supports renewable energy grid-connected power generation: grid companies should fully acquire the on-grid power of renewable energy grid-connected power generation projects within their grid coverage and provide Internet access for renewable energy generation. . Support the construction of renewable energy independent power systems in areas not covered by the power grid to provide electricity services for local production and living; encourage clean and efficient development and utilization of biomass fuels, encourage the development of energy crops; encourage units and individuals to install and use solar water heaters Solar energy utilization systems such as systems, solar heating and cooling systems, and solar photovoltaic systems; encourage and support the development and utilization of renewable energy in rural areas.

In addition, in terms of price management and cost sharing: the on-grid price of renewable energy power generation projects will be determined in accordance with the principle of promoting the development and utilization of renewable energy and economic rationality, and timely adjustment according to the development of renewable energy development and utilization technologies; The cost incurred by the grid enterprise for the purchase of renewable energy by the on-grid electricity price is higher than the difference between the expenses calculated according to the average on-grid price of conventional energy generation, and is apportioned among the sales electricity price; the reasonable payment by the grid enterprise for the acquisition of renewable energy The cost of network connection and other reasonable related expenses can be included in the transmission cost of the grid enterprise and recovered from the sales price; the price of renewable energy and gas entering the urban pipeline network is beneficial to promote the development and utilization of renewable energy and economy. Reasonable principles are determined based on price management authority.

Finally, in terms of economic incentives and supervision measures: the state finance will set up special funds for renewable energy development, support scientific and technological research, standard setting and demonstration projects for renewable energy development and utilization; and support renewable energy utilization in rural and pastoral areas. Project: Support the construction of independent power systems for renewable energy in remote areas and islands; support resource exploration, evaluation and related information system construction for renewable energy; support the localization of renewable energy development and utilization equipment. For renewable energy development and utilization projects that are included in the national renewable energy industry development guidance catalogue and eligible for credit, financial institutions can provide preferential loans with financial interest subsidies. The state grants tax concessions to projects listed in the Catalogue for the Development of Renewable Energy Industries

From the content, it should be said that the Renewable Energy Law is a very advanced law. The current urgent task is to formulate supporting implementation policies and mechanisms to effectively implement the requirements of the law.

Ecological agriculture policy

Compared with China's long history of ecological agriculture practice, the relevant policy construction is relatively lagging behind. In 1993, the Ministry of Agriculture, the State Planning Commission, the State Science and Technology Commission, the Ministry of Finance, the Ministry of Forestry, the Ministry of Water Resources and the State Environmental Protection Administration, seven ministries and commissions jointly organized 51 eco-agricultural demonstration counties nationwide. After more than ten years of hard work, the national, provincial and pilot counties have basically formed a three-level ecological agriculture management and extension system, and ecological agriculture practices have gradually embarked on the path of institutionalization and standardization.

Chinese existing policies related to eco-agriculture are mainly normative and management policies, such as the Notice on Piloting the Construction of National Ecological Demonstration Zones (National Environmental Protection Agency, 1995) and Measures for the Management of Pollution-free Agricultural Products (National Certification) Accreditation Supervision and Management Committee, General Administration of Quality Supervision, Inspection and Quarantine, 2002), Opinions on Accelerating the Development of Green Foods (Ministry of Agriculture, 2002), Implementation Opinions on Comprehensively Promoting the "Non-Pollution Food Action Plan" (Ministry of Agriculture, 2002)), "Administrative Measures for Pollution-free Agricultural Products Signs" (Ministry of Agriculture, National Certification and Accreditation Administration, 2003), "Notice on Further Regulating the Work of Originating and Product Certification of Pollution-free Agricultural Products" (Ministry of Agriculture, National Certification and Accreditation Supervision and Administration) Committee, 2003) and so on. The focus of these normative documents is to accelerate the construction of ecological agriculture, promote the production of pollution-free food, and strengthen management.

In general, China's current eco-agriculture policy has three characteristics or deficiencies.
(1) the existing policies are mainly based on administrative norms and macro guidance. The policy system including laws and regulations, management systems and economic incentives has not yet been established at the national level.
(2) the existing policies mainly start from the end of ecological agriculture construction, that is, pollution-free agricultural products, and lack relevant policies in the process of ecological agriculture construction.
(3) insufficient support for the construction of ecological agriculture technology systems and service systems.

Environmentally friendly product related policies

Environmentally friendly products are still a relatively new concept in China. At present, there is no unified extension and connotation definition. Generally it refers to those products that are produced with environmentally friendly raw materials or have high resource and energy utilization rate. In the case of products with low environmental pollution, products with low environmental pollution after use, and products that can improve environmental quality, the form of the product may be either a product in a form of matter or a service in a non-material form.

China's environmentally friendly product policy is primarily a sign (or logo) system and procurement system. The labeling system includes six categories: environmental labeling system, green food labeling system, organic food labeling system, pollution-free food marking system, environmentally friendly enterprise marking system and energy efficiency labeling system. Among them, the first four marking systems are currently more commonly used in China. The system; the environmental labeling system has a 10-year history of practice; the environmentally friendly corporate marking system has been tested for less than two years. An energy efficiency label is an information label attached to the smallest package of a product or product. It is used to indicate performance indicators such as the energy efficiency rating of the energy-using product. It provides necessary information for users and consumers to purchase decisions to guide users and consumption. Choose energy efficient products.

The Measures for the Administration of Energy Efficiency Labels jointly issued by the National Development and Reform Commission and the General Administration of Quality Supervision, Inspection and Quarantine, stipulate that the National Development and Reform Commission, the General Administration of Quality Supervision, Inspection and Quarantine and the National Certification and Accreditation Administration are responsible for the establishment and organization of the energy efficiency labeling system. The Product Catalogue of the People's Republic of China for the Implementation of Energy Efficiency Labeling stipulates that all products listed in this catalogue shall be marked with a uniform energy efficiency label in the obvious part of the minimum packaging of the product or product, and shall be stated in the product manual.

The Ministry of Finance and the National Development and Reform Commission issued the "Opinions on the Implementation of Government Procurement of Energy-Saving Products" (hereinafter referred to as "Implementation Opinions") issued in December 2004, which unveiled the history of green procurement by the Chinese government. The "Implementation Opinions" require that state organs, institutions and organizations at all levels (collectively referred to as "purchasers") to use fiscal funds for procurement, should preferentially purchase energy-saving products and phase out low-efficiency products; government procurement is a product in the energy-saving list. When the technical, service and other indicators are equal, the energy-saving products listed in the energy-saving list shall be preferentially purchased; if the purchaser or its entrusted procurement agency fails to purchase according to the above requirements, the relevant departments shall comply with relevant laws, regulations and rules. Processing, the financial department can refuse to pay for procurement subject to availability.

In summary, China's environmentally friendly products related policies are still in their infancy. In the future, the direction of policy construction should first expand the scope of environmentally friendly products and formulate relevant catalogues: second, establish legal basis; third, formulate taxes, prices, and Purchasing preferential policies to promote the development and application of environmentally friendly products through market mechanisms: Fourth, on the basis of the "Opinions on Implementation of Government Procurement of Energy-Saving Products", expand the scope and intensity of procurement of environmentally friendly products and accelerate government green procurement legislation.

2.3 Key Policy Adjustments for China's Circular Economy Development

Since the 1990s, China's circular economy-related policies have gradually established a relatively complete framework, and policy capacity building has also made great progress, but overall there are still directional and structural defects, and cannot meet the sustainable development. Needs, especially in the rational development and recycling of resources, as well as the comprehensive utilization of waste resources and related environmental protection industries, further policy support and continuation are needed.

Policy recommendations for resource development and utilization

In the 1990s, China has achieved good results since the implementation of the resource development and utilization policy. However, in terms of its existing problems and challenges in the future, the current resource development and utilization policies are still unable to meet the needs of developing circular economy. The direction of management and the policy structure need to be adjusted.

1. In order to ensure the rapid growth of the economy, China has given more preferential policies to the development of mineral resources, which has ensured the demand for natural resources in economic construction in a certain time and promoted economic development. However, developed countries have begun to adopt restrictive policies on non-renewable resources, especially those with heavy environmental pollution (such as coal), to reduce the development and utilization of such resources as much as possible, and to reduce the ecological environment and economy. The extent of the impact of continued development. However, China's resource development policies that endanger the ecological environment and affect sustainable development have not yet changed.

2. Mineral development is the starting point of resource utilization, and the level of development efficiency directly affects the degree of overall resource utilization. In most of China's mineral development process, the development loss rate is very high and the resources are wasted.

Although China's mineral resources policy is based on encouraging development, it lacks support for the development and application of high-efficiency mining technology and lacks management of mining rate. At present, China does not have a specific economic policy to increase the rate of resource exploitation. The government cannot regulate the exploitation rate of resources through market means, which is an important reason for the low rate of resource development in China.

3. Insufficient constraints and incentive policies to improve resource utilization. As mentioned above, China's resource policy pays more attention to the development process, ignoring the use of the link: pay more

attention to the amount of mining, less attention to mining efficiency and utilization efficiency in the production process. In 2007, the General Office of the State Council issued the "Notice on Resource Conservation Activities", and proposed specific targets and policy measures, but the actual results will depend on the formulation and implementation of relevant supporting policies. Therefore, it is urgent for the state to improve the policy system for the development and utilization of China's resources from the two aspects of encouragement and restriction, and efficiency as the core. Restrictions and penalties for production with backward technology and low resource utilization rate, encourage enterprises that adopt technology with high resource utilization rate, and establish specific preferential policies such as finance, taxation and credit.

Finally, China must transform the existing resource management policy direction and structure in the future, reduce preferential policies for the development and utilization of non-renewable resources or serious environmental pollution resources, gradually change from support policies to restraint policies, and increase the development of mineral resources efficiently. Support for technology research and development, strengthen the management of mineral development rate, formulate some necessary economic policies, regulate the resource utilization behavior of enterprises, and ensure the efficient and sustainable use of mineral resources.

Suggestions on the adjustment of comprehensive utilization policy of waste resources

The most important feature of China's comprehensive utilization of waste resources and related environmental protection industry policies is that the policy structure is gradually shifted from the initial macro-guided policy to the economic incentive policy, and the management mechanism is transitioned from government-led to market-based. Synchronized with China's planned economy to the market economy reform process, and maintained a good continuity. The transformation of government administrative means is of great significance to the industry in the early stage of development.

But China's comprehensive utilization of waste resources and related environmental protection industries objectively are still in the initial stage of development, facing the problems of small industrial scale, unreasonable structure, and imperfect market environment. They are far from competent to develop circular economy and integrate waste resources. Use and related environmental protection industry requirements. The existing policies show four weaknesses, which is also a key link in establishing and improving relevant policies.

Integrating resources and establishing a unified recycling industrial system and management system

Due to the different stages of development, there have been two industries of recycling and utilization of waste resources and environmental protection industries. Before the 1980s, the recycling of waste resources was often referred to as the recycling of waste materials. It involved industrial production and consumption of households. Waste products that can be processed or used directly or by conventional technical processes, belonging to the materials department and supply and marketing cooperatives. System Management. After the emergence of the environmental protection industry, the scope of waste resources has been extended to all solid, gas and liquid waste discharged from industrial production, rather than being limited to waste materials. Especially after the concept of circular economy emerged, the types of waste available in domestic waste are also expanding. The depth of processing and utilization and the requirements for technology are also constantly improving, and even many of the technologies used are in the high-tech category. In short, today's waste concept actually is a waste of resources, no waste in the traditional sense. Therefore, the two concepts of comprehensive utilization of resources and environmental protection industries, which are currently in use, have a large crossover and overlapping of connotations, causing many confusions and ambiguities in government management and market operations.

Therefore, according to the development requirements of the circular economy, the two should be unified into the recycling and utilization of waste resources and safe disposal industries.

In addition, in the process of market economy transition, the waste materials recycling and utilization agencies under the supply and marketing cooperatives and materials departments (now changed materials companies) still exist in many places. Although these institutions have been restructured into independent accounting enterprises, they are still state-owned enterprises and even public institutions in nature, and there is no clear business guidance and management part that faces many management malpractices and personnel burdens left by the planned economy era. At present, most of these enterprises are concerned about the recycling of industrial bulk waste resources (such as metals), and basically do not involve domestic consumption waste. Residents' consumption waste is occupied by mass unorganized "picking out the army", which has caused many social problems. The comprehensive utilization of industrial "three wastes" is generally undertaken by the production enterprises themselves or private specialized enterprises. In short, China's current comprehensive utilization of waste resources and related business entities are very complex, and the management system is not uniform, which restricts the healthy, orderly and rapid development of the industry.

Therefore, under the premise of unifying the comprehensive utilization of waste resources and the title of safe disposal industry, the existing private specialized enterprises will be the main body, and the existing state-owned recycling enterprises will be reformed, and the "picking army" will be organized to establish a unified comprehensive utilization of professional waste resources. The market operation entity that is safely disposed of can be attributed to the Development and Reform Commission in industrial management and to the environmental protection department in environmental supervision.

Establish a special law and industry standard for recycling and recycling of waste resources as soon as possible

In the past few decades, in addition to the relevant environmental protection laws, the comprehensive utilization of China's waste resources and the emergence and development of environmental protection industries mainly rely on the government's macro-policy guidance and economic policy incentives. There is no specific laws and regulations for strong promotion, and there is no industry standard norm. And improve the level of comprehensive utilization of resources. According to the requirements of circular economy, the comprehensive utilization and safe disposal of waste resources is a connected industry in the field of grafting production and consumption. It is an important new industry in the national economy. It is called "venous" industry in Japan; it is also an environmental pollution treatment and disposal industry. , has a strong public welfare nature. According to the experience of developed countries, the promotion of the recycling of waste resources and the development of safe disposal industries need to be based on market mechanisms, but must first have special legal guarantees. The Circular Economy and Waste Management Law, implemented in Germany in 1996, is a comprehensive law for the comprehensive utilization and safe disposal of waste resources. Similarly, the Japanese circular economy legal system is composed of two comprehensive laws and five individual laws. The comprehensive approach includes the Waste Disposal Act and the Resource Effective Use Promotion Act, which includes waste recycling methods for container packaging, household appliances, construction materials, food, and automobiles. Therefore, the main body of the legal system of the Japanese recycling society is composed of the comprehensive utilization of waste resources and the law of safe disposal.

It should be said that the German and Japanese legislative models can be learned in China, but from the perspective of the existing legal system framework and administrative management system, the Japanese model may be more suitable for China's national conditions, that is, based on the revised solid waste law, a number of parallels are formulated. Comprehensive utilization of different types of waste resources (see Chapter 6).

Strengthening credit support and related charging policies

As mentioned above, in China's comprehensive utilization of waste resources and environmental protection industry policies, tax incentives are relatively complete, but credit policies are weak and lack of pertinence. Especially for most small and medium-sized enterprises in the industry, the credit support policy with general appeal is basically unable to play a substantial role. Therefore, specific credit support policies should be enacted in accordance with the relevant provisions of the SME Promotion Law to support the development of related enterprises. In addition, although the garbage and sewage charging policy has been established, the implementation is not satisfactory. It is estimated that the current urban sewage treatment fee in China is about 60%, the charging standard is 0.2-1.2 yuan/ton, and most of the charges are lower than the treatment cost; the garbage disposal fee is only about 16%, and the charging standard is also Generally lower. According to the conclusions of the relevant research of the China Council for International Cooperation on Environment and Development, the solution to this problem is to integrate the existing charging policies issued by relevant ministries (published in the form of notices and opinions) and publish them in the form of decisions or regulations of the State Council. Improve the authority and enforcement of policies.

Formulating technology research and development policies

The comprehensive utilization and safe disposal of waste resources under the circular economy system is a new type of industry with high technical content and even high technology support. Technology policy has always been a weak link in China's relevant industrial policies. Industrial technology policies for comprehensive utilization and safe disposal of waste resources should focus on three ways: First, the government must invest a certain amount of funds to establish a special R & D team; Second, rely on policy concessions to encourage enterprises to carry out technology research and development and introduce and digest international advanced technology; It is to implement specific technology research and development and promotion projects in the industry's five-year plan.

The construction of China's circular economy development policy system

According to the connotation, development model and strategic focus of China's circular economy, as well as relevant international experience, the circular economy is not a sustainable development practice in some areas and parts, but a thorough transformation and transformation of traditional production and consumption patterns. Therefore, circular economy the policy system includes not only core policies in key areas, but also innovations in social and economic basic policies. It also needs an eco-cultural education policy that is compatible with the development of circular economy. The core policy, basic policy and publicity and education policy are circular economy. The basic policy, environmental management policy and its supervision and management and sustainable development policies are the direct driving force for promoting the construction and practice of all circular economy policies.

Basic policies for the development of circular economy

It is the basic policy of circular economy that leads the core policy, basic policy and publicity and education policy. The basic policy is the most fundamental and universally applicable guiding policy for the development of circular economy. Its purpose is to determine the strategic position of circular economy in social and economic development, and propose the overall strategic objectives, steps, main systems and measures for the development of circular economy in order to use the cycle. Economic concepts, principles and methods guide all aspects of social and economic development and form the legal basis for core policies and basic policy innovation. According to Japanese experience, the basic policies of the circular economy include the Basic Law and the Basic Plan. The basic plan for the development of circular economy in China can be composed of two parts: one is to formulate a strategic plan for the development of medium and long-term circular economy; the other is to incorporate the development goals, tasks and measures of circular economy into the five-year plan for national economic and social development as a stage plan. According to China's development planning system, the development stage of circular economy or short-term planning should not be independently formulated to avoid disconnection from mainstream planning of social and economic development.

The core policy of circular economy development

The core policy directly promotes the policies in the key areas of the circular economy. The policy forms can be basically divided into laws and regulations and standards, economic incentives and administrative supervision and management systems. Special planning is also a very important policy tool.

According to the current construction of China's relevant policies, policies that are more favorable to the development of circular economy include: eco-industrial policy, energy conservation and renewable energy policy, and environmentally friendly product mark (logo) policy; weak policies include: recycling of used resources, Utilization, resource and harmless industrial policies, ecological agriculture policies, resource development and utilization policies; basic absent policies include: green consumption and service industry policies, government green procurement policies, environmentally friendly and resource-based energy-saving infrastructure construction Policy, etc.

The overall principle in the core policy construction of circular economy is to effectively implement and use the existing policies that are conducive to the development of circular economy, improve the weak policies, and supplement the lack of policies.

1. Effectively implement and use existing policies

The types of policies that can meet the needs of circular economy development are: industrial restructuring policy, cleaner production policy, comprehensive utilization of waste resources and VAT preferential policies, sewage and garbage charging policies, energy conservation and renewable energy development policies, environmental signs. Environmentally friendly product mark (marking) policies such as organic food signs, green food signs, pollution-free food signs, environmentally friendly corporate appraisals and energy efficiency labels, resource development tax and fee policies, and resource price (such as water price) reform policies.

2. Improve weak policies

The current circular economy related policies that need to be improved as soon as possible are:

Resource recovery, reuse, resource and harmless industrial policies: The direction of resource recovery, reuse, resource utilization and harmless industrial policies is: first, rationalize and reform the management system and industrial system, and establish a unified waste. The resource recovery, reuse, resource and harmless disposal management system and industrial system, and establish a market operation mechanism based on the market mechanism and with a high degree of organization. Learn from the Japanese legislative model and establish a legal system for the comprehensive utilization and safe disposal of waste resources. While continuing to implement tax incentives, we will focus on strengthening credit support and related charging policies. Formulate technology research and development policies and implement specific technology research and development and promotion projects through five-year industrial development planning.

Eco-industrial park construction policy: China's eco-industrial park construction policy is basically in a state of vacancy. The direction of its establishment and improvement is to upgrade the existing eco-industrial demonstration park to a national demonstration park, expand the number of demonstrations, and provide funds and tax incentives; While encouraging the construction of new eco-industrial parks, the focus should be on transforming existing economic development zones, especially economic and technological development zones and high-tech industrial parks into eco-industrial parks; setting eco-industrial park standards and establishing incentive systems.

Ecological agriculture policy: In terms of ecological agriculture, the direction of policy adjustment and improvement is to simultaneously focus on the green (non-polluted) product end and ecological agriculture construction process to fill ecological agriculture legislation, economic policy, ecological agricultural base construction and technical policy. blank. Resource development and utilization policy: In the resource and energy development and utilization policy system, change the policy structure of re-development and light utilization; focus on improving the resource pricing policy and the basic policies of taxation and compensation, so that resource prices tend to fully reflect resource production costs and scarce costs. And environmental costs, to create a good market environment for improving resource extraction efficiency, utilization efficiency and recycling rate; gradually modify existing relevant resource laws and regulations to reflect the concepts and principles of sustainable development and circular economy; Means, determine specific targets, implement specific projects, and steadily promote energy conservation and comprehensive utilization of resources.

Policies related to environmentally friendly products: China's environmentally friendly products related policies are still in their infancy. In the future, the direction of policy construction should first expand the scope of environmentally friendly products and develop relevant catalogues; second, establish legal basis; third, establish taxation, preferential policies on pricing and procurement, and the development and application of environmentally friendly products through market mechanisms.

3. Supplementary absence policy

The policy that needs to be established in China is focused on environmentally friendly and resource-saving and energy-saving infrastructure construction policies. It is possible to start with the construction of energy-saving standards for building houses and various infrastructure resources, and gradually establish economic incentives, information release and new government supervision. Management system, etc. Green consumption and service industry policies can actively carry out pilot projects of green communities and green hotel hotels and develop equipment and equipment leasing industry on the base of increasing publicity and education. The government's green procurement policy is based on the implementation of the "Opinions on Government Procurement of Energy-Saving Products", expanding the scope and intensity of procurement of environmentally friendly products and accelerating the government's green procurement legislation.

Basic policies for the development of circular economy

The circular economy basic policy refers to a policy that creates a good institutional environment for the practice of circular economy focus areas to a greater extent. The basic policies of circular economy can be broadly divided into three categories: macroeconomic policies and basic economic systems, basic incentive policies and assessment policies. Macroeconomic policies and basic economic systems include economic restructuring policies, green trade policies, and property rights systems that are conducive to resource environmental protection. Basic incentives include green finance, green finance, green taxes and green pricing policies. The assessment policy includes the green national economic accounting system, the green accounting system, the green auditing system and the green one-central assessment system. Since the implementation of the socialist market economic system, the reform of such basic policies in China has been carried out with great intensity and progress, and has gradually adapted to the market economic mechanism. After implementing the transformation of economic growth mode and sustainable development strategy, basic policies and systems such as economic restructuring, partial resource and energy prices, some taxes, and finances have begun to move toward environmental protection and sustainable development. Especially after implementing the scientific development concept and taking the road of new industrialization, China has begun to actively study advanced green systems such as green national economic accounting and green cadre performance evaluation.

At the same time, however, we must be soberly aware that the transformation of the basic economic system will take a long time, and the resistance and difficulty of change will be great. The task of policy reform in the future is to apply the theories and principles of sustainable development, circular economy and resource environmental protection under the guidance of the scientific concept of development, and unremittingly gradually green China's basic economic policies and systems.

Chapter 3 Analysis of the Extraterritorial Experience of Circular Economy Development Model

The essence of circular economy is a new economic development model proposed by the international community in the process of seeking to resolve the contradiction between resource environment and economic growth. The biggest feature of this new development model is the recycling of materials, efficient use and environmental friendliness, that is, the economic development model of "resources, energy consumption, high economic benefits, and low pollution emissions".

Sustainable development in both developed and developing countries requires the development of high and effective use of resources as part of an important strategy to avoid future development crises. The goal of improving energy efficiency is achieved through the entire life cycle of the product, not just the production process. To this end, the Johannesburg Summit on Sustainable Development in 2002 proposed an action framework for building sustainable consumption and production systems to achieve the goal of efficient use of resources and reduction of environmental load. Some countries and regions have begun to respond, including improving resource efficiency in Germany, building a recycling-oriented society in Japan, industrial park networks, and building sustainable production and production systems in European countries. At present, China's vigorous development of circular economy is completely consistent with the sustainable consumption and production system proposed by the international community.

This section first reviews the main practices of EU countries in building sustainable consumption and production systems, improving resource efficiency, and developing circular economy. It focuses on the practice of developing circular economy in Germany and Japan, which are at the forefront in the development of circular economy. And policy; at the same time, it also studied the practical activities related to circular economy in other developed countries; finally, through comparative analysis with China, it put forward the reference and enlightenment of international experience on China's development of circular economy.

3.1 International experience in sustainable production and consumption

Europe's economic model is based on higher consumption of natural resources such as energy and raw materials. From an environmental point of view, the annual per capita raw material consumption in industrialized countries is 31 to 74 tons (calculated according to the total consumption of raw materials), and the raw materials consumed in food, housing and transportation are the most consumed. The average raw material concentration of the EU-25 is slightly lower than that of the United States, but twice that of Japan; the same is true for energy intensity, but the energy efficiency of the Japanese economy is more significant.

There are also big differences between EU countries. The energy output per unit of resources in Western Europe is several times higher than the energy output per unit of resources in emerging EU countries in Central and Eastern Europe. The intensive concentration of raw materials per unit of GDP is also different, with Estonia at 11.1 kg/EUR and France at 0.7 kg/EUR.

Relatively speaking, many EU countries have achieved economic growth and resource and energy consumption decoupling in the past 10 years, but this does not necessarily lead to an absolute reduction in environmental pressure, because the absolute use of resources has remained basically stable over the past 20 years. Part of the reason for this decoupling may be to increase the import of natural resources, thereby reducing the exploitation of Europe's own resources. Human wealth is mainly based on the consumption of natural resources, including raw materials, energy and land resources. However, the increasing use of resources and their environmental impacts will have many negative impacts leading to ecological crises and security threats. For example, over-exploitation of natural resources can increase resource supply pressures (such as maintaining resource supply to ensure sustainable production) and causing land subsidence (such as controlling the environmental impact of resource use and considering whether ecosystems can carry pollution emissions).

In Europe, it is recognized that resource constraints affect the continued growth of the economy. Since the Rio de Janeiro summit in 1992, the sustainable use and management of natural resources has gradually become the focus and theme of national policy discussions. The EU is also paying more attention to the sustainable use and management of resources, especially after the adoption of the EU Sustainable Development Strategy and the Sixth EU Environmental Action Plan (6EAP) in 2001. The Sixth Environmental Action Plan clearly stated that "it is necessary to decouple economic growth from resource utilization". Improving resource utilization efficiency is a core part of circular economy activities. Practices, policy implementation and activities to improve resource utilization efficiency have been in Europe for a long time. As mentioned earlier, the EU Sustainable Development Strategy and the Sixth Environmental Action Plan aim to provide strategic guidance to EU countries, influence EU policy development and ensure policy coherence. Specifically, many policy initiatives will facilitate the development of circular economy activities.

For example, different policy instruments are used to manage resource utilization. Some countries have begun to impose raw material taxes on mining (sand, gravel, limestone, etc.). The collection of raw material taxes can encourage the full use of resources. Other policy instruments affecting the exploitation of resources are the specific raw material mining permit system and the legal provisions on the amount of exploitation.

The Integrated Product Management Policy is another policy approach to production and consumption. It is designed to stimulate product design that effectively utilizes raw materials in the production process and enhance product recyclability. Building energy efficiency directives are primarily for energy efficiency. There is also an economical tool for managing energy demand, with water pricing being a prime example.

The policy measures for waste disposal mainly include discharge standards for waste treatment facilities, such as landfill and incineration directives. There are other restrictions and taxation policies for specific waste landfills that encourage enhanced recycling of waste.

In 2005, the European Union officially implemented the Waste Electrical and Electronic Equipment (WEEE) Directive to address the rapidly growing waste of electrical and electronic equipment. It mainly relies on manufacturers and producers to carry out end-of-product management and is responsible for the recycling of the products sold, thereby reducing the amount of landfill for waste electrical and electronic equipment. This also leads manufacturers to consider factors such as environmental protection and reusability when producing electronic equipment. Consumers can also return e-waste to manufacturers free of charge. In conjunction with WEEE, there are also restrictions on the use of certain hazardous substances (Robs) in electrical and electronic equipment, which mainly limit the use of certain harmful substances, such as lead on printed circuit boards.

In December 2005, the European Union promulgated the thematic strategy on the sustainable use of natural resources, a new European strategy for the sustainable use of natural resources. The strategy aims to mitigate the environmental impact of European resource use and global economic growth. Unsustainable use of resources has many negative effects on the environment, such as overexploitation of water, land, minerals and fish resources due to climate change caused by the use of fossil fuels. The strategy focuses on raising awareness, developing monitoring tools, and promoting sustainable use of strategic approaches in specific economic sectors, European member states, and internationally.

The main objectives of the thematic strategy for the sustainable use of natural resources can be summarized as follows:

1. Multiple values   – use less resources to create more value (improve resource productivity);
2. Less impact - reduce the overall impact of resource utilization (improve ecological benefits);
3. Good choice If you can't achieve the effect of clean and resource utilization, replace the existing resources with better clean resources.

The above objectives are to be achieved through the entire cycle of resource utilization, while avoiding the transfer of environmental impact from one cycle phase to another or to other regions and countries. Since waste generation represents the final phase of the resource utilization cycle, the resource strategy will provide important information support for waste prevention and reuse thematic strategies to reduce waste generation.

3.2 Practice and Policy of German Circular Economy Development

The background and policy evolution of the development of circular economy in Germany

In Germany, the circular economy was brewing in the late 1980s, and the practice of the system appeared in the mid-1990s, marked by the Circular Economy and Waste Management Law, enacted in 1994 and implemented in 1996. China's circular economy is also called "junk economy", which is derived from the reuse and disposal of domestic and industrial waste. It then extends to the production field through the extension system of production responsibility, and promotes sustainable production and consumption patterns. set up. At present, further experiments are carried out to promote the development of circular economy in the region through the overall material flow management method.

Stage1: from chaos to order (1945-1972)

After the end of World War II, health care became the focus of waste management. Germany has set up research groups and associations to undertake research on data on waste management planning, such as the composition and quantity of garbage. At the same time, research centers have been set up in some universities to study waste disposal from a scientific perspective.

In 1965, Germany established the Central Waste Disposal Bureau of the Federal Ministry of Health. Through the systematic research, the statistics on the composition and quantity of garbage make people better understand the garbage problem and, to a certain extent, promote some cities. Measures have been taken to optimize waste disposal.

In the mid-1950s, in order to improve waste treatment and disposal technology, Germany established a pilot plant that uses waste and waste sludge for composting, with the aim of putting waste recycling into practice. By 1970, 11 composting points had been built. At that time, 22 large and medium-sized waste incineration facilities capable of comprehensive utilization in terms of heat and electricity were put into use.

However, overall, the waste disposal management at the time was still in a state of chaos. In 1970, there were 50,000 messy and irregular dumping sites in Germany, where various types of garbage were dumped, causing more serious secondary pollution, threatening the surrounding environment and people's health.

Based on these circumstances, in 1972, Germany introduced the first waste disposal law, which determined the important principles that the waste-free disposal and disposal business can be undertaken by private enterprises. The purpose of the law is to close many poorly managed dumps, build garbage center treatment stations, and be managed by counties and cities. About 300 domestic waste disposal stations still in use are established after the law was enacted.

It is worth noting that by the early 1970s, German waste disposal was orderly and legalized, but there was no regulation and practice regarding garbage reuse.

Stage 2: From waste dumping to material closed loop management (1973-1996)

With the implementation of the first Waste Disposal Act (1972), the "economic" principle of waste management activities has become increasingly important. After the oil crisis of 1973, the purpose of burning garbage has also changed. Since then, garbage is no longer just incinerated, it is also used directly to harvest energy to save energy and resources. In this context, the German government issued the first national waste management plan in 1975, which first proposed the important principles of "prevention, reduction, recycling and reuse", "sharing disposal costs according to the polluter pays principle" and aims. Through this program, waste management is transformed from a safe disposal to a waste economy. However, because these goals are not legally enforceable, the practice process is very slow and the effect is not obvious.

Higher environmental standards in Germany have correspondingly increased the cost of waste disposal, which has led to more and more problems, as commercial or industrial waste producers want cheaper disposal methods. The waste disposal area in Europe has been expanded and the waste may be transported in the name of "economic goods" to other European countries that are not strictly regulated.

In addition, in densely populated Germany, as garbage became more and more in the mid-1980s, it became increasingly difficult to find suitable locations for landfills or waste incineration.

Therefore, Germany enacted the Waste Disposal Act in 1986, proposing two groundbreaking regulations: first, for the first time, prevention priority and reuse after garbage disposal; second, for the first time, the responsibility of product producers was regulated. (Responsibility of the oil industry to recover waste oil). At the same time, the law also promotes the extraction of secondary materials with market value.

In the early 1990s, Germany introduced a number of new regulations aimed at improving the level, operation and organization of waste treatment technologies, with the aim of solving the secondary pollution problems in the waste treatment process. In 1991, Germany enacted the Regulations on the Avoidance and Recycling of Packaged Garbage and the Packaging Regulations, which expanded the scope of waste recycling and strengthened the product producer responsibility system. At the same time, the Packaging Regulations, by requiring the recycling of packaged waste, transferred responsibility from the government to the private sector, and established a collection system based on market economic mechanisms.

On the basis of summarizing the experience of the implementation of these laws and regulations, Germany officially promulgated the "Material Closed Cycle and Waste Management Law" in 1994, and it came into effect in 1996. This marks the first appearance of the term "circular economy" in the legal text.

The important principles and ideas of the Material Closed Cycle and Waste Management Law are embodied in eight aspects: the waste management is extended to the European scope on the basis of independent treatment in the country; the waste management is carried out in a closed manner; Ecological or economic reasons cannot be reused; the main purpose of recycling activities should be to conserve natural resources and protect the climate; to equalize the reuse of substances and energy in specific situations; to promote the participation of private enterprises in waste management (Product recycling / binary system); enables producers to undertake recycling responsibility through classified collection systems or existing public systems, including waste oil, packaging waste, batteries, scrapped vehicles, and future e-waste, to establish new ecological changes in industrial society mode.

Stage 3: Exploring the new order (since 1997)

After the entry into force of the Closed Circulation and Waste Management Act, there has been a major change in the state of waste management in Germany: the shift of waste management from the principle of government responsibility to the principle of private economy or producer payment. Waste management is increasingly becoming an integral part of production and consumption. Economic factors in waste management have received priority attention. The integration of industrial incineration and heat treatment plants is facilitated by the possibility of reuse of waste in the form of energy. Europeanization of waste management. In terms of waste management, the EU is constantly promoting the unification of environmental standards in Europe.

Since 2004, Germany is experimenting with a holistic material flow management strategy to promote different levels, especially regional circular economy or economic and social sustainable development. Material Flow Management (MFM) is a new sustainable development policy tool adopted by the European Union after the Rio Conference in 1992. The German Federal House of Representatives initially formulated an outline of material flow management.

According to the definition of the German Parliament, material flow management is a goal-oriented, sustainable management of resources and energy centered on the efficient use of materials, material flows and energy. Material flow management combines economic benefits, regional integrated value added (such as employment) and environmental protection. Material flow management has different forms at different levels: material flow management at the national level (national level); material flow management across regions (between regions, provinces and counties); material flow management within the region; inter-company Material flow management; material flow management within the company.

At present, typical success stories of material flow management in Germany focus on resource and energy flow management in the food production sector. Through the management of material flow, the garbage flow in this field has become a resource flow, which not only avoids the secondary pollution caused by the traditional practice of urban garbage transportation to the suburbs, but also classifies, collects, transports, and biogas in the regional garbage flow. The operation of the plant and the power plant increased employment opportunities and increased regional added value.

The main practices and policies of developing circular economy in Germany

The main practices of developing circular economy in Germany include: establishing a sound legal and regulatory system; establishing an implementation mechanism based on the charging system and enterprise operation; and testing the material flow management model from the enterprise to the regional level.

The core part of the German circular economy law and regulation system is composed of the Material Closed Cycle and Waste Management Law and several special regulations under it. The special regulations include both German-developed regulations and EU directives on electronic waste management, abandoned motor vehicle management, packaging waste management, chemicals and dangerous goods management. The Material Flow Management Law currently under study will become another iconic law of the German circular economy.

The Material Closed Cycle and Waste Management Act stipulates that producers are responsible for the entire life cycle of a product, from raw material into production to final recycling of the product, including transportation of energy. The law stipulates that the waste owner or manufacturer is primarily responsible for the reduction, recycling, reuse and safe disposal of waste. In order to promote the development of an environmentally friendly and circular economy, a balance sheet of different material materials should be developed. Based on this law, the German federal government has issued a number of decree regulations and voluntary agreements to create conditions for waste regulation, transportation permits, specialized waste management companies and associations, waste management concepts, waste cycle analysis and waste recycling. There are specific regulations for the following items, including: packaging, discarded vehicles, electronic equipment, waste oil, waste wood, commercial waste, biodegradable waste, sewage sludge, and toxic waste. There are voluntary agreements for construction waste, demolition waste and special paper. In addition, the federal government has enacted waste incineration regulations under the Federal Emission Control Act. Therefore, the bill is a firm implementation of the polluter pays principle in the field of waste.

In September 1990, Germany's 95 packaging companies and factory companies and retail traders established the German dual recovery system (DSD). DSD is a non-governmental organization that specializes in the recycling and utilization of packaging waste. It accepts the entrustment of the enterprise, organizes the consignee to recycle and classify the packaging waste of the enterprise, and then sends it to the corresponding resource recycling manufacturer for recycling. Packaging waste that can be directly recycled is returned to the manufacturer. In 1997, the organization became a non-listed company (DSDAG) represented by nearly 600 trade and industrial companies.

The environmental label used by Germany for the packaging industry is the "Green Point" logo. If the manufacturer or distributor wants to use the "Green Point" mark, it must pay a certain registration fee. The cost depends on the packaging material, weight and volume. The fee charged is used as the charge for the recycling and classification of packaging waste.

The establishment of the DSD system has greatly facilitated the recycling of German packaging waste. At present, there are 210 sorting workshops in Germany, which can classify 2.5 million tons of light packaging.

The policies mentioned above have enabled Germany to establish a modern closed-loop waste management system that has a significant positive impact on resource conservation, climate, soil, water and human health. Today, 240,000 people are engaged in waste management, with an average annual output of 50 billion euros. The highest raw material recovery rate that helps protect raw materials and major energy sources demonstrates the contribution of waste management to the sustainable development of the German economy. Almost 60% of municipal waste and 40% of production waste are recycled. For some waste types, the recovery rate is even higher, such as 86% of construction waste, 81% of packaging waste, 77% of batteries, and about 82% of waste paper.

Modern waste management models contribute to climate protection. In the past 15 years, greenhouse gas emissions have been reduced by an average of 30 million tons of carbon dioxide per year.

The environmental goal of the German federal government is to further develop a closed material recycling waste management system in the future. By strictly distinguishing waste types, pre-treatments, and energy recycling, Germany plans to make full use of material resources until the landfill is completely abandoned.

Experience in developing circular economy in Germany

From the decades of policy evolution in Germany and the active efforts of the participants in the circular economy, the following main conclusions can be summarized:
1. It is very effective to explore the public potential. Most Germans are proactive in coordinating the implementation of various waste reduction and recycling measures. Individual citizens and NGOs are important supporters for the successful implementation of these policies.
2. It is critical to attract more stakeholders and call for them to take responsibility. It has been proved that voluntary participation and other active participation activities are very important for the smooth implementation of waste policy. Active communication with pressure groups such as industrial enterprises and related institutions can also bring important support to policy implementation. For example, in 1997 the

German paper industry took the initiative to take responsibility for improving the recycling rate of waste paper. After the investment efforts of the following years, the recycled paper utilization rate of paper production in 2001 reached 65%.

3. Use market mechanisms and market instruments to improve resource utilization. The implementation of the polluter pays principle helps to reduce pollution from the source. For example, the one-off beverage bottle deposit system introduced in early 2003 was very effective in reducing packaging waste, and it has been completely transformed into sustainable consumption suitable for repackaging.

4. Adjust production rules as early as possible to reduce hazardous waste and reduce long-term costs. For example, the Closed Circulation and Waste Management Act provides for priority recycling of waste prior to waste disposal, which will result in hazardous waste being landfilled into abandoned mines; technically a legal means of recycling. In order to meet the development requirements, in 2002 the German government promulgated the "Underground Waste Accumulation Regulations", which detailed the types of underground waste accumulation, rock formations and related documents.

5. The use of circular economy principles can also bring long-term economic benefits. Focusing on improving energy efficiency greatly reduces the cost of the enterprise and the entire economic development. In addition, exploring ecological benefits in the production process can also stimulate innovation and create unlimited business opportunities for domestic and international competitiveness.

3.3 Practices and policies for establishing a recycling society in Japan

Despite the different titles, the historical background and development process of establishing a recycling society in Japan is basically consistent with the circular economy of Germany. In the historical process of dealing with the relationship between resource environment and economic development, the concept and practice of recycling society have been created and developed to solve the problem of living and industrial waste.

Compared with the concept of circular economy in Germany, the concept of recycling society in Japan is more in-depth and broad, emphasizing the establishment of a society with the least resource and energy consumption and environmental load, which is equivalent to China's current advocacy. A resource-saving and environment-friendly society. This difference has a certain relationship with Japan's use of "post-development advantage" to learn and develop German experience.

The background of establishing a recycling society in Japan

From the economic development priority strategy to the proposal to build a recycling-oriented society, Japan is closely related to the environmental problems it encounters in the development process. Since the late 1960s, after more than 20 years of efforts, Japan has successfully solved the problem of very serious industrial pollution and some urban life-type pollution. In the late 1980s, Japan began to enter post-industrial society and consumer society. The sharp increase of industrial and domestic waste has become one of the important issues facing Japan's environmental protection and sustainable development, which is manifested in five aspects:

First, a large amount of waste is produced. After a high economic growth in the 1960s and 1970s, Japan gradually formed a social system that realized economic growth through mass production, mass consumption, and mass abandonment, and a wasteful social structure. As a result, a large amount of waste was generated every year. Things.

Second, new environmental issues and the generation of difficult-to-handle waste. The increasing number of toxic, toxic and hazardous hazardous wastes such as chemicals, pesticides, tires, batteries, and small gas tanks has made it difficult for many local governments to manage.

Third, the final disposal of waste is seriously inadequate. The large amount of waste generated each year is a huge challenge for Japan, a country with a small land area, and it is increasingly difficult to build new landfills.

Fourth, illegal dumping of waste occurs frequently. The illegal dumping of waste has continued to occur. In 2001, 1,150 cases occurred and 240,000 tons of waste were illegally dumped.

Fifth, the recycling rate of waste cannot be improved. Maintaining the current level of social and economic development, Japan's annual resource input is about 2.1 billion tons, inventory (social material accumulation) is 1 billion tons, consumption and abandonment of 1.1 billion people in 600 million tons of waste, 200 million tons of Recycling, accounting for about 10% of total resource input. If the world lives in the way of the Japanese, humans need 2.7 planets to sustain themselves. It shows that Japan has formed a social and economic structure of waste of resources.

In addition, Japan's pressure on fulfilling the Kyoto Protocol's commitment to reduce greenhouse gas emissions is also an important driving force for its establishment of a recycling-oriented society to alleviate the dependence of social and economic development on resources and energy and related documents.

The practice model of establishing a recycling society in Japan

The practice model of establishing a recycling society in Japan can be summarized into three sentences: environmental industrialization, that is, the development of "venous" industry; industrial environmental transformation that is, development of environmentally friendly "arterial" industry; "artery" and "venous" combined or connected and tend to balance material flow.

The vein industry is a key area and entry point for Japan to establish a recycling-oriented society. The main practice is to establish an ecological industrial park for the waste recycling industry. The vein industry system has established, in theory, the material recycling system between the dynamic and intravenous industries or the entire society will naturally form.

Japanese vein industry

Japan's vein industry mainly includes packaging waste recycling industry, waste home appliance recycling industry, construction waste recycling industry, food recycling industry, automobile recycling industry, and recycling, transportation and recycling associated with the above-mentioned waste recycling. Technology research and development.

1) Waste appliance recycling industry. In Japan, discarded electrical products mainly include televisions, washing machines, air conditioners and refrigerators. About 18 million units and 600,000 tons of household appliances become garbage every year, of which 100,000 tons can be recycled. In response to this problem, Japan began implementing the Appliance Recycling Law on April 1, 2001. Under this law, producers, sellers, and consumers are each obligated to handle responsibilities and use resources efficiently. The waste household appliances to be recycled, as stipulated in the Household Appliances Recycling Law, include televisions, washing machines, air conditioners, and refrigerators. The legal recycling rates are 55%, 50%, 60%, and 50%, respectively.

2) Automobile recycling industry. About 5 million cars are scrapped every year in Japan. Because scrapped cars contain available metals and components, they have a high resource value. Japan promulgated the "Automobile Recycling Law" in 2002 and officially implemented it on January 1, 2005. The promulgation and implementation of the "Automobile Recycling Law" provides legal guarantee for the recycling of scrapped automobiles in Japan, and puts forward higher requirements for the recycling technology of scrapped automobiles.

Development status and management mode of Japanese eco-industrial parks
Development status

The Japan Eco-Industrial Park aims to build a resource-recycling society and vigorously cultivate and introduce environmental protection industries based on the regional industrial advantages, strictly control waste discharge, and strengthen recycling. Japan has been planning and building eco-industrial parks since 1997 and has made it an important measure for building a recycling-oriented society. As of October 2004, 23 ecological industrial parks have been approved.

The main features of the Japanese eco-industrial park:

（1）taking the vein industry as the main component is the biggest feature of the construction of the Japanese eco-industrial park. The existing 23 eco-industrial parks mainly focus on waste recycling, with more than 40 related facilities, and dozens of wastes recycled and recycled.

（2）most of the waste used in eco-industrial parks falls within the scope of individual regeneration laws. For example, waste household appliances, used automobiles, and waste containers in general waste are covered by the Household Appliances Recycling Law, the Automobile Recycling Law, and the Container Packaging Recycling Law. The recycling of building mixed waste is as stipulated in the Law on the Recycling of Building Materials.

（3）a special experimental research area is opened in the park. Enterprises, schools and governments jointly research waste treatment technology, reuse technology and environmental pollution control technology, and provide technical support for enterprises to carry out waste recycling and recycling.

（4） the construction of eco-industrial parks is characterized by distinct features and distinct features. In general, the industrial activities in the Japan Eco-Industrial Park are mainly based on waste recycling. However, depending on the type of waste used, there is still a difference between the parks, that is, each park has its own main body. direction. In addition, the same type of waste recycling business may be implemented in different eco-industrial parks.

（5） the eco-industrial park is a multi-functional vehicle. In addition to conducting routine industrial activities, it is also a window for regional environmental undertakings. For example, in the Kitakyushu Eco-Industrial Park, in addition to various waste recycling facilities, it also has the following functions: organizing environmental knowledge learning for citizens; organizing environmental-related training and lectures; receiving study tours; supporting experimental research activities; Comprehensive environmental management; display environment, recycling technology and recycled products; display and introduce the city's environmental protection industry.

Management model for the construction of Japanese eco-industrial parks

The construction of Japan's eco-industrial parks is dominated by local governments, and the state and local governments jointly assist and manage. Enterprises, research institutions, and administrative departments actively participate in the formation of a park management and operation model that integrates production, education, and government.

At present, the construction and management of the Japanese eco-industrial park is mainly the responsibility of the Ministry of the Environment and the Ministry of Economy, Trade and Industry, and implements a dual management system. The Ministry of the Environment is responsible for the reasonable disposal of waste, while the Ministry of Economy and Trade is mainly managed from the industrial side and is responsible for the management of recyclable resources such as iron and waste plastics.

The central government has formulated a compensation system for eco-industrial parks, which is implemented by the Ministry of the Environment and the Ministry of Economy, Trade and Industry. Among the 40 venous industrial facilities in the existing park, the Ministry of the Environment mainly supports the construction of software and hardware facilities and scientific research and technology development in eco-industrial parks; the Ministry of Economy, Trade and Industry mainly supports the construction of hardware facilities, the development of "3R" related technologies and ecological products. Development and so on. Individual facilities projects are jointly undertaken by the two provinces. For more than 40 intravenous industry enterprises in 23 existing parks in the country, about 20% are supported by the provinces and the provinces support about 30%. In the past few years, as the technology matured and the situation opened, the support funds of the two provinces were decreasing.

The technical level of the enterprises entering the park must be advanced and leading in the same industry, and they can obtain financial assistance from the state and local governments. The state subsidies for the enterprises entering the park account for 1/3~1/ of the total initial construction funds. 2. Local governments also have less subsidies for enterprises entering the park, but the amount of subsidies varies.

The local environmental protection department's management of the eco-industrial park is to monitor the sewage discharge of the enterprise; the second is to provide information and technical guidance for the rational use of resources by the enterprise, to approve the enterprises entering the park, and to help the enterprises entering the park to go through other formalities; Subsidize eligible enterprises; Fourth, be responsible for publicizing information to the public and citizens.

Japan's legal system and policy for establishing a recycling society

1. The framework system of circular social policies and regulations

From the perspective of laws and regulations, Japan's legal and regulatory system for promoting the development of a recycling-oriented society consists of three levels: one basic law, namely, the Basic Law for the Formation of a Recycling Society; and two comprehensive laws, the Waste Disposal Act and "Efficient Use of Resources": 6 special laws, "Container Packaging Recycling Law", "Home Appliance Recycling Law", "Building Materials Recycling Law", "Food Recycling Law", "Automobile Recycling Law" and "Green" Procurement Law.

"Basic Law for the Formation of a Recycling Society"

The main content of the law has the following six aspects:

1) Establish the concept of a "circular society". Simply put, the so-called "circular society" refers to a society in which natural resources are consumed and the environmental burden is minimized.

2) For substances that are called "junk" without considering their value, they are defined as "recyclable resources" and promote their recycling.

3) The "priority processing" sequence is: garbage reduction-reuse-recycling-energy utilization-safety processing. "Reduction" refers to reducing the generation of waste; "recycling" refers to the reuse of "recyclable resources", using waste as a product or part; "recycling" means using "recyclable resources" as raw materials. Further use; "energy utilization" refers to the recovery of heat from "recyclable resources"; finally, the safe disposal of non-useable waste.

4) Clarify the responsibilities of the central government, local governments, enterprises and the public, and encourage everyone to make efforts to establish a recycling-oriented society. In particular, it is clear that companies and the public are responsible for "garbage producers" and increase "producer responsibility", that is, producers are primarily responsible for the production of their products from the place of origin to disposal.

5) The government is responsible for formulating the "basic rules for promoting the establishment of a recycling society".

6) Identify government measures to establish a recycling society. These measures include: reducing the amount of waste generated; stipulating "residence of waste generators" in the form of regulations; increasing "producer responsibility" throughout the process of product recycling to evaluation; encouraging the use of recycled products; impeding environmental protection and pollution The company levies environmental compensation fees.

Law on the Effective Use of Resources

The Law on the Promotion of the Effective Use of Resources is a revised law on the Law on the Promotion of Recyclable Resources, promulgated in 1991, which was implemented in April 2001. The law is committed to building an economic system with higher resource and environmental efficiency and is a leader in the world. The law requires seven industrial enterprises to implement the principles of waste reduction, reuse and recycling at all stages of the production, distribution and consumption processes. At the same time, the law proposes five specific measures: reducing waste generation by saving production resources and extending product life; recycling parts; companies recycling used products and recycling them; Collect labels; reduce by-products and take other revolving measures.

Waste Disposal Act

The law was enacted in 1970 and was revised three times in 1991, 2001 and 2003. The newly revised law adds provisions for minimization of waste generation, waste sorting and recycling: stricter management provisions for toxic solid waste (such as medical waste); establishment of a waste disposal center system; sharing of responsibility for selective treatment The public; local governments set up a committee to promote waste reduction.

"Container Packaging Recycling Law"

The purpose of the law is to establish a container and packaging recycling system, and to develop specific provisions for the recycling of glass bottles, PET bottles, paper products, plastic packaging products.

"Household Appliance Recycling Law"

The Act stipulates the obligation of manufacturers and importers to recycle household appliances and re-commoditize them according to the re-commodification rate standards. The law stipulates that the re-commodification rate (resource recovery) of refrigerators and washing machines must reach 50% or more; the re-commodification rate of TV sets must reach 55% or more; the re-commodification rate of air conditioners is over 60%.

"Building Materials Recycling Law"

It was promulgated in 2001 and implemented in 2002. The law requires that wastes such as asphalt blocks and waste wood should be recycled. In 2010, the recycling rate of the above three kinds of wastes was 96%.

"Food Recycling Law"

The law was implemented in April 2001. The law stipulates that food factories, distribution and export enterprises have the obligation to convert food waste into feed and feed.

Green Procurement Law

The law was implemented in April 2001. The law stipulates that state agencies and local governments have the obligation to prioritize the procurement of environmentally friendly products. In 2001, environmentally friendly products were purchased from a total of 101 categories of 14 categories including stationery, office automation equipment and automobiles.

"Automobile Recycling Law"

The law was partially implemented in April 2002 and was fully implemented in January 2005. The law stipulates the obligations that the relevant parties must fulfill. The automobile manufacturer must recycle and recycle the residue after the crusher treatment; the automobile seller and the automobile repair enterprise must recycle and deliver the used automobile; the automobile owner must deliver the final disposal fee. After use, the scrapped car should be handed over to the recycling company.

The characteristics of the Japanese circular economy legal system can be summarized as follows:

（1） the coverage is wide. The law has clear regulations on production, consumption, recycling, reuse, and safe handling. For example, domestic waste includes household appliances, automobiles, food, packaging containers and other wastes, and industrial waste includes industrial wastes such as mining, metallurgy, chemicals, and water treatment.

（2） the operability is strong. In the formulation of laws, it is easy to adopt the method of first easy and then difficult, that is, first to legislate for the recycling of wastes with less relevant interests. For example, the Law on Recycling of Household Appliances only targets air conditioners, refrigerators, televisions, washing machines, etc. 》 Recycling and recycling only for car body, plastic, air bag, etc.

（3） the responsibilities of all parties are clear. The law clearly stipulates the responsibilities and obligations of the government, local governments, enterprises, and the public. For example, the Appliance Recycling Law stipulates the costs to be borne by manufacturers, consumers, and recyclers; Intermediaries and responsibilities for managing disposal fees were designed.

Japan's economic policy to promote circular economy

In order to promote the development of a recycling society, Japan has adopted a series of economic policies. One of the main policies is the compensation system for eco-industrial parks. The compensation system is implemented by the Ministry of the Environment and the Ministry of Economy, Trade and Industry. Projects involving other departments are supported by the competent authorities. For example, the food waste treatment research project of the Kitakyushu Eco-industrial Park has received financial support from the Ministry of Agriculture, Forestry, and Culture. In 2003, the Ministry of the Environment and the Ministry of Economy, Trade and Industry provided 1.5 billion yen each. In addition, the Ministry of the Environment also provides substantial financial support for research units, enterprises and intermediaries in waste disposal technology research and development, industrial demonstration, and policy investigation.

In the implementation of the special regeneration law, Japan has formulated a detailed economic system to ensure that waste can be collected, handled, and recycled. For example, in the recycling of household appliances, the handling fee for the disposal of a household appliance by the residents is clearly stipulated; the waste automobile law stipulates the handling fee payable by the new owner and the old owner; the local government stipulates the fees payable by the enterprises and institutions for the disposal of the waste (comparison The fees charged by residents are much higher).

Japan's main measures for promoting technological research and development in a recycling-oriented society are to open up specialized experimental research areas in eco-industrial parks. Production, learning, and government jointly research waste treatment technologies, reuse technologies, and environmental pollution control technologies. Provide technical support for waste recycling and recycling

Performance Objectives and Achievements of Japan's Recycling Society Construction

In the basic plan for the construction of a circular society, Japan proposed the numerical target of the assessment index system. The target mainly includes two aspects. The first aspect is the material flow (raw material flow) target. There are three main sources: resource productivity (inputs of GDP/natural resources, etc.), indicating how to obtain the maximum wealth with the least resources. By 2010, it will reach approximately 390,000 yen/ton (up 40% compared with 2000); recycling utilization will reach approximately 14% by 2010 (up 40% compared with 2000); final treatment volume, to In 2010, it was reduced to about 280 million tons (50% less than in 2000). The second aspect is the target of measures, that is, the amount of garbage discharged per person per day is reduced by 20%, and the relevant commercial market and employment scale of the recycling society is doubled. The establishment of the evaluation index system and the formulation of numerical goals have played a very good policy guiding role in the practice of Japanese recycling society and enhanced operability.

After less than 10 years, the Japanese recycling society has entered a period of benign development, and the recycling rate of many wastes has reached or exceeded the statutory target.

3.4 Practical experience in other countries

Although other countries do not have a clear definition of circular economy, many practices reflect the concept and principles of circular economy, especially the application of "3R" principle in waste disposal, clean production carried out by enterprises and construction of ecological industry.

Circular economy practice at the enterprise level

Cleaner production is widely considered to be a concrete form of practice for circular economy at the enterprise level. Since the United Nations proposed the concept of cleaner production in the late 1980s, many countries in the world have established national cleaner production centers to promote cleaner production. In general, due to the advanced nature of the technology and economy, most enterprises in developed countries have basically reached the requirements of clean production or environmentally friendly production.

The material circulation inside the enterprise is the basic performance of the circular economy at the micro level. Companies participating in the World Business Council for Sustainable Development (WBCSD) and adopting eco-economic benefits as a criterion generally value the material circulation within the enterprise. A typical example is DuPont Chemical, the leader in chemical manufacturing. In the late 1980s, DuPont researchers used the factory as a laboratory to test the concept of circular economy, creatively developing the "3R" principle into a "3R manufacturing method" that was combined with the actuality of the chemical industry to achieve less emissions or even zero. Environmental protection targets for emissions.

Construction experience of eco-industrial parks

The clean production and internal circulation of a single enterprise have certain limitations, because a part of the waste and by-products that cannot be dissolved in the factory will inevitably occur in the production process, so it is necessary to organize the material circulation from outside the factory. Eco-industrial parks are the rule of implementing circular economy on a larger scale, connecting different factories to form an industrial symbiosis combination of shared resources and interchange by-products, making the waste gas, waste heat, waste water and waste of this factory another. The raw materials and energy of the factory. Since 1990, the eco-industrial park has become the theme of the development of the world's industrial parks, and has accumulated rich experience in the specific practice of each country.

Kalundborg, Denmark, is the most typical representative of the world's industrial ecosystems. The main enterprises of this eco-industrial park are power plants, oil refineries, pharmaceutical plants, and gypsum board production plants. Taking these four enterprises as the core to utilize the waste and by-products generated by the other party's production process through trade, not only reduces the amount of waste generated and treated, but also produces better economic benefits and forms economic development and environmental protection and virtuous circle.

Since the 1970s, with the support of the US Environmental Protection Agency (EPA) and the Presidential Council for Sustainable Development (PCSD), the US Eco-Industrial Park project has emerged, involving bioenergy development, waste disposal, clean industry, solids and Recycling of liquid waste and other fields. At present, there are nearly 20 eco-industrial parks in the United States, each with its own characteristics. For example: the modified Chattanooga Eco-Industrial Park. In the park, DuPont's nylon thread recycling as the core to promote zero-emissions reform of enterprises not only reduced pollution, but also promoted the development of environmental protection industry, and developed new industrial space in the old industrial area. The new Choctaw Eco-Industrial Park. For example, Oklahoma uses a large amount of waste tires as a resource, and uses pyrolysis technology to recycle these waste tires to obtain products such as carbon black, plasticizers, and waste heat, which can further derive different product chains. The virtual Brownsville Eco-Industrial Park. On the base of the original members of the park, new members are constantly added to take on the role of "chain-linking network" in the industrial ecological chain, such as the introduction of thermal power stations, waste oil, waste solvent recycling plants.

Since 1995, the eco-industrial park project has been gradually launched in the Portland industrial area in Toronto, Canada. This industrial area brings together a wide range of manufacturing and service industries with potential for waste and energy exchange.

Comprehensive recycling of waste

1. French packaging waste recycling system

Under the pressure of the Packaging Act, in August 1992, French manufacturers and importers and exporters set up a recycling system and a household classification packaging center. The environmental packaging trademark company manages the packaging of packaging products, product manufacturers, and importers to promote environmental protection. In addition, there are some packaging recycling organizations in France.

For example, the bottle manufacturer of the wine and beverage industry has established Adephe, whose mission is to collect pharmaceutical packaging waste. In the same year, the timber industry set up Eco-bois with the task of collecting wood packaging. Manufacturers and importers can also entrust third parties to choose a deposit system or an independent recycling system to recycle packaging waste.

2. US packaging waste recycling system

The recycling system in the United States has roadside recycling, scattered recycling and dispersion recovery systems. Roadside recycling is to require residents to put wastes that can be recycled as renewable resources, such as newspapers, metal, glass, plastic bottles, etc., to be collected by the local authorities, and then sorted, sorted, and sent to the corresponding factories. use. Roadside recycling is often considered the most efficient method of recycling. In 1996, the total number of roadside recycling stations reached 8,917, serving 135 million people. The cost of scattered recycling is almost the same as the cost of roadside recycling, but because it is not convenient, usually only a small number of people participate. The decentralized recovery system can complement the roadside recycling system and work together. In terms of economic policy, it mainly adopts the returnable security policy, garbage charging policy, raw material tax, landfill and incineration tax, which effectively promotes the reduction and recycling of waste such as packaging waste.

3. Recycling of used household appliances

According to the US Environmental Protection Agency, the use of scrap steel recovered from waste household appliances instead of mining, transportation, and smelting of new steel can reduce 97% of mine waste, reduce 86% of air pollution, 76% of water pollution, and reduce 40%. Water consumption, saving 90% of raw materials, 74% of energy, and the performance of scrap steel and new steel is basically the same.

In waste electronic products, the disposal of used computers has been a big problem in the United States. In March 2004, Massachusetts enacted the first law in the United States prohibiting private disposal of obsolete computer monitors, televisions, and other electronic products from landfills and incinerators.

Relevant laws, regulations and policies of the circular economy

In the face of waste, many countries have laws and regulations to solve problems. Since the 1990s, many countries have developed their own policies and regulations to promote the reduction, recycling and safe disposal of waste. In summary, there are: voluntary recycling system, producer responsibility system, industry fee reduction system, waste classification system, market means, financial and taxation policies, waste recycling fund, waste incineration recycling energy, environmentally responsible procurement methods, Environmental labeling system and business principles for sustainable development.

All states in the United States have their own laws and regulations. The early circular economy law can be traced back to the 1970s, but there is no national circular economy regulation. In 1976, the United States enacted the Solid Waste Disposal Law, which was revised several times. In 1990, the Pollution Prevention Act was passed. In 1991, the US Environmental Protection Agency established the priority of waste disposal, namely, reduction. Reuse - recycling - incineration - landfill. Since 1980, some states in the United States have enacted laws and regulations to promote recycling of resources; Oregon, New Jersey, and Rhode Island have successively enacted regulations to promote recycling of resources; more than half of the states have developed different forms. Regenerative recycling regulations.

Enlightenment of international experience on China's development of circular economy

1. Comparative analysis of Chinese and foreign concepts of circular economy

Although the term "circular economy" is an exotic product, the development of China's circular economy has a unique momentum in the world, regardless of the degree of government attention, social propaganda, practice, or the connotation of circular economy. This is mainly due to the different national conditions and the urgency of the problem to be solved. The circular economy advocated by the developed countries represented by Germany and Japan starts from the recycling of wastes, expands the circular economy to the production and consumption fields through the extension system of production responsibility, promotes the regional production through material flow management, and changes the traditional mass production. The pattern of social and economic development with a large amount of consumption and a large amount of abandonment. In comparison, the concept of "circular economy" advocated by China is broad and rich in content, involving both production and consumption. It is a big concept for transforming the entire economic growth mode to regulate the material between the socio-economic system and the ecological environment system. The (resources/waste) flow pattern is the starting point, with the core of improving eco-efficiency as the core, and the goal of establishing an economic growth model of "low resource consumption, high economic efficiency, and low pollution emissions". Of course, from the pursuit of the goal, the advanced nature of the technological economy and eco-efficiency of the developed countries in the production field, and the development trend of the circular economy in developed countries, the connotation of circular economy in China and developed countries is not essentially different, but only practical. The focus and time series are different. Therefore, the current circular economy advocated by China can be linked to the sustainable production and consumption that is currently being promoted internationally and the "3R" strategy advocated by the G8 conference.

Sustainable production and consumption are theories of sustainable development, especially the normative documents of the Johannesburg World Conference on Sustainable Development, which are common concepts in the international community. The implementation plan adopted by the Johannesburg World Conference on Sustainable Development calls for countries to encourage and promote the development of a 10-year framework to support regional and national accelerated shifts to sustainable consumption and production, and to promote socio-economic development within the carrying capacity of ecosystems, In response to the spiritual requirements of the implementation plan of the Johannesburg Summit, sustainable production and consumption have become hot issues in the international community.

The main objectives of the "3R" strategy are twofold: first, to improve resource efficiency, and second, to prevent pollution, that is, to maximize resource efficiency and at the same time minimize pollution load. The international community has already vigorously promoted the "3R" strategy as an important way and strategy to achieve sustainable production and consumption.

At the national level, the UK launched a government framework for sustainable consumption and production in 2003; Germany has embarked on a national strategy; Finland commissioned a committee to draft a national plan for sustainable consumption and production; countries in Central and Eastern Europe and Central Asia also It is recognized that sustainable consumption and production are essential requirements for sustainable development and are reflected in the national policy framework.

From the perspective of the nature of China's circular economy, it mainly covers two key areas of production and consumption. Therefore, sustainable production and sustainable consumption have become two important dimensions of the development of circular economy. The main purpose of sustainable production is to improve the efficiency of resources and energy use, improve resource productivity, and transform traditional industrial production systems. In practice, it is mainly reflected in the promotion of cleaner production at the enterprise level, the construction of ecological industrial parks at the industrial park level, and the construction of Eco-industrial network.

The sustainable consumption system provides a variety of consumer goods and services by reducing natural resource consumption and creating a good living environment to meet the basic needs of human beings, including not only the production and consumption of green products, but also the recycling of waste materials and resources. Effective use, living environment and species protection cover all aspects of production and consumption behavior.

Experience in developed countries shows that production and consumption are mutually causal, but in the buyer's market, consumption orientation and consumption behavior have a decisive influence on the way and content of production. For example, the choice of environmentally friendly products in the consumer sector can effectively foster circulation. The economic market, the scale of the circular economy, the correct economic incentives to the production sector, the formation of a circular economy system in the production sector, the stimulation of the development and application of circular economy technology, so that the prices of circular economy products and services tend to be reasonable A reasonable price can promote consumers to adopt an environmentally friendly consumption pattern, and finally form a cycle of benign interaction between the two. In addition, sustainable consumer behavior and other related industry activities provide 'renewable resources and green services' for production activities. For example, the recycling and reuse of waste in the consumer sector can provide a large amount of renewable resources to the production field, reduce the pressure of end processing, lengthen the industrial chain, and create new employment opportunities. At the same time, enterprises can be extended through the system of production responsibility extension. Strengthen the reduction, reuse, recycling and harmlessness of resources. Therefore, sustainable consumption plays an important guiding role in establishing a sustainable production model. From the perspective of coverage, building a sustainable consumption model is an important part of developing a circular economy. From the perspective of the mechanism of action, sustainable consumption is the intrinsic driving force for the development of circular economy. To sum up, China has five aspects to develop a circular economy and establish a sustainable consumption system. The first is the certification of environmental labeling products, organic foods, and energy-saving products; the second is to vigorously develop the green service industry, that is, the tertiary industry; the third is the creation of ecological buildings and green communities; the fourth is to raise public awareness and advocate public green consumption; Promote government green procurement.

2. The significance of international experience for China's development of circular economy

Through comparative research, we can find that the international practice of developing circular economy and building a recycling-oriented society has many implications for the circular economy that China is currently vigorously promoting, mainly reflected in regulations and policies, management systems and mechanisms, practice models and evaluation methods, and priority areas. Choices, technology and information, publicity and public participation.

(1) Laws, regulations and policy implications

A sound legal system of circular economy is the basic basis and guarantee for the development of circular economy. In order to implement the recycling of resources throughout the process and realize the development model of circular society, Japan has established a set of perfect laws and regulations on the three levels of "basic law, comprehensive law and special law", which is worth learning from China.

The promulgation of the "Clean Production Promotion Law" indicates that China's environmental protection legislation has shifted from the end pollution control to the production process control, but this legislative idea is not fully reflected in other resources and environmental laws. In addition, in the important areas of circular economy such as resource recycling and sustainable consumption, China's legislation is basically in a blank. Therefore, China should re-engineer the existing resource and environmental legal system and build a system of circular economy laws and regulations covering the areas of production, consumption and resource recycling, covering the basic law, comprehensive law and special law, including the basic law of circular economy. The Waste Disposal Law, the Resource Conservation and Comprehensive Utilization Promotion Law, and the special laws and regulations that promote the recycling of various specific substances and the safe disposal of wastes make the development of China's circular economy legally compliant and coordinated with existing resources and environmental laws.

To comprehensively promote the development of circular economy, China should gradually establish and improve the following four key systems and policies:

（1） the circular economy market system. The circular economy market system refers to the constraint and incentive system that regulates the individual economic behavior of the industrial economy from the perspective of circular economy with the aim of using price as a lever to activate resource utilization efficiency in various fields of industrial economic production, circulation and consumption.

（2） the circular economy normative system, including the clean production system, the green consumption system, the green trade system, the green procurement system, the green packaging system, and the green sign system. The establishment and implementation of these systems will enable resources to recycle resources in the economic fields of production, exchange, distribution, consumption, etc., and forcefully regulate and regulate various resource recycling behaviors. The producer responsibility extension system is an important circular economy norm system. During the product life cycle, producers are not only responsible for the quality of products, but also responsible for the recycling and recycling of used products. Use economic instruments and market mechanisms to establish mechanisms for producers to be responsible for their collection, recycling and recycling after the use of their products.

（3） the circular economy accounting system, including the green accounting system, the green audit system, and the green national economic accounting system. These institutional arrangements include the inventory consumption and depreciation of ecological resources and the protection and loss costs into the assessment of resource recycling and economic performance, evaluate the real economic performance of social economic activities, and implement effective quantitative assessment of economic behavior of economic individuals. And supervision.

（4） in view of improving the efficiency of resource and energy utilization, it is the core content of the development of circular economy. In the development of circular economy, the international community also attaches great importance to improving the efficiency of resource and energy utilization, and adjusting and optimizing the energy structure. Therefore, it is established and improved. The supporting resources and energy utilization policies are very important. In view of the current situation in China, it is necessary to focus on formulating policies to promote comprehensive utilization of resources, policies to improve eco-efficiency, energy conservation and emission reduction in key industries, water conservation policies, and e-waste recycling and recycling policies.

(2) Economic policy implications

Economic incentives under the market mechanism can effectively promote the development of China's circular economy. From international experience, it is precisely because of the overall resource prices (energy, water, land, etc.) and services (disposal of waste) in Germany, Japan and other OECD countries. The high cost of environmental liability (litigation, fines, etc.) has become a major factor in promoting resource efficiency.

From this point of view, the circular economy incentive system, including the green fiscal system, green financial system, green tax system, green investment system. These incentive institutional arrangements will provide an effective incentive mechanism for resource recycling and environmental protection activities.

(3) Management system and mechanism enlightenment

Appropriate institutional arrangements can ensure that the various departments of the government coordinate with each other and perform their duties to jointly promote the development of circular economy. Countries such as Germany and Japan can smoothly promote the development of circular economy and build a recycling-oriented society. They have a close relationship with the government departments to establish a circular economy management system that is harmonious, efficient, and has its own functions and cooperation. Therefore, China needs to establish a coordinated management system to promote the development of circular economy.

The circular economy management system should be established according to the connotation and essential characteristics of the circular economy. First of all, the circular economy is an economy, a social production and reproduction activity, and the economic comprehensive department should naturally play a leading role. That is to say, from the perspective of macroeconomic regulation and control measures such as industrial policy, resource and energy price policy, fiscal and financial policy, and national social and economic development planning, we will guide the adjustment of economic structure and the development of microeconomic activities in the direction of circular economy.

Secondly, the circular economy is different from the traditional economic development model. It starts from the resource and environmental issues, and the whole process of economic activities is the main line of improving resource efficiency and protecting the environment. It is a sustainable production and consumption activity, resources and environmental protection. The department is an indispensable part of the circular economy management system. Otherwise, in the operation management and guidance methods, there is no guarantee that the development of the circular economy will be different from the traditional economy. The environmental protection department has two main functions in promoting and guiding the development of circular economy: First, it supervises and evaluates the development of circular economy from the perspective of resource and environmental performance of economic operations. The development of indicator systems and standards in different fields and levels of the circular economy is the basis and prerequisite for the environmental protection department to play this role. The second is to strengthen environmental supervision and management, grasp the environmental impact assessment of projects, policies and plans, and form the driving force for the development of circular economy from the outside.

In sum, the development of circular economy is the responsibility of the government department. It requires the economic comprehensive department and the resource and environmental departments to play a leading role from different angles according to their respective functions. The relevant departments of science and technology, finance, finance, taxation and national economic construction work closely together. . This requires a unified coordination mechanism between the state and governments at all levels to coordinate the management functions and actions of the major departments.

International experience shows that establishing a circular economy operation mechanism and clarifying the respective responsibilities and obligations of the government, enterprises and the public are the key to ensuring the smooth development of the circular economy. In the development of circular economy, the government has both guiding responsibilities and funding and policy support through the formulation of various economic incentives. As the practice subject of circular economy, enterprises should be aware of their social responsibilities, and encourage enterprises to be responsible for the production, use, collection, recycling, recycling and treatment of their products during the life cycle of the products through the polluter pays system and the producer responsibility extension system. . Public participation is not only to create a good social atmosphere for the development of circular economy, but also the public has direct responsibilities and obligations in many areas of circular economy development (such as green consumption, resource conservation and recycling of waste), as consumers, Pay for collecting and disposing of household garbage.

(4) Evaluation method and practice mode: material flow analysis and management
Japan, Germany and other EU countries have adopted a material flow analysis method to improve resource efficiency and develop a circular economy performance evaluation. The specific practice mode is to comprehensively introduce the concept and method of material flow management, and its evaluation method and practice model are worthy of China. Learn from. Material flow analysis and management can play a methodological guidance role in circular economy practice in five aspects. First, reduce the total amount of material input. In social and economic activities, the amount of material input directly determines the amount of resources extracted and the degree of impact on the ecological environment. Especially for non-renewable resources, the reduction of material input directly means the increase of the useful life of resources, and its significance to the whole social economy and environment is extremely significant. Therefore, the circular economy emphasizes the need to achieve social and economic goals while reducing the total input of materials. Decoupling or decoupling of economic growth and material consumption and environmental degradation by reducing total input of materials. Second, improve resource utilization efficiency. Resource utilization efficiency reflects the level of conversion between substances and products, and production technology and processes are the core to improve resource utilization efficiency. Through material flow analysis, the relationship between material input and product output can be analyzed and mastered, and the transformation efficiency between materials and products can be improved through technology, process modification and renewal, and resource utilization efficiency can be improved to achieve as little as possible. The purpose of material inputs to achieve the desired economic goals. Third, increase the amount of material circulation. By increasing the recycling rate and recycling rate of waste, it is possible to increase the recycling amount of materials, prolong the service life of resources, and reduce the initial resource input, thereby ultimately reducing the total amount of material input. Fourth, reduce final waste emissions. In essence, in social and economic activities, by increasing the efficiency of resource utilization and increasing the amount of material circulation, not only can the total amount of material inputs be reduced, but also the goal of reducing final waste emissions can be achieved. Therefore, in the process of developing a circular economy, the progress of production technology and technology, the development of the ecological industrial chain and the development of the vein industry can reduce the final waste discharge by improving resource use efficiency, increasing material circulation and reducing total material input. The purpose of quantity. Fifth, develop circular economy indicators and standards. To develop a circular economy, how to evaluate the development

performance of the circular economy is an important content, which requires the establishment of a scientific and feasible indicator system. Material flow analysis provides a scientific method for analyzing the efficiency of economic activities, resources and environmental pressure. Therefore, the indicator system based on material flow analysis is an important indicator for evaluating the efficiency of economic activities and the development of circular economy. There are six main indicators based on material flow analysis: resource input indicators; economic output and waste output indicators; resource consumption indicators; resource balance indicators; eco-efficiency indicators; reflecting the correlation between material consumption, environmental degradation and economic growth The composite index of the relationship.

(5) Priority area selection

Despite the same or similar nature, due to the different stages of development in China and developed countries, China's differences in the priority areas of circular economy and specific modes of practice are determined. China's circular economy construction must solve the resource bottlenecks and environmental pressures encountered in China's rapid industrialization process. Therefore, China's circular economy faces the complex environmental problems arising from China's unique compression-type industrialization. Very rich, almost including the various industries of the national economy.

Renovating the existing industrial system and constructing the eco-industrial system are the key points in the development of circular economy in the production field. We must closely seize the links of resource exploitation and utilization, product production and recycling of waste resources, and follow economic, resource recycling, environmental and social employment. The principle of unifying benefits, selecting "double high" industries with high pollution and high resource and energy consumption, such as steel, coal, petroleum, petrochemical, chemical, building materials and other industries, to improve their resource productivity, reduce their pollution load, and make them ecological Transformation.

Although China and developed countries have focused on the selection of priority areas for the development of circular economy, the recycling of waste resources in the priority areas of developed countries and the recycling of recycling industries (the so-called intravenous industry) have special significance for China, and should also become China's priority areas for developing a circular economy.

(6) Technology and information support system

The main technical carrier of the contemporary knowledge economy is high-tech led by information technology and biotechnology. International experience shows that the circular economy also needs advanced science and technology as the support. If there is no input of advanced technology, the economy and environment pursued by the circular economy The goal will be difficult to achieve at all. The supporting technical system of circular economy consists of five categories: alternative technology, reduction technology, reuse technology, resource technology, and system technology.

At the same time, the circular economy is a complex economic reproduction system, which can only be analyzed and managed by material flow using modern information technology. The ecological and economic benefits of the circular economy will ultimately be reflected in the material flow changes of the economic system. A circular economy system should significantly reduce resource input flows while drastically reducing waste output streams. From the perspective of circular economy, the analysis and evaluation of the output input and environmental impact of an economic system (whether enterprise, household or city, country) must be based on the whole process and the whole system, not just one of them. One part. Therefore, material flow analysis constitutes the basic idea of   circular economy information management technology. It requires the analysis of the system's resource consumption and pollution emissions from the whole process of material and energy circulation, namely mining, processing, transportation, use, recycling and final disposal, so as to obtain the whole process of the whole system. Environmental impact, establishing a virtuous cycle of environmental and economical regional circular economy systems.

(7) Publicity and education and public participation

The circular economy system includes both production systems and consumer systems. Without sustainable consumption methods, it is impossible to form sustainable production methods, and the circular economy cannot be discussed. Therefore, the development of circular economy requires not only the government's advocacy and corporate self-discipline, but also requires all members of the whole society to start from me and participate together. Carrying out circular economy propaganda and education and raising public awareness is to create a good social atmosphere for promoting the development of circular economy. At the same time, it is more important for the public to build a circular economy.

Japan attaches great importance to the use of various means to carry out propaganda work on the establishment of a recycling-oriented society. The public has actively participated in the construction of a recycling-oriented society and achieved very good results. The public can participate in the construction of a circular society from three aspects. First, to prevent over-packaging, reduce packaging waste, correct shopping and environmentally friendly consumption; second, to bear part of the collection and recycling of used electronic products, scrapped motor vehicles, etc., to improve the recycling rate of waste resources; With disposable consumables, you can give it to others without using it for life durable goods such as clothes, old appliances, furniture, etc., and do not discard them. The German public and non-governmental organizations have also become the backbone of the promotion of circular economy.

China is a nation that advocates diligence and thrift, but we must also see that with the deepening of the industrialization process, especially after the per capita GDP exceeds 1,000 US dollars, the pace of consumption upgrading is accelerating, the consumption structure has changed significantly, and the characteristics of consumer society are revealed. China must learn from the lessons of Japan, vigorously promote the lifestyle of circular economy, advocate green consumption, widely publicize, carry forward fine traditions, and establish an environmentally friendly and resource-saving social consumption model.

Part 4　The Role of Circular Economy Theory in Eco-environment Design

Chapter 1 Analysis of the relationship between circular economy theory and ecological environment

With the development of social economy and the gradual improvement of various aspects of the system, people pay more and more attention to the ecological environment. The introduction of the theory of circular economy has played a significant role in the ecological environment. Therefore, explore the circular economy. The relationship between theory and the ecological environment is significant.

1.1 Relationship between ecological environmental impact assessment system and circular economy theory

The ecological environment impact assessment system plays an institutional role in the design of ecological environment. The analysis of the ecological environment impact system under the circular economy can help us explore the relationship between circular economy theory and ecological environment design.

Since the implementation of the eco-environmental impact assessment system in China in the 1970s, it has played a positive role in controlling new pollution and promoting old pollution control. However, with the development of social economy and the change of environmental protection concept, China's current ecological environmental impact assessment has been unable to meet the requirements of environmental protection and social development. China's traditional environmental impact assessment mainly focuses on the end control and end treatment of pollution. This passive approach to environmental management is far from meeting the requirements of the times. To this end, the State proposes in the Clean Production Promotion Law that "new construction, reconstruction and expansion projects should conduct environmental impact assessments, analyze and demonstrate the use of raw materials, resource consumption, comprehensive utilization of resources, and generation and disposal of pollutants, giving priority to resource utilization. Clean production technologies, processes and equipment with high rates and low pollutant production." Therefore, the environmental impact assessment can analyze the whole process from the raw materials, production process and final product of the project, and complete the initial transition from the end treatment to the whole process control. However, clean production technology is limited to one project, but not between enterprises and between industries.

With the establishment of the scientific concept of development, China's government and academia have invariably regarded the development of circular economy and the establishment of a conservation-oriented society as an important means for China to implement sustainable development and implement the scientific development concept. Some areas in China have begun to establish eco-industrial parks with enterprise symbiosis as the mainstay, and established a national circular economy pilot province (city) in Liaoning Province and Guiyang City, which laid the foundation for the development of circular economy in China. This model is rapidly spreading throughout the country, and there are more and more closely related enterprise groups such as eco-industrial parks, ecological agriculture, and ecological enterprises. This requires China's environmental impact assessment to jump out of the circle of projects, in a larger area. In the evaluation and coordination among multiple enterprises and industries, more consideration is given to the coordination and complementarity between enterprises and industries, and the concept of circular economy is further applied to environmental impact assessment. Starting from the principles, objectives and the connotation of circular economy of environmental impact assessment, we focus on the need to adapt to the rapid development of circular economy in China, the adjustment of a series of adjustment directions and evaluation methods of environmental impact assessment, and at the same time, the development of circular economy to China The eco-environmental impact assessment system puts forward new requirements, and the eco-environment system also promotes and promotes the development of China's circular economy. The two mutually promote each other.

Since the implementation of environmental impact assessment in China, China's environmental management has completed the transition from traditional management to scientific management and from decentralized management to system management. China's environmental impact assessment has also gone from single factor evaluation to comprehensive evaluation, from concentration control to total quantity control, from end treatment to cleaner production, from construction project environmental impact assessment to planning environmental impact assessment. China's environmental impact assessment is gradually maturing and standardizing, and it has also played an increasingly important role. Specifically, China's environmental impact assessment has experienced the following important stages:

Stage 1: the environmental impact assessment system was implemented from scratch and implemented at the end. Since the 19th century, especially after the middle of the 20th century, the expansion of environmental pollution and serious public nuisance incidents have directly led to the emergence of environmental impact assessments. Its emergence has changed the old "social development, economic development, that is, the overall development of mankind" The concept emphasizes that the environment is the foundation of human existence and opposes the idea that man dominates and rules nature. In 1979, the environmental impact assessment system was established in China. It was first applied in the evaluation of construction projects. At that time, it was a passive control and partial governance, mainly for the treatment and control of pollutants. The core goal was to achieve emission standards. For the process of pollutant production, the cause of the analysis is not deep enough, which is a limitation that must exist under the conditions at that time.

Stage 2: the end control is transferred to the whole process control. By the end of the 1980s, the concept of cleaner production emerged as the main way to achieve sustainable development, which was widely accepted by various countries. The proposal of this concept provides a new idea for the environmental impact assessment system. Clean production requirements are environmentally friendly from the acquisition of raw materials, to the use of products, and scrapping. This inevitably requires environmental impact assessment to shift from terminal governance to full process control. Environmental impact assessment is required for product design, raw material extraction, process flow and pollution control, and appropriate environmental protection measures are taken. The application of cleaner production in environmental impact assessment makes the environmental impact assessment of construction projects tend to be perfect, and the pollution control measures are more scientific and reasonable. In the third stage, pollution control is turned to source control. In 2003, after the enactment and implementation of the Environmental Impact Assessment Law, China planned the environmental impact assessment in a statutory form, and planned to control environmental pollution and ecological damage from the planning level, thus shifting environmental impact assessment from the end treatment to the source. control. In the decision-making four-stage "policy-planning-planning-project", the level of planning is mentioned from the project level. Although the evaluation of the policy has not been included, it has taken a big step toward source control. This transformation is in line with the requirements of sustainable development and has changed the passive situation in the past when the project environmental impact assessment. Considering environmental issues during the planning phase of development can avoid many major environmental pollution incidents and ecological damage problems, making decision-making more scientific.

1.2 The relationship between ecological environment design and circular economy theory

The introduction of circular economy theory in recent years has put forward higher requirements for the design of ecological environment in China. It is also imperative to explore the relationship between ecological environment design and circular economy theory. We can call the relationship between circular economy and ecological environment design, complement each other and promote each other.

What is mean it by "complementing each other and promoting each other"? This is not to say that without a circular economy, it is impossible to develop an ecological environment design, or that without the ecological environment design, a circular economy cannot be developed, and it can be said that it is the same as our left and right hands. Our left and right hands are part of our body. Some people are born without left or right hands, but relying on one hand after training cannot affect life, but it is much less than those born with hands. convenient. The relationship between circular economy and ecological environment design is like this. With the theory of circular economy, the design of ecological environment will develop better, it is more suitable for the trend of social development, and the design and improvement of ecological environment will be correspondingly improved and transformed. The development of circular economy will be more rapid, and the speed of popularization will also accelerate, and people's life and production will be accelerated. The meaning is also very favorable.

Chapter 2 Analysis of the Role of Circular Economy Theory in Ecological Environment Design

2.1 Circular economy promotes the improvement of various aspects of China's ecological environment design

According to the principle of ecology, the circular economy grasps the "3R principle", through rational design of industrial chains and products, scientific use of resources to achieve the optimal use of environmental resources, to produce the best environmental and economic benefits, and achieve sustainable development.

According to the requirements of circular economy, there are still some defects in China's environmental impact assessment, such as the management of heavy facilities in environmental impact assessment, the scientific use of light natural resources, the discharge of heavy pollutants, the comprehensive utilization of light pollutants, and the implementation of heavy policies. Management, light economy, and effective scientific guidance. That is to say, China's current environmental impact assessment does not comprehensively consider the four links of natural resources, process flow, waste utilization and economic benefits. Therefore, China's environmental impact assessment should pay more attention to the utilization of source resources and the end-of-production management. It should actively promote the use of energy-saving and pollution-reducing processes, adhere to clean production technologies, promote comprehensive utilization of waste, and actively develop product life cycle. Evaluation and promotion of environmentally sound technologies.

From this point of view, under the guidance of circular economy, China's environmental impact assessment will certainly be further improved: from linear control to cross-over, comprehensive control. The concept of circular economy with "the most effective use of resources" as its core content is just right for China's current resource shortage and serious environmental pollution. After experiencing the pursuit of "the most effective use of labor" and "the most effective use of capital", people finally realized To natural resources is the foundation of human survival. It is necessary to make full use of resources, make good use of its capacity and carrying capacity, and pursue the "most effective use of resources". It must not violate the general laws of nature and carry out supernormal mining, utilization and discharge. In this context, the environmental impact assessment should break through the boundaries of the original individual enterprises and individual industries. It is necessary to conduct comprehensive evaluation and analysis of multiple enterprise industries along the industrial chain, and propose the most reasonable "reduction, reuse, recycling". Measures: At the same time, to break through the limitations of the original pollutant discharge standards and total control, it is necessary to highlight the optimal use of resources, emphasize the efficiency of resource utilization, and effectively reduce the energy consumption and consumption of unit products.

2.2 Circular economy theory provides theoretical guidance for China's ecological environment design

In these years, China's environmental design theory has undergone great changes. The biggest change is to pay more attention to the protection of the ecological environment and pay more attention to the recycling and development of resources. However, the speed of social economy and situation renewal far exceeds the update speed of ecological environment design theory and principles. After the theory of circular economy was put forward, it provided direction guidance for the next ecological environment design in China. China now advocates the ecological development of circular economy, and the ecological development of circular economy is a systematic project that integrates many fields such as economy, society and science and technology. It needs a series of profound changes to form a strong innovation support. system.

1. Circular economy theory helps us update the concept of ecological environment design

Concept is a kind of thinking, a kind of consciousness, which determines the behavior of human beings. The innovation of ideas is to replace the old ideas with new ideas, which is also the need to adapt to the new situation and new changes. In the design of ecological environment, we should replace the traditional concept of circularity with the concept of circular economy, establish a sense of worry and overall concept, and guide people to update the concept of ecological environment design once and achieve harmony between man and nature.

2. The theory of circular economy requires us to carry out the technology and management innovation of ecological environment design.

Science and technology as the primary productive force is the core competitiveness of circular economy and ecological environment design and development. This requires us to give full play to the role of science and technology in the process of developing ecological environment design under the circular economy, and develop and establish including clean production and resources. The green eco-environment design technical system, such as recycling and ecological management, accelerates the application and promotion of key industries and key enterprises, and promotes the development of eco-environment design technology.

As a basic function of the government, in the process of developing the ecological environment design under the circular economy, it is necessary to give full play to the functions of the government's macro-control. On the one hand, it is necessary to carry out circular economy theory learning for ecological environment designers through public opinion and publicity and education. The whole society understands the circular economy and recognizes the importance of the ecological development of circular economy. On the other hand, it is necessary to set up an intermediary organization for the development of circular economy, and play its unique role in the management innovation of ecological environment design.

Chapter 3 Research on the Value and Significance of Ecological Environment Design to Circular Economy

While the circular economy plays a role in promoting and perfecting various aspects of ecological environment design, it is also of profound significance and value for the development of circular economy and the improvement of circular economy theory.

3.1 Strengthen environmental impact assessment and promote the development and implementation of circular economy

Sustainability requires people to consider their environmental consequences before they act to avoid environmental pollution and ecological damage caused by blindness and ignorance, thus affecting the sustainability of development. Circular economy is an effective way to achieve sustainable development. It is an innovative economic growth model. It is the only way for us to break the growth nightmare and guarantee the ultimate realization of China's modernization on the basis of sustainable development. However, due to various factors such as inaccurate understanding of the meaning of circular economy or lack of understanding of the meaning of implementing circular economy and lack of practical experience in the implementation process, the circular economy encountered such problems in the implementation process. The main reason for this is that there are no corresponding regulations, standards, etc., and thus lack legal binding. Environmental impact assessment is one of the important tools for integrating the principles of sustainable development into human development activities and strategic decision-making. Since the promulgation of China's "Environmental Protection Law" in 1979, the environmental impact assessment system has become a legal system, which is mandatory and must be violated. It is also included in the basic procedures of project construction, and the environmental impact after the investment system reform in China. Evaluation has become the forefront of the approval process and has become the first pass for the project to be launched. It is precisely because environmental impact assessment has such status and legal coercion. Under the circumstances that China has not yet established or built regulations and standards for implementing circular economy, it is better to promote the implementation of circular economy through environmental impact assessment. select. Environmental impact assessment is a means and a system, which technically realizes the sustainability of our society; circular economy is an idea, a way, which provides ways and means for sustainable development. The mutual complementation and mutual promotion are two indispensable aspects for China to achieve sustainable development and build a well-off society in an all-round way. Through the environmental impact assessment, the feasibility analysis of the implementation of cleaner production and circular economy, and the corresponding implementation recommendations and measures, so as to implement the concept of circular economy in the construction project and planning.

3.2 Adjust the goals and content of the eco-environment design to meet the needs of the new situation

The implementation of circular economy requires construction projects or planning to focus on the optimal use of resources. While meeting the environmental feasibility, we must also consider the reuse of resources and the cascade utilization of energy. Therefore, in the future goal of eco-environment design, the goal of rational use of resources should be added on the base of emission standards and total amount control, and the analysis and evaluation of the industry chain should be emphasized in the content.

In the current ecological environment design process, resource utilization is often excluded from environmental impact, and ignoring resources and environment is also the basic condition for human survival. Even if the implementation of the project or plan can meet the pollutant discharge standards and meet the total control indicators, if the consumption of too much resources will directly lead to unsustainable development. Therefore, according to the requirements of the circular economy, the future environmental impact assessment should make the rational use and optimal utilization of resources as the target of its evaluation.

The key to the smooth implementation of the circular economy lies in the formation and stable existence of the industrial chain. The eco-industrial parks actively promoted in China are carried out around the industrial chain. The environmental impact assessment should also focus on the industrial chain, and at least the evaluation content should be The following points should be included:

1. Excavation and feasibility evaluation of potential industrial chain

The key to the realization of circular economy is whether it can achieve "reduction, reuse, recycling". In a single enterprise, it mainly implements clean production audit, while in the enterprise group or the whole society, it should span a single enterprise or industry. Grasp the establishment of the industrial chain, so that the waste generated by the enterprise will become the raw material and resources again, so as to achieve the purpose of "reduction, reuse and recycling". After incorporating the concept of circular economy into environmental impact assessment, environmental impact assessment should adopt a cross-over (industry crossover, enterprise cross) evaluation method to find possible industrial chains, and at the same time evaluate whether the industrial chain is feasible, stable, and technically feasible. Economic feasibility and environmental feasibility are fully demonstrated in three aspects. Among them, technical feasibility is the premise, economic feasibility is guarantee, and environmental feasibility is the purpose. At present, there is such a problem in the eco-industrial parks in China and even in the world. Although some enterprises can use the waste generated by other companies, it is technically feasible, but the economy is unreasonable or will produce more serious secondary pollution. Therefore, the feasibility of the industrial chain in the evaluation is the focus and difficulty of the evaluation.

2. Stability evaluation of ecological industry chain

The general eco-industrial chain has a leading industry. For example, the Guigang Eco-industrial Park takes sugarcane sugar as the core and leads to alcohol plants, papermaking, cement and other enterprises. Therefore, whether the eco-industrial chain can be stable and sustainable, the core industry (enterprise) is the key. When evaluating the stability of the eco-industrial chain, the core industry (enterprise) should first be evaluated for stability. This evaluation should include the development prospects of the industry, the development potential of the enterprise, and the amount of waste (raw materials of downstream enterprises) and waste. Stability of ingredients and properties, etc.

After analyzing the stability of the core enterprise, it should also analyze the anti-interference ability of the chain of the industrial chain.

It is necessary to fully consider the viability of downstream enterprises when there is fluctuation in upstream enterprises. In the case that the waste of the upstream enterprise (the raw material of the downstream enterprise) is insufficient or the composition is changed, whether the downstream enterprise has a good solution or not, how to solve it. For example, in the Kalundborg Eco-Industrial Park in Denmark, due to changes in the source of coal fuel used in power plants, the amount of vanadium in the fly ash produced by the power plant is too high, resulting in the downstream wall material plant having to undergo process modification.

Chapter 4 Analysis of the Legal System Framework of Circular Economy

4.1 Circular Economy Ecological Design System

Legislative necessity

Eco-design is a new concept in the field of environmental management proposed by the Dutch public authorities and the United Nations Environment Program in the early 1990s. It combines multidisciplinary theories of economy, environment, management and ecology, and is an effective way to promote economic development. . Eco-design refers to the integration of environmental factors into the design of products. In every bad section of the product life cycle, the environmental load that may be generated is taken into account, and the environmental impact of the product is minimized by improving the design. To put it simply, eco-design is the systematic process of environmentally plunging into the design process of energy-using products. The main purpose is to improve the environmental performance of the product during its life cycle. The life cycle refers to the continuous, interlocking aspects from the design of the energy-using product to the final treatment, covering the aspects of product design, transportation, energy use, and disposal after scrapping.

Although ecological design is only a kind of idea and concept in the specific production process, it is also of great significance to the overall and long-term development of China's economy and society.

It is conducive to building a resource-saving society and achieving sustainable economic and social development. With the continuous deepening of the construction of China's primary stage of socialism, the contradiction between natural resources and economic development has become increasingly acute. Only by taking the connotative development path, expanding the role and influence of science and technology in production, and establishing the ecological design concept of products can we effectively alleviate and finally resolve this contradiction. As people's demand for material culture is increasing and the level is getting higher and higher, it is impossible for China to take the road of "inaction" in the development of the economy. It is impossible to achieve the least possible use of resources in terms of quantity. . At the same time, China does not have the resources that developed countries have had, and the historical conditions for the development of industry that are "inexhaustible and inexhaustible". Therefore, in addition to the idea of ecological design in the process of industrialization, "3R" is adopted. In principle, there are no other roads to choose from. China's catch-up strategy for developed countries can only be achieved by giving full play to the systematic characteristics and high-tech characteristics of ecological design.

In today's world economic integration, if China is to be based on the international market, it must change the place where the original supply of raw materials, low-level and low-tech products in the world economic structure, and the sales of high-end foreign products. Status. After China's accession to the WTO, although traditional tariff barriers are gradually being broken, the green trade barriers such as high-tech and global environmental protection have not been eliminated, but there has been a growing trend. The international competition environment, we only constantly improve the scientific and technological content of products, improve the production process, implement the green concept in the design of products, use green technology, can break the international green trade barriers, and truly integrate Chinese products and markets into the international unification. Go in the big market.

Ecological design has certain guiding significance for China's agriculture to take the industrialization road and win the international and domestic markets with its characteristics. The situation of industrialization of Chinese agriculture is very serious, mainly manifested as: limited quantity of land resources and declining quality; agriculture The infrastructure is weak, the advantage of latecomer is not obvious, or even not at all; the human resources situation is too much and the quality is very low; the competition in international agricultural products is becoming increasingly fierce. All these shortcomings indicate that China's agriculture will only have a good development prospect if it takes a special road. With the rise of nature and the emphasis on healthy lifestyles on a global scale, the agricultural industry based on ecological design ideas and concepts has great potential for development. This is also one of the important ways for China to solve the "three rural issues" and the road to prosperity in the central and western regions.

The ecological design idea is conducive to forming a good consumption habit in the whole society and cultivating people's good moral sentiments. "Investing in quantity" and "diligence and thrift" are good traditional habits of the Chinese people. With the development of the market economy and the deepening of reform and opening up, the phenomenon of extravagance and waste has risen. Especially the blind comparison psychology, advanced and conspicuous consumption are incompatible with the national conditions and folk customs of the primary stage of Chinese socialism. While vigorously developing the economy, we should vigorously carry forward the excellent traditional moral style, from production to distribution, exchange and final consumption, leading the ecological design concept and running through it, and finally settled in the green consumption trend of the whole society.

Both mainstream economic theory and modern management ideas and methods contain the idea of "people-centered". The ecological design concept in product production is the concrete and concentrated expression of this kind of thinking. People should change the stupid and arrogant attitude of overcoming nature in the early days of industrialization. They will no longer continue to expand and deepen the breadth and depth of the claims of nature. The result of production should not form human and nature. Sharp opposites. The core content of ecological design is to reflect the "people-oriented", the harmonious unity of human society and the natural environment.

European Union (EU) ecological design legislation practice

In 2003, the EU Commission's WEEE directive and ROHS directives have made companies feel exhausted. On April 13, 2005, the European Parliament approved the Eco-design Framework Directive for

Energy-Efficient Products (hereinafter referred to as the Ecological Directive) and reached a consensus with the representative of the Member State (Coreper) on the Eco-Directive.

The scope of the Eco-Directive covers an unprecedented range.

1. Overview of the EU Ecological Directive

The directive will focus on improving energy efficiency. It defines key principles and standards for product design with the aim of minimizing the negative impact of the product on the environment. Although the Directive itself does not set technical requirements for specific products, it paves the way for future implementation of technical specifications (standards) for various products. The various products included will be discussed by the European Commission and the supervisory committee established for this purpose.

The main idea behind this directive is that for any particular device, its design will have an impact on the environment throughout its lifecycle. Therefore, the European Commission will have the right to take appropriate measures (standards) to develop ecological design standards for each product. The eco-design criteria will cover the raw materials, production methods, water supply or energy consumption, product life expectancy and final disposal or recyclability of the product at the end of its useful life.

The purpose of the European Commission's directive is to include the following four points.
First, ensure the free flow of energy-using products in the EU market. The ecological design is mainly to formulate a unified committee directive at the EU level to eliminate trade barriers between member states due to the different laws and regulations of each member state.

Second, comprehensively improve the environmental performance of these products to achieve the goal of protecting the environment. One aspect of ensuring sustainable development is to minimize the impact of products on the environment, but the impact of products on the environment is multifaceted. Some industry policies may focus on one or more aspects and stages, but on product life. The aspects or stages of the cycle are harmful, so that conflicts or effects between policies are mutually offset.

Third, ensure the supply of energy and improve the competitiveness of the EU economy. The EU market is very dependent on energy. This is especially true after the EU has expanded. The EU's impact on external energy sources is limited. Therefore, it is necessary for the EU to intervene in internal energy demand. This intervention is not an economic intervention, but is achieved by improving energy efficiency.

Fourth, protect the interests of the industry and consumers. This directive is for all Energy-using Products (EUP). In the Directive, energy-using products are defined as products that depend on energy (electrical, fossil fuel, and renewable energy) and are used to generate, Products that transport and measure these energy sources, including those that are directly purchased by the end users of these products, can be individually evaluated for their environmental impact.

Since the ecological directive is only a framework directive, there is no specific ecological design requirement in the directive. It only specifies the energy product standards for the implementation measures, the ecological design indicators for the products (including the general ecological design requirements and the special products). The overall requirements of special ecological design requirements, the basis and standards for product evaluation, the requirements for products that meet the requirements of ecological design directives, and the market supervision system.

2. EU Ecological Directive countries implement measures

The EU countries are actively implementing the ROHS Directive, and the implementation of the ROHS Directive is inextricably linked to the implementation of the WEEE Directive.

(1) Netherlands

National Decree: The Netherlands converted the ROHS and WEEE directives into the "Electricity and Electronic Equipment Waste Regulations", which came into effect on August 13, 2004. The provisions on restrictions on toxic substances entered into force on July 1, 2006.

(2) Hungary

National Decree: The ROHS Directive was translated into National Decree on October 8, 2004 by Ministerial Decree No. 16/2004 and became effective on July 1, 2006. The WEEE Directive has also been translated into a national decree and has entered into force. The manufacturer has been registered since January 1, 2005, and the manufacturer's regulations for the disposal of commercial electrical waste were implemented in August 2005.

Competent department: The Ministry of the Environment is responsible for the transformation of the decree. The National Environment, Natural and Water Authority is responsible for implementing the WEEE Act and handling national registration matters.

Main provisions: Manufacturers are required to register and report to the National Environment, Natural and Water Authority and pay a product tax to finance the collection of various electrical waste such as mobile phones, refrigerators and freezers. However, the manufacturer may apply for an exemption from the delivery of the product tax as a result of its compliance with the law. Manufacturers are required by law to properly label electrical and electronic equipment manufactured after August 13, 2005. Hungary was allowed to delay until December 31, 2008, the date of collection of electrical waste, which was extended by 24 months compared with the deadline set by the WEEE Directive.

Plan: The responsibility for collecting electrical waste is solely the responsibility of the manufacturer. Established a ROHS laboratory. If the local government implements a private residential electrical waste collection program, the producer is responsible for funding

Fine: If you violate the WEEE and ROHS directives in Hungary, you must pay a fine for waste management.

(3) Spain

National Decree: Spain has adopted the Royal Decree of February 25, 2005 to convert the WEEE and ROHS directives into national decrees.

Main provisions: Since January 2006, all electrical and electronic equipment manufacturers are required to register with the National Industrial Registration Office or the local registration department. All electrical and electronic equipment manufacturers are responsible for financing, recycling, processing and re-engineering products that have withdrawn from the market after August 13, 2000. For products that exit the market before that date, producers are responsible for their market share. The new product will be implemented on July 1, 2006 with the ROHS directive.

4.2 Suggestions on Ecological Design System in Circular Economy Legislation

Principles of ecological design

Generally ecological design must follow the following principles:

First, the closed-loop design principle of parallel product life cycle. This is because the green level of the product is reflected in all stages of the product's life cycle.

Second, the principle of best use of resources. First, when selecting resources, we must consider the regenerative capacity and inter-period configuration problems, and use renewable resources as much as possible. Second, we must ensure that the selected resources are used to the maximum extent throughout the product life cycle; Under the premise of functional quality, the product structure is simplified as much as possible to maximize the detachability and recyclability of the parts of the product.

Third, the principle of minimum energy consumption. First, try to use clean energy or primary energy; second, strive to minimize energy consumption during the entire life cycle of the product.

Fourth, the principle of zero pollution. At the time of design, we will implement environmental protection strategies such as "prevention-based, governance-assisted" clean production, and fully consider how to eliminate pollution sources and fundamentally control pollution.

Fifth, the principle of advanced technology. In order for the design to reflect the specific effects of green, it is necessary to use the most advanced technology and creatively apply it to obtain the best ecological and economic benefits.

The main content and mode of ecological design

According to the above principles, to achieve the expected goals of green products, the main content of the design should include: the choice of ecological design materials, product detachability design, product recyclability design, green product cost analysis, green product design database and Knowledge base (including all data and knowledge related to the environment, economy, technology, objects, etc. in the product life cycle). The whole design mode is based on the environment and utilizes the product life cycle assessment technology to unify the many local design methods in the contemporary design method into a whole to achieve the overall optimality. Fluorine-free refrigerators are a successful example of ecological design. At present, although some important achievements have been made in the fields of quality function development, material selection design, manufacturing and assembly design, disassembly design, cycle design, life cycle assessment, and eco-design tool software development, it is far from meeting the needs of ecological design.

Ecological design system conception

First, ecological design requirements. Ecological design requirements are the core content of implementing ecological design, and also an important guarantee for achieving ecological design goals, which are divided into common ecological design requirements and special ecological design requirements. General products only need to formulate common ecological design requirements, and products with relatively large environmental impacts must also have special ecological design requirements according to needs. Eco-design requirements should be based on technical, economic, and environmental analysis, and the flexibility of these requirements must be ensured, which means that the environmental performance of the product can be improved more easily.

Ordinary ecological design requirements are ecological design requirements that are proposed to enhance the ecological appearance of a product. These requirements do not limit specific values for an environmental factor. In the process of formulating common ecological design requirements, the product life cycle, environmental factors, environmental impact factors and their changes are mainly considered. Manufacturers should evaluate the environmental impact of energy-using products throughout their life cycle based on normal conditions of use and design use. The assessment should focus on and prioritize factors that can be significantly improved through product design. Based on a consistent assessment, the manufacturer should establish an ecological profile of the product model, identifying product characteristics related to the environment and the inputs and outputs during the product life cycle.

Special ecological design requirements are quantifiable ecological design requirements that are specific to the environmental factors specific to an energy product. The purpose is to selectively improve or improve the environmental performance of the product. Special requirements are mainly achieved by reducing the consumption of a resource at various stages of the life cycle of the energy-using product, such as by setting a resource consumption limit (such as the water consumption limit value in the use phase, the number of materials used in the product). The value, the minimum amount of the recyclable substance is used, etc.).

Second, the products are placed on the market and in circulation. If a product has no specific implementation measures, the ecological design is not binding on it. If a certain type of product already has implementation measures, then the product can fully enter the market or be put into use after fully complying with these implementation measures.

Products that have been eco-designed must be certified by the relevant authorities before being placed on the market, and their manufacturer or authorized representative will issue a compliance statement to ensure that the product complies with the relevant provisions of all eco-designs.

Third, the implementation of the supervision system. Relevant departments of the state supervise products that have obtained eco-design certification. For products that do not comply with the applicable implementation measures, the manufacturer or authorized representative of the product must take action to comply with its applicable implementation measures. If no action is taken in time, the relevant state department should restrict or prohibit the product from entering the market or order it to withdraw from the market.

Producer responsibility extension system

1. The necessity of legislation

The producer responsibility extension system advocates a product from the cradle to the grave, always pays attention to it from an environmental point of view, regulates the responsibility of the producer and its extension, and regulates the responsibility of the government and consumers. Under the producer responsibility extension system, producers are not only responsible for the environmental pollution caused by the production process, but also bear certain responsibilities for the environmental management after the product is abandoned, that is, to undertake all or part of the waste product recycling, utilization and disposal. responsibility.

The producer responsibility extension system does not simply shift the waste management responsibility from the traditional government management to the producer completely or partially, but organically links the waste management with the production consumption. Implementing an appropriate producer responsibility extension system will help motivate producers to design more environmentally friendly products, promote the recycling and recycling of waste products, and develop a circular economy. Usually, the responsibility of the producer extends to the following types of economic responsibility, which refers to the economic cost of the producer to bear the recycling, recycling and final disposal of the product after the waste; the specific behavioral responsibility means that the producer directly participates in the management of the discarded product and is responsible for the product. Recycling and disposal, prohibiting the use of certain toxic and hazardous materials or substances; information responsibility means that the producer should provide information about the environmental impact of the product and how the product can be reused or disposed of in an environmentally acceptable manner.

In addition, there is a more thorough producer responsibility to separate the right to use and ownership of the product. The producers produce products and satisfy the customer's demand for the products through the Product Service System (PSs). The producer sells the right to use the product but retains ownership of the product, and the customer purchases the right to use the product. Producers are completely responsible for their products.

The environmental management responsibility of waste products in various forms of responsibility is linked to producers, requiring manufacturers to bear economic and specific responsibility for the environmental impact of their products after circulation, use and end of life, which is an important part of the extension of producer responsibility.

Under the previous product waste management model, the government bears the responsibility for the economic responsibility of product waste management and the responsibility for recycling and disposal. The management cost after the product is abandoned is borne by the government from the producer to the whole society. Under the extended responsibility system of producers, the responsibility for managing product waste is transferred from the local government to the producers in whole or in part, so that the environmental costs of product waste recycling, treatment and disposal currently undertaken by the whole society can be transferred to the producers. In order to maximize profit, producers have the incentive to design products that are easier to recycle and reuse, to reduce the cost of product waste management, thereby promoting producers to design environmentally friendly products, achieving efficient use of resources and reducing environmental hazards. purpose. The producer responsibility extension system has changed the mode of post-pollution governance, emphasizing the transition from "end management" to "source control", clarifying producers' responsibility for product waste management, and comprehensively using legal and economic means to encourage producers to carry out Eco-design, development of green products and green processes, on the one hand, encourages companies to reduce the substances and energy entering the production and consumption process, and no waste is generated or produced from the production to the consumption process, thereby reducing waste generation from the source. On the other hand, product waste can be more easily recycled and safely disposed of, which is beneficial to the "reuse" and "recycling" of waste products. Under the producer responsibility extension system, the nature of capital chasing profits has become the most powerful driving force for the development of circular economy. Therefore, the producer responsibility extension system provides the driving force for the development of circular economy by changing the structure of producer cost, prompting enterprises to adopt the production mode that meets the requirements of circular economy, embodying the concept of circular economy, and is the institutional guarantee for establishing circular economy.

Nowadays, for many products such as packaging materials, batteries, automobiles, tires, lubricants, electrical and electronic equipment, many developed countries have implemented the producer responsibility extension system through legislative enforcement, government guidance or enterprise spontaneously. The implementation of the extension of producer responsibility system in developed countries and the expansion of producers' responsibilities have formed an irreversible trend. Germany, Sweden, Japan and other countries have implemented legislation to extend the producer responsibility system. Their laws on wastes such as packaging waste, used cars and used electrical and electronic products have been in force and implemented. In China, the drivers of the development of circular economy are mainly government and enterprises. Under the conditions of market economy, the government cannot simply adopt the means of administrative means or call to make the Chinese economy realize the transition to a circular economy. This requires adapting to the world trend, implementing the extension system of producer responsibility, and comprehensively applying legal and economic means. Encourage enterprises to assume their due responsibilities and make enterprises truly become the main body and the first promoter of the development of circular economy. Of course, this change will increase the economic burden of some enterprises in the short term, but in the case of increasingly scarce resources and deteriorating environment, the pain of experiencing such changes is inevitable. In the long run, gradually expanding the responsibility of producers and implementing the extension system of producer responsibility is an inevitable way for China to develop a circular economy.

2. Legislative practice and experience of "extending producer responsibility" in developed countries and regions

At present, the countries that have successfully implemented the producer responsibility extension system are Germany and Japan. The EU's directives in the electro-mechatronics field that require member states to establish a producer responsibility extension system have not yet taken effect. The Taiwan region of China has taken the lead in establishing producer responsibility in the world. The system is extended, but the effect of implementation is not ideal. So far, the United States has no federal legislation on the extension of producer responsibility or a national e-waste management law. The Environmental Protection Agency has put forward some principled recommendations, including the application of the producer burden principle in waste recycling issues. The basic policy orientation is to promote the corresponding legislation of the states according to local conditions. Since 2000, more than 20 states have begun planning for the development of e-waste. In addition to a few related laws that have already entered into force, most of them are still in the stage of proposal and review.

(1) EU

Since the early 1990s, the European Union has begun a legislative attempt to establish an extension of producer responsibility. In 1994, the European Union issued a directive on packaging materials, requiring the recycling rate of package waste in its member countries to reach 25% to 45%, and the recovery rate of each waste is not less than 15%; in February 2000, the EU passed the "automobile production". The Responsibility Extension Regulation requires automotive manufacturers to use recyclable materials and is responsible for the final disposal of the vehicle.

At present, the EU has extended the responsibility of producers to the management of electro-mechanical waste. The total amount of e-waste generated by EU countries is 6.5 million to 7.5 million tons per year, accounting for about 1% of the total solid waste in the EU, accounting for 4% of the total amount of municipal solid waste, but the growth rate is much higher than other solid waste. The growth rate.

In view of the continuous growth of the total amount of e-waste, it has the characteristics of being reusable, and the recycling cost is low, which has great potential harm to the environment. The EU listed e-waste together with waste packaging materials and construction waste in the early 1990s. Waste stream project for priority treatment. In 1998, the European Commission proposed a draft of a draft directive on the disposal of waste electronic and electrical products, listing the objectives of electronic and electrical waste treatment and the corresponding policy principles. After discussion by EU member states, after five revisions, it was finally passed in 2000. The proposal for electronic waste disposal is divided into two parts: the "Proposal for the Disposal of Waste Electro-Electromechanical Products" and the "Proposal on Restricting the Use of

Hazardous Substances in Electro-Mechanical Products". The former proposal stipulated the producer's obligation to recycle electronic and electrical waste. The latter proposal focused on "source control", requiring producers to reduce the content of harmful substances in electronic and electrical products, and adopt materials that are beneficial to the recycling of electronic and electrical waste. Production process, etc. The European Parliament approved the two bills in October 2002 and officially implemented on January 1, 2006.

The "Proposal for the Directive on the Disposal of Waste Electro-Electromechanical Products" first specifies the types of waste that are specifically applicable to the extension of producer responsibility and the timetable for each Member State to achieve a specific target. In addition, the EU also stipulated that by December 31, 2005, the per capita recycling index of e-waste in each member country must reach 4kg. Although the EU has a higher recycling ratio for recycled products, the overall recycling rate is also affected because the specified recycling ratio is actually low.

The Directive on the Directive on the Disposal of Waste Electro-Electromechanical Products also stipulates the basic principles for the recycling and disposal of electro-mechanical and electrical waste: Member States must establish collection systems for the ultimate holders and distributors to return electronic and electrical products free of charge; Member States must ensure distribution To provide new free electronic and electromechanical products that are free of contaminants from private households, producers must provide for the collection of non-private household electronic and electrical waste; Member States must ensure that all electronic and electrical waste is transferred to approved disposal facilities, waste The disposal facility must be approved by the competent authority, and the producer of the electromechanical product must establish a waste disposal system; the private user of the electromechanical product must obtain the necessary information about the return and collection system, and the producer must provide the user with the ingredients contained in the product. Information on substances, substances and hazardous substances; Member States must inform the European Commission each year of the quantity and quality of electronic and electrical products in the market, and the quantity and quality of skin recycling and reuse. Member States are also required to submit the implementation of the directive to the Commission every three years. Report of the proposal; after the proposal is effective In five years, producers must compensate for the recycling, disposal, and ultimately disposal of environmentally-friendly electronic and electrical waste in private homes. The recycling of non-private home electronics is handled by producer and consumer agreements. At present, some member states of the European Union (such as the Netherlands, Switzerland, Norway, Sweden, etc.) have passed domestic legislation that establishes statutory recycling obligations for producers in the field of electronic waste.

The scope of application of the "Proposal on Restricting the Use of Hazardous Substances in Electromechanical Products" is the same as the "Proposal for the Directive on the Disposal of Waste Electro-Mechanical Products". It serves the effective implementation of the former from the perspective of "source control". The proposed directive requires producers from member countries to start with lead, mercury cadmium, hexavalent chromium and polybrominated biphenyls (PBBs) polybrominated diphenyl ethers (PBDEs) in electromechanical products starting January 1, 2008. Other substances are substituted, except for the exceptions specified in the proposed Directive.

It can be seen that these two EU directives only stipulate the objectives of the reduction, recycling, recycling and disposal of electronic and electrical waste in member countries, as well as the basic legal relationship between producers, sellers, consumers and the government and the laws they bear. Responsibility, there is no specific measures specified. Its reference is that the relationship between the central government and the local government can be determined in the process of implementing the producer responsibility extension system.

(2) Germany

In 1972, Germany enacted the Waste Management Law, which for the first time unified management of waste disposal nationwide. The law has made great contributions to the management of solid waste. Its basic principles and systems are basically the same as those of China's Solid Waste Pollution Prevention and Control Law (1995). Although it has been revised many times, it still cannot meet the needs of actual management. To this end, Germany enacted the "Package Management Regulations" in 1991, and officially entered into force on June 12, 1991.

The Packaging Management Regulations require producers and distributors to be fully responsible for their product packaging, recycling their product packaging, and reusing or recycling the active portion. The goal of the implementation of the regulations is to minimize unnecessary packaging, reduce the consumption of packaging materials, reuse the packaging multiple times, and recycle packaging that is unavoidable. In short, the regulations require reduction and recycling, while limiting direct landfill disposal. In terms of financial guarantees, the Packaging Management Regulations stipulate that enterprises must invest in recycling and recycling of product packaging. The related costs are shared by producers and distributors, thus reducing the burden on the government.

The Packaging Management Regulations provide two options for producers and distributors to manage their packaging waste: one is that producers recycle their product packaging through wholesale and retail channels; the other is established nationwide. A private system to recycle and recycle all of these packaging waste from different manufacturers. In order to meet the requirements of the regulation, the relevant producers and distributors spontaneously organized together to establish a "Dual Disposal System", which operates in parallel with the public waste. The functioning of the system is the German Dual System Corporation (DSD), which was established on September 28, 1990 under the German Industrial Union (BDI) and the German Business Enterprise Association (DIHT). The founder is 95. The company involved retail, daily necessities production and sign production companies. By the end of 1997, about 600 companies had joined, which constituted the main body of the German business community. The Dual System Company (DSD) is a completely non-profit organization, and the participating companies do not extract any profits. The mission of the Dual System Company (DSD) is to establish a system for packaging recycling, sorting and recycling for households and small groups across Germany, and to recycle and regenerate packaging waste with the "Green Point Mark". The operating capital is derived from the registration fee charged when the producer is awarded the "Green Point Sign". Since October 1, 1994, the Dual System Company (DSD) has used the type of material used for the total weight of the package and the additional congratulations related to the volume and footprint as a basis for the core. In other words, the processing costs of various packaging materials are reasonably reflected in the registration fee. For example, the charge per gram of glass, iron, aluminum and plastic is 0.15 mark, 0.56 mark, 1.50. mark 2.95 mark. These registration fees are all used for the management of packaging waste.

The operation of this system has received significant results. In 1991-1995, the consumption of packaging materials for residents and small group users fell from 7.6 million tons to 6.7 million tons, a decrease of 12%. However, before 1991, especially in 1988-1991, this figure had risen sharply. In 1995, each resident consumed an average of 82 kg of packaging, a decrease of 13 kg compared to 1991. At the same time, the proportion of material recycling in waste packaging has increased significantly. In 1996, the recycling ratios of various packaging materials were: paper and cardboard boxes 94%, glass 85%, aluminum products 81%, plastic 6%, iron 81%, composite packaging 79%.

Due to the successful implementation of the Packaging Management Regulations, Germany has further expanded the scope of application of the extension of producer responsibility. In 1996, the new Closed Matter Circulation and Waste Management Act came into effect, and producer responsibility was extended in the fields of used batteries, waste paper, used cars, and construction waste. The core idea of this law is to encourage producers to be responsible for the entire life cycle of their products, namely the management of "cradle to graveyard". The responsibility of the producer must be consistent with the design and production of the product, including transportation, sales, after-sales service, and waste disposal until the end of the life of the product. At the same time, consumers are also obliged to avoid waste generation during the use of the product and return it to the recycling process after the product has been scrapped. Only those who are truly unable to re-circulate can use the safest method to date. The Closed Matter Circulation and Waste Management Act stipulates that starting from 1999, all enterprises above a certain size must conduct their own material life cycle analysis. The purpose of this initiative is to significantly promote material recycling within and between firms, thereby essentially achieving the goal of a closed material cycle.

German successful experience in extending the responsibility of producers includes paying attention to cost-benefit analysis and combining the mandatory provisions of the law with the voluntary behavior of enterprises. At the beginning of the extension of producer responsibility, not only to reduce environmental damage, but also to reduce industrial processes and macroeconomic costs, the business community can continue to reduce waste and increase the proportion of internal recycling. Gaining huge potential benefits is the fundamental driving force behind the active participation of business enterprises in waste management. In addition, a system for collecting and recycling packaging waste with sufficient capacity for the whole society should be established. Producers' packaging of their products through their wholesale and retail channels is a form of extension of producer responsibility under the Packaging Management Regulations, but the cost of this model is too high. The establishment of the German Dual System Company (DSD) has achieved the goal of scale operation, which not only improves recycling and reuse, but also greatly reduces the economic burden on producers.

(3) Japan

The extension of producer responsibility in Japan is part of the plan to build a recycling society. In June 2000, the Japanese government promulgated the "Basic Law on the Promotion of the Formation of Recycling Society". Its fundamental purpose is to form a virtuous circle of "resources-products-renewable resources" and fundamentally resolve the long-term contradiction between environment and development. As one of the plans to promote the formation of a recycling society, on April 1, 2001, Japan began to implement the "Household Appliances Cycle Law", which stipulates that waste air conditioners, refrigerators, washing machines and televisions must be recycled by producers, and consumers pay producers. A small fee. As of 2005, 600,000 tons of household appliances have been recycled and utilized. The reason why Japanese implementation of producer responsibility extension has achieved great results is mainly because it has chosen home appliances as the cutting point for implementing the responsibility of producers. The cost of home appliance recycling is relatively low, and producers can only rely on their sales channels to complete. The Household Appliances Circulation Law stipulates that the recycling costs are shared by producers and consumers, which further reduces the economic burden on producers.

Based on the successful experience of the Household Appliances Circulation Law, the Japanese government has naturally introduced the concept of a recycling society into the field of automobile production and consumption. In April 2002, the Japanese government submitted the "Automobile Recycling Act (Draft)" to the National Assembly, which is basically the same as the legislative framework of the Appliances Recycling Law. It stipulates that automobile manufacturers are obliged to recycle used cars and then recycle them. The owner of the car will have to pay a recycling fee of about $150. Because the cost of car recycling is far greater than the recycling of home appliances, car manufacturers are worried about increasing indirect costs and affecting consumers' desire to purchase, thus weakening the market competitiveness of products. At present, there are more than 70 million vehicles in Japan. The owners have to pay more than 1 billion US dollars. The transparency of fund management is difficult to guarantee. The recycling of used automobile resources also requires the establishment of a new metal smelting and recycling system. However, Japanese society still generally The bill is highly regarded as the axis of establishing a "circular society".

(4) Taiwan, China

The Taiwan Waste Area amended the Waste Disposal Act (1974) on November 11, 1988 and March 28, 1997. Article 10.1 of the Act states: After the product or its packaging or container is consumed or used If there are components that are difficult to remove and contain, which are not susceptible to corrosion for a long period of time, contain harmful substances or have the value of recycling and reuse, and are seriously polluted by the environment, the manufacture, import and sale of the articles or their packaging and containers shall be responsible for recycling and removal. Dispose of and specify the type of waste that should be recycled by the competent authority. This is the first legislative practice in the world to extend the responsibility of producers. Article 10.1 of the "Waste Cleaning Law" (1974) also stipulates the economic responsibility of the producer:

the manufacturer should follow the current business volume, and the importer should report the import volume and container material to the "General Administration of Customs". Before each business tax declaration and payment, according to the rate approved by the "Central Competent Authority", the collection and removal processing fees shall be paid as a resource recovery management fund, and the financial institutions shall be entrusted to keep in charge of the revenues and expenditures. The competent authority" stipulates. For the use of the fund, Article 10.1 of the "Waste Repair Law" (1974) stipulates that: the fund is used to pay the actual recycling and disposal costs, the subsidy recovery system, the recycling, the implementation agency's cleaning costs, and the "Central Competent Authority". The selected impartial group performs the audit certification fee and other purposes approved by the "Central Competent Authority". It can be seen that there are two forms in which the producer bears the responsibility for extension: one is responsible for recycling and disposal; the other is to pay a certain fee. For the revision of the "Waste Cleanup Law", the recycling organization of the self-organized organization of the enterprise, the law stipulates that the remaining related expenses of such organization shall be transferred to the resource recovery management fund, and shall not continue to engage in the profit-making behavior of the waste recycling business. Taiwan's "Environmental Protection Agency" has successively announced 15 categories of recyclables or containers such as iron, aluminum and glass containers. The "Resource Management Fund Management Committee" promoted the producer responsibility extension system and achieved certain results. The amount of garbage in the day dropped from 1.135kg in 1987 to 0.828kg in 1991. In 1991, it recovered 15.5%, and in May 2003 it broke 16.5%.

However, this specific system has been widely criticized by the business community, and it has not played its due role in extending the system of producer responsibility. First of all, the company believes that it should not bear the dual responsibility of payment and recycling. At the same time, the practice of recycling by the production company will have the drawbacks of unregulated declaration rate recovery and evasion of recycling responsibility. It is difficult to accurately verify the recycling amount of the recycling enterprise or the processing enterprise, which often causes the recycling and processing enterprises to defraud the consequences of the resource recovery management fund subsidy through false reporting. Secondly, producers believe that Taiwan's implementation is not a real extension of producer responsibility. The processing fee paid by it is essentially an environmental tax. The payment of the fee is the responsibility of recycling and disposal. The fund established by the Environmental Protection Department Management Committee is co-ordinated. This provision has no incentive for producers to use materials and technologies that reduce product waste generation and facilitate recycling. The extension of the main producer responsibility is to require producers to participate in the whole process of production, consumption, recycling and disposal of products, while the Taiwanese producer responsibility extension system does not fully assume the responsibility of producers.

It can be seen that the extension of the producer responsibility system established by Taiwan in China has generally failed, and a new "recycling and recycling law" is currently being drafted.

3. The embodiment of the extension system of producer responsibility in the legislation of circular economy

Article 15 of the Circular Economy Promotion Law stipulates that enterprises that produce products or packaging materials that are listed in the compulsory recovery list must be responsible for the recycling of discarded products or packaging materials; for those that can be used, the production enterprises are responsible for the use; If it is not suitable for use due to lack of technical and economic conditions, the production enterprise shall be responsible for the harmless disposal.

The purpose of this legislation is to pass legislation and enact relevant regulations to clearly extend the producer responsibility. Producers, manufacturers, importers, and distributors are responsible not only for the environmental pollution caused by the production process, but also for the responsibility of protecting the environment during the entire life cycle of the product, for scrapped products or used packaging. Responsibility for recycling or disposal.

The packaging industry, household appliances and electronic products manufacturing industry, and automobile manufacturing industry can be selected as breakthroughs. In the packaging industry, manufacturers must recycle the sales package of the product, which can be recycled jointly with the seller, or can be entrusted to a special packaging waste recycling agency for recycling. The seller is obliged to recycle the consumer's secondary packaging and sales packaging, set up recycling points in or near the store, and set up obvious signs. In the home appliance and electronics manufacturing industries, manufacturers are encouraged to produce environmentally friendly products, reduce or even eliminate the use of hazardous substances from the source, and use materials and designs that are more conducive to recycling, and promote the recycling of electronic waste in an environmentally sound manner. And processing.

Establish a matching waste recovery deposit return system in accordance with the requirements of the producer responsibility extension system. Considering the feasibility of operation, the deposit system for beverage packaging such as beer bottles, soft drink bottles, wine bottles, liquid bottles, cans, etc. can be implemented first, and the deposit system for bulk waste such as used household appliances, electronic waste, and used tires is also explored.

First, actively promote the system of responsibility extension, so that the public and enterprises have a correct understanding of the producer responsibility extension system, so that they recognize the great significance of the producer responsibility extension system.

Second, formulate and implement effective producer responsibility extension laws and regulations as soon as possible, especially the regulations on the recycling of used household appliances and electronic products.

Third, for products with high specificity for recycling or recycling, encourage enterprises with good conditions to build their own recycling systems for waste products, and the state will provide sufficient support for policies, funds and risk compensation; for highly versatile recycled products, Relying on the relevant national departments to build a common product recycling system, and develop a strict "producer responsibility organization" management system, and establish a recycling network system.

4.3 the environmental safety system of the resource recycling industry

the necessity of environmental safety legislation for China's renewable resources industry

1. Legal status of environmental safety legislation in renewable resources industry

Since 1979, the National People's Congress of China has reviewed and passed more than 330 laws, including one comprehensive environmental resource protection law, five pollution prevention laws, nine natural resource management laws, and one clean production. The law of the aspect, but there is no basic law that specifically regulates the recycling of renewable resources.

The current Environmental Protection Law of the People's Republic of China does not have corresponding regulations on the recycling of renewable resources. Article 3 of the Law on the Prevention and Control of Environmental Pollution by Solid Wastes promulgated in 1995 only stipulates the principle of reduction of solid waste and the decontamination of resources. Articles 17 and 18 only specify packaging and agricultural film separately. Recycling. Article 9 of the Clean Production Promotion Law promulgated in 2002 is only a principled requirement to develop a circular economy, promote cooperation between enterprises in the areas of comprehensive utilization of resources and waste, and achieve efficient use and recycling of resources; Governments at all levels and relevant competent authorities provide recyclable waste supply and demand information and services to the society; Article 13 provides for the formulation of product marks and standards for energy conservation, water conservation, waste recycling, etc. Article 16 provides that the government gives priority to Purchasing and encouraging the public to purchase energy-saving, water-saving, waste recycling and other products; Article 26 stipulates that enterprise waste and waste heat are transferred to other enterprises and individuals with conditions; Article 35 provides for the use of waste to produce products and Depreciation tax relief for recovered raw materials in waste. However, these regulations do not cover the professional recycling of major industrial wastes, agricultural waste, waste packaging, waste plastics, waste glass, used household appliances, used electronic products, construction waste, food waste, used automobiles and their accessories.

Although there are some regulations on the comprehensive utilization of resources in the existing administrative regulations and regulations, such as the "Interim Provisions on Several Issues Concerning the Comprehensive Utilization of Resources" promulgated by the State Council, the State Council approved the transfer of the State Economic and Trade Commission and other departments to further develop resources. Notice of the use of opinions, but we believe that the concept of "comprehensive utilization of resources" widely used in China is not equivalent to the recycling of renewable resources. It should be said that the extension of comprehensive utilization of resources is greater than the recycling of renewable resources. Judging from the provisions of existing administrative regulations and rules, the comprehensive utilization of resources can refer to the conservation and utilization in the process of resource exploitation, production and use of resources, and can also refer to the development and reuse of resources after functional destruction. The recycling of renewable resources mainly refers to the development and reuse after the original functions are eliminated. The definition of renewable resources in the "Notice on Strengthening the Management of Recycling Resources Recycling" promulgated by the State Council in 1991 is too narrow, referring only to scrap metal resources. In addition, since most of these specifications appear in the form of "regulations", "trials", "temporary", "decisions" and "opinions", they lack the validity and standardization of the law. The long-term existence of this situation is obviously inconsistent with the responsibility of the recycling and recycling laws and the status of the legal system. The result is that the recycling system of renewable resources is seriously lacking in authority and stability. At the same time, since the implementation of the "Administrative Licensing Law of the People's Republic of China" (hereinafter referred to as the "Administrative Licensing Law") since July 1, 2004, some of the original ministry regulations have lost their effectiveness, and the management blanks for regulating the recycling of renewable resources are more .

Since there are neither basic regulations for the management of renewable resources and management methods for different types of waste, China is far from developed countries in terms of recycling of renewable resources. In recent years, the number of household appliances, used dry batteries, used computers, used tires, waste paper, and scrapped automobiles that need to be recycled has increased. Due to the lack of corresponding laws and regulations, the above-mentioned wastes are randomly disposed or used at a low level. Bibi is the first, which makes China's waste of resources and environmental pollution problems quite serious. The value of resources that are not recycled in Chinaese annual renewable resources is more than 50 billion yuan. In China, about 5 million tons of scrap iron, 200,000 tons of waste non-ferrous metals, 14 million tons of waste paper, and a large amount of waste plastics, waste glass, and waste rubber are not recycled every year. The recycling rate of China's renewable resources is only equivalent to the world. About 30% of the recycling rate in developed countries.

2. Legal Analysis of Environmental Security Legislation in Renewable Resources Industry

The basis for China's renewable resources legislation is the relevant provisions of Articles 9, 14 and 26 of the Constitution of the People's Republic of China. These provisions stipulate that the state guarantees the rational use of natural resources; implements conservation and opposes waste; and protects and improves the living environment and ecological environment. These provisions are clear to the state that the corresponding obligations should be assumed. At present, the Chinese economy has not fundamentally changed the extensive growth mode of "high investment, high consumption, high emissions, low circulation". The establishment of the legal system for renewable resources will fully reflect the state's commitment to the aforementioned obligations, and is the premise and basis for the country to build a resource-saving society, improve the efficiency of resource utilization, and protect and improve the environment. Jurisprudence believes that the legislator's enactment of any law is not fabricated out of thin air. Any law has a certain value orientation and lacks a clear value orientation. The establishment of the legal system will lose its meaning and will not understand the value orientation of the law. It is impossible to understand and use the law accurately. As far as the legislation on renewable resources is concerned, it can be combined with the requirements of the state's obligations in the Constitution to seek the value orientation pursued by the legislation from the following perspectives.

First, environmental benefits. This study believes that renewable resource legislation first reflects the value orientation of environmental benefits. Environmental science research tells us that waste is actually another form of existence of resources. When humans recycle them effectively, they will meet human needs. The form is expressed; when humans do not use them effectively and do not deal with the laws of nature, they will manifest themselves in forms that are not needed by humans and cause harm to the environment. Therefore, the root cause of environmental problems is the lack of effective use of resources. In view of this, a value concept based on harmony with nature is emerging. This concept advocates that human beings should make rational and effective use of natural resources, implement resource recycling strategies in economic activities, and achieve "zero emissions" to the environment. Under the guidance of this value concept, since the 1990s, developed countries have adopted legislation to develop a circular economy, implement resource recycling, and put economic operations into a closed-loop feedback process of "natural resources – products – renewable resources". The discharge of waste does not exceed the environmental capacity limit, thus achieving good environmental benefits.

Second, security interests. Security as used here refers to resource security. The issue of resource security is of great significance to China, which is determined by China's national conditions. First of all, China's natural resources are relatively scarce, the per capita resources are small, the resource security threshold is small, and most resources are approaching the security warning line. Secondly, the 16th National Congress of the Communist Party of China put forward the goal of building a well-off society in an all-round way. The total value has quadrupled from 2000. The rapid economic growth poses a severe challenge to China's resources. Whether the supply of resources has practical guarantees and whether resources can continue to meet the requirements of national economic development has increased China's resource security. Concerns about the problem. To solve the problem of resource security, it is necessary to establish a legal system for recycling of renewable resources, guide the transformation of traditional production methods and traditional consumption views, and promote the transformation of economic growth from excessive consumption of resources to sustainable use of resources, prompting consumers to fully use the goods. After that, the manufacturer recycles the waste.

Third, economic benefits. Renewable resources have great economic value. According to calculations, for every ton of scrap steel, 850kg of steel can be used. Compared with iron ore steelmaking, it can save iron ore 2 and save 0.4 tons of standard coal. For every 1 ton of waste paper, 800kg of pulp can be produced, compared with wood pulp. Papermaking can save 3 tons of wood, save 1.2 tons of standard coal, save 600kW, and save 100m3. However, the economic value of renewable resources is a potential economic value that can only be manifested through effective development and utilization. Due to the lack of legal norms, renewable resources cannot be recycled, discarded, or extensively recycled by unsuitable subjects. Economic value is not only impossible to achieve, but also causes secondary pollution. Through the legislation of renewable resources, we will adjust various social relations in the process of recycling and recycling of renewable resources, and guide the recycling of renewable resources to the scale, and fully develop the economic value of renewable resources. This has been practiced in western developed countries. It has been proved. For example, the annual recycling value of the renewable resource industry in the United States reached 100 billion US dollars, and the growth rate is 15%-20% per year. The renewable resource industry has played a big role in promoting the development of the US economy.

Fourth, maintain the interests of market order. For a long time, many renewable resources in China (such as waste batteries, waste plastics, and waste household appliances) have been disposed of at will, and there is no channel for recycling. Although there are a large number of self-employed and individual processing households in the streets, these operators The pursuit of economic benefits is the sole purpose, the management is not standardized, the management is unregulated, and the processing technology is backward, resulting in a series of problems such as poor quality of renewable resources and chaotic market order. On the one hand, the establishment of the legal system of renewable resources will guarantee and realize market freedom, on the other hand, it can restrict and intervene in the market freedom to ensure the formation of a good market order. For example, the establishment of a market access system can regulate non-standard and non-scale operators, and prohibit individuals or units that do not have the conditions to engage in the recycling of renewable resources and avoid secondary pollution. Another example is the producer responsibility system that is being implemented in some countries, which imposes restrictions on the freedom of manufacturers and requires them to assume more obligations. What proportion of materials are recycled by the manufacturer and which materials cannot be used at the time of design can pass.

Legislation is clear. Introduction to Environmental Safety Legislation of Recycling Resources in Other Major Countries

Since the 1970s, countries such as Germany, the United States, and Japan have started waste recycling legislation, and have standardized, institutionalized, and procedural management of renewable resources recycling. The recycling rate of renewable resources in these countries is quite high. The achievement of these achievements is closely related to the awareness of environmental protection and the high degree of civilization of the public. But more importantly, developed countries have established a comprehensive recycling law for renewable resources. system. Summarizing the experience of implementing legal regulation of renewable resources around the world is indispensable for improving China's legal system for resource recycling.

1. Legal regulation of environmental safety in the recycling of renewable resources in Germany

German resource recycling has always been at the leading position in Europe. The German Waste Disposal Law was first formulated in 1972, but the dominant idea at that time was still at the end of waste disposal. It was not until 1986 that Germany changed it to the Waste Restriction and Waste Disposal Act. The dominant idea was to increase the "how to deal with waste" to "how to avoid waste generation" and to avoid waste generation as waste. The primary goal of management.

In 1991, Germany first formulated the "Packaging Waste Treatment Law" in accordance with the circular economy concept of "resources, one product and one resource". The law stipulates that the manufacturer must be responsible for recycling packaging materials or entrusting professional companies to recycle, realizing the goal of full use of the packaging materials not to be transferred with the transfer of goods, and legally ensuring the full recycling of packaging materials. This is the producer responsibility system now adopted by most countries.

On July 8, 1994, German new Circular Economy and Waste Act was passed by the Bundestag. The bill clarifies new measures in waste management policy. The central idea is to systematically extend the circular economy idea of closed-loop resources from packaging to all production departments, so that more material data can be kept in the production circle. The new bill draws on the plans of the European Union, the Organization for Economic Co-operation and Development and the United Nations, surpassing the simple amendments to the previous Packaging Waste Treatment Act proposed by the Bundestag, raising the treatment of waste to the height of the development of circular economy.

The Circular Economy and Waste Law clearly and clearly defines the respective responsibilities of the parties. It requires manufacturers, distributors, and individual consumers to consider the issue of waste recycling from the outset. In the initial stages of production and consumption, focus not only on the use and suitability of the product, but also on the problems that will occur at the end of its life cycle. Fundamentally, any organization that produces and sells consumer goods is responsible for the avoidance, recycling, reuse, and proper disposal of the resulting waste. The owner or producer of the waste is primarily responsible for avoiding or recycling and disposing of the waste. The above-mentioned legal system design in Germany has created a new situation in environmental protection legislation. To sum up, the main German regulations on waste management are divided into three levels: bills, regulations and guidelines. Related bills include the Circular Economy and Waste Avoidance Act (1994), the Environmental Obligations Act (1991), the Waste Avoidance and Recycling Act (1986), and the German Waste Act. (1972). Relevant regulations include: classification regulations for toxic waste and residual waste, waste and residue control regulations, waste disposal regulations, packaging and packaging waste management regulations, and sewage sludge management regulations. Relevant guidelines include: Waste Management Technical Guide, Waste (Urban Solid Waste) Management Technical Guide.

2. Legal regulation of environmental safety in the recycling of renewable resources in Japan
In Japan, not only the individual regulations for resource recycling and utilization have been formulated, but also a highly realistic and forward-looking circular economy legal system has been formed.

Japanese rapid economic development in the decades after the war, but also led to frequent environmental pollution and public nuisance incidents. Among them, wastes remain high, and the continuous disposal of wastes continues to increase to Japanese air, water, soil and other environments. A major crisis has seriously undermined the normal material cycle in nature. In order to solve these problems and change the social status quo of "mass production, mass consumption, and mass abandonment", Japan has established a relatively complete legal system that promotes the recycling of resources and the establishment of a recycling-oriented society. This legal system can be divided into three levels: the basic level is a basic law, namely the Basic Law of Recycling Society; the second level is a comprehensive two-part law, namely Solid Waste Management and Public Cleansing Law and The Law on Promoting the Effective Use of Resources; the third level is five specific laws and regulations based on the nature of various products, namely, the Promotion of Container and Packaging Separation and Recycling Act, the Household Appliances Recycling Act, and the Building and Materials Recycling Act. Food Waste Recycling Law and Green Procurement Law.

Japanese "Complete Waste Management and Public Cleansing Act" was first enacted in 1970, but legislation from the perspective of circular economy is later than Germany. In 1991, Japan enacted the Law on Promoting the Use of Renewable Resources, which was determined to reduce waste, promote recycling, and ensure proper disposal of waste. Unlike Germany's circular economy legislation, which first implements circular economy ideas in specific areas and then establishes a system as a whole, Japan is the first to have a total recycling law, and then to advance to specific areas. In the 1990s, Japan proposed the slogan of "Environmental State" and concentrated on a series of regulations on waste disposal, recycling of renewable resources, recycling of packaging containers and household appliances, and management of chemical substances. On the basis of establishing laws and regulations on environmental protection and waste recycling, the Japanese government drafted the Basic Law on Recycling Society (Draft) in 2000 and submitted it to the National Assembly for consideration and approval. Japan's "Basic Law on Recycling Society" describes the "circular economy society" as follows: "According to the principle that the relevant parties play a fair role, promote the circulation of materials to reduce the environmental load, and thus seek to achieve sound economic development, and build A society that is constantly evolving. The law deals with the responsibility of the state, local governments, enterprises and the general nationals in dealing with "circular resources" (available waste): the government is responsible for formulating basic plans for building a recycling-oriented economy and society; Enterprises have the obligation to reduce the recycling and recycling of "recycling resources"; local governments implement measures that restrict waste discharge, classify it, store, collect, transport and recycle; Extend the use of consumer goods and coordinate the recycling of local governments or enterprises.

In 2000, at the same time as the promulgation of the "Basic Law on Recycling Society", a number of supporting regulations were promulgated: "Promoting the Effective Use of Resources" (the revised Law on the Promotion of the Use of Renewable Resources in 1993), requiring products The resource conservation and recycling of raw materials are the responsibility of the manufacturer, and the target products include 69 computers and photocopiers. The office computer was implemented in April 2011, and the home computer was implemented in April 2002. Due to the recycling fee when the computer is recycled, the development of the second-hand computer market has been promoted. The Food Waste Recycling Law is aimed at the severe situation of up to 20 million tons of organic waste based on food waste and 1.6 years of landfill life. It requires more than 10 million food processing industries, and food stores and supermarkets are making great efforts to reduce food. At the same time as waste, the conversion of food waste into fertilizer, feed and biogas for recycling, from April 2001, requires a recycling rate of 60% in 2006. Due to the attention of the society, food waste disposal has formed an industry. The Building and Material Recycling Law, for the large amount of construction waste materials, requires the improvement of life expectancy and the reduction of waste materials, while focusing on the recycling of three large waste materials, such as smashing blocks, asphalt slabs and waste wood chips, from April 2002. Since implementation, the recycling rate in 2010 reached 95%. The "Green Procurement Law" requires the government and its affiliates to purchase recycled products and less polluting green products in order to expand the market for recycled products. It has been implemented since April 2001 and is targeted at stationery and office machines. There are 101 types of 14 types of automobiles. Enterprises are also actively responding to the call, and the results are good.

Although the content and treatment methods of wastes in different laws are different, the laws of each ministry are issued in a timely manner. The names of the laws of different ministries are different, but the basic spirit and principles are the same, that is, the "3R" principle, that is, the reuse of resources. (Recycle), reuse of used products or parts (Reuse) and reduction of waste (Reduce). The main purpose of enacting and implementing these laws is to establish a system of corporate, administrative, and consumer trinity, and to establish a system that curbs the generation of waste, promotes the regeneration of resources, and prevents the illegal placement of waste, and finally establishes a sustainable use of resources. A recycling society that reduces environmental load.

Through the restrictions and guidance of the above regulations, the national industrial waste in Japan in 2000 was 400 million tons, of which the recycling rate of broken glass was 77.8%, the recycling rate of paper was 57.0%, and the recycling rate of plastic bottles was also 35%. . From this group of Japanese corporate waste recycling data, we can see that the recycling rate of Japanese waste resources is very high.

3. Legal regulation of environmental safety in the recycling of renewable resources in the United States
As early as the 1960s, the United States had noticed the dangers of waste, and some state governments began to take legal measures to force the recycling of these wastes. As the state government emerged, the situation gradually eased, which led to a protection campaign entitled "Protect the beauty of the United States." In terms of waste recycling, the United States established the Solid Waste Disposal Act in 1965 and became the first country to determine waste utilization in legal form. The law was amended to the Resource Recycling Act in 1970 and was further renamed the Resource Conservation and Recycling Act in 1976. It was subsequently revised four times in 1980, 1984, 1988 and 1996 respectively. For the first time, the law gives the US Federal Environmental Protection Agency the power to control the hazardous waste from the "cradle to the grave" and builds a management system for harmless waste. It has established the "4R" (Reduction, Reuse, Recycle, Recovery) principle. Waste management is extended from a simple clean-up work to a comprehensive plan that combines recycling, reduction, and resource reuse. That is, resource recycling should start from the source control of product manufacturing, and seek to use easily recycled resources to reduce waste manufacturing. Instead of focusing only on end waste or garbage. At the same time, the law also establishes and improves laws relating to the recycling of solid waste, including information disclosure, reporting, resource regeneration, demonstration of regeneration, technological development, recycling

standards, economic incentives and use priorities, occupational protection, citizen participation and litigation. system. In 1984, the Resource Conservation and Recycling Act emphasized that Congress should fund the state government's Environmental Protection Agency to establish research and development on waste treatment, resource recovery, environmental protection planning and recycling technologies and equipment, and fund professional training. The Federal Hazardous Solid Waste Amendment provides for the prohibition of landfill disposal of hazardous waste.

With the help of the American recycling concept and a large number of fruitful legislation, the domestic recycling of renewable resources has developed rapidly and has received strong technical and financial support from the state. For example, in the "Extra Fund Amendment and Authorization Act" promulgated in 1986, detailed provisions were made on waste treatment technologies, coordination of regulations between states, expansion of EPA authority, and increase of state capital investment. It has greatly promoted the environmental protection and comprehensive recycling of waste in the United States. In 1990, the United States promulgated the "Pollution Prevention Law," which implemented the theory of cost-benefit analysis, starting with four aspects: reducing resources, expanding the use efficiency of clean energy, recycling waste, and sustainable agriculture. The pollution prevention policy supplemented by the prevention policy and replaced by the end-of-pipe treatment clearly stipulates that the pollution source must be prevented or reduced in advance, and those who cannot recycle it should be treated as much as possible, as for discharge or final disposal. It is the last resort. In this way, it can not only control the generation of pollution, but also protect the recycling and sustainable use of resources. At the same time, in order to raise public awareness of environmental protection, the United States has designated November 15th as the "Recycling Day". Each state has also established a variety of Recycling Materials Utilization Associations, and has established a website to list the use of regeneration. Manufacturers of substances for production, and organize various activities to encourage people to buy recycled products. Taking the recycling of US newsprint as an example, its recycling rate has been at a relatively high level. In recent years, it is still in a rising trend, which is very beneficial for the United States to save wood and protect forests.

4. Korea's renewable resources recycling industry environmental safety system

South Korea has a small land area and a dense population, which consumes a lot of energy every year. Therefore, the Korean government pays great attention to environmental protection and recycling of resources. In 2002, South Korea's fiscal expenditure on environmental protection reached 13 trillion won (about 11.1 billion US dollars), accounting for 2.3% of its GDP. In 1992, South Korea began to implement the "waste prepayment system", in which producers prepaid a certain amount of funds to the government according to the quantity of their products, and according to their final abandoned resources, the government returned some of the prepaid funds. The government's return of funds to producers is generally 40% to 50%, and the rest of the funds are used for environmental protection. The "waste prepayment system" has played a role in controlling the discharge of wastes and pollutants, but at the same time it has brought many drawbacks, such as local governments using prepaid funds as tax collection.

Since 2002, South Korea has changed the "waste prepayment system" to "recycling responsibility system". The so-called "recycling responsibility system" is to require the reuse of restricted sewage to waste resources. 18 kinds of waste products such as electrical appliances, tires, lubricating oils, fluorescent lamps, batteries, paper bags, plastic packaging materials, metal cans, glass bottles, etc. must be recycled and recycled by the production unit. In 2004 and 2005, the "Recycling Responsibility System" was successively implemented in food boxes, instant noodle foam bowls, synthetic resins, and packaging materials. If the waste products recycled and recycled by the producers do not reach a certain proportion, the government will impose fines on the relevant enterprises, and the fines will be 1.15~1.3 times of the recycling costs. The "Recycling Responsibility System" has played a positive role in reducing waste emissions and promoting recycling of waste. Production units can take three forms of recycling and disposal of waste when implementing the "Recycling Responsibility System". The first type is that the production unit recycles and disposes the waste by itself, and the recycling and disposal costs are self-paying, and the benefits of recycling the waste are enjoyed by themselves. The second form is "the producer reuses the business combination", which is the responsibility of the cooperative that recycles the waste. The producer transfers the responsibility for waste recycling to the cooperative, and pays the contribution according to the weight of the waste. The third form is that the production unit signs an entrustment contract with the waste recycling enterprise, and pays the commission amount according to the quantity of the waste, and the latter is responsible for the waste recycling and disposal.

5. Legal regulation of environmental safety in the recycling of renewable resources in Australia

The Australian Government attaches great importance to the recycling of renewable resources and defines the concept of renewable resources as waste generated throughout production and living. As a developed country, Australia's annual per capita waste is second only to the United States, ranking second in the world. In order to solve this problem, in 1992, the Australian Federal Government and the state governments identified a solid waste reduction plan, which is to reduce the percentage by 50% in 1992 by the year 2000. On the one hand, the Australian Government has set a planning goal of reducing waste year by year, and has increased the proportion of waste utilization year by year. On the other hand, it has actively played the role of industry associations, and has conducted good communication with urban residents and industrial and commercial enterprises through various waste recycling professional committees. Relevant policies actively guide and encourage people to reduce waste and promote the use of renewable resources. Australia's states have their own legislation, and Queensland enacted the Waste Management Strategy (Draft) in May 1994, which has had a major impact on the country's important government agencies and has established both businesses and consumers. Should be responsible for the disposal of waste. 60% of the residents of the state participated in the waste recycling system project, which created a good living environment for 3 million residents. Therefore, the Australian government has listed this state as a model to promote the recycling of waste throughout the country.

The legislative practice of recycling and recycling of renewable resources abroad has important reference significance for China's environmental protection legislation, especially in establishing relevant legislation for sustainable development. China is a developing country, and social development and economic construction are at a critical crossroads. Therefore, it is very helpful for China to avoid the advanced experience and practices of other countries and avoid detours in social development.

The experience of other major countries has important implications for the development of China's renewable resources recycling industry. First, the improvement of laws and regulations is fundamental to the management of recycling of renewable resources. The reason why the recycling of renewable resources in western developed countries is done well is inseparable from the perfect laws and regulations of various countries and the legal awareness of citizens. China must formulate a sound legal system for recycling of renewable resources. Second, we should take the market as the guide and use economic means to recycle and recycle renewable resources as an industry. Third, renewable resource management 朋 policy objectives are environmental protection and resource conservation. Fourth, actively play the role of industry organizations. In foreign countries, renewable resource industry organizations (such as the Renewable Resources Industry Association) have played an important role in the recycling, utilization and management of renewable resources. Reproductive resource industry organizations can strengthen communication between governments, enterprises and individuals, and promote the development of renewable resources policies. And strengthen the supervision of renewable resources industry. Fifth, the key to promoting the recycling of renewable resources is the concept of bone circulation economy. In the legislation for the protection of environmental resources, the establishment of a sound environmental resource protection laws and regulations, the establishment of a recycling resource recycling legal system to ensure the development of renewable resources recycling.

Suggestions on Environmental Safety System of Recycling Resources Industry in Circular Economy Legislation

1. Implement market access and qualification system

The market access system is regulating the market access for renewable resources. The people's governments at all levels shall, in accordance with the principle of overall planning and rational distribution, plan the construction of recycling enterprises, renewable resource recovery outlets, renewable resource trading markets and renewable resource industrial parks in urban construction and development. Recycling resources recycling mainly includes renewable resource recycling and utilization enterprises, renewable resource recycling and utilization sites, renewable resource sorting and sorting enterprises, production and processing enterprises that use renewable resources as raw materials, and individual industrial and commercial households engaged in recycling and recycling of renewable resources. For renewable resource recycling enterprises, we should stipulate in the legislation that qualifications must be carried out, and the technical conditions and means for implementing recycling of renewable resources should be stipulated. Recycling resources recycling practitioners should also have certain conditions, such as vocational training and vocational skills appraisal, and have local resident or temporary residence. The administrative department of renewable resources shall encourage the establishment of a renewable resource trading market and implement total control over the renewable resource trading market.

2. Market order management system

Market order management aims to regulate the order of operation and management of the renewable resources market. In the renewable resources market, it is forbidden to issue and transfer renewable resources recycling business, prohibit forced trading, prohibit abuse of market dominance, prohibit competition restrictions, and prohibit administrative monopoly. Recycling resource recycling outlets shall be fixed locations, listed operations, clearly marked prices, and standardized services. Recycling resource recycling outlets set up in the community must promptly clear and recycle materials, keep the community environment clean and hygienic, and do not carry out processing activities that generate noise, dust, odor and other pollutants in the community.

3. Legal liability

Legal liability is the sanctioned consequence of the offenders recognized by laws and regulations. If the legal liability provisions do not understand, the rights of the subject of legal relations are difficult to achieve, and the illegal acts are not sanctioned accordingly. China's existing laws and regulations are extremely incomplete in terms of legal liability for violations of recycling laws for renewable resources. The operability is not strong, and those who violate the law can take advantage of it. Some of the legal liability costs are far less than the benefits of polluting the environment, and the subject prefers It is illegal to assume relatively light legal responsibilities and is reluctant to adopt environmentally friendly recycling technologies. Therefore, the provision of legal liability is closely related to the implementation effect of recycling of renewable resources. The legal liability for violation of laws and regulations should be based on economic sanctions. However, economic sanctions cannot be understood as the replacement of the obligations of the obligation by the fine. The economic sanctions cannot exempt the obligations of the obligor. The purpose of the legislation is to achieve regeneration. The recycling of resources, and legal liability is only a means to achieve legislative purposes. Therefore, economic sanctions are old means, and it is the goal of obligors to fulfill their obligations and implement recycling of renewable resources.

Part 5 Analysis of Ecological Environment Quality Evaluation Based on Circular Economy Mode

Chapter 1 Analysis of China's Eco-environmental Quality Evaluation Index System and Method

The United Nations Agenda for Sustainable Development 21 emphasizes the important role that local governments play in promoting national and global sustainable development. The first problem that local governments need to solve is to evaluate the sustainability of the local ecological environment, and use various relevant indicators to construct an integrated ecological environment index to provide more intuitive and clear information for the digital decision-making of the ecological environment management and the public. Since the 1970s, researchers at home and abroad have conducted extensive research on how to select evaluation indicators and build a comprehensive eco-environment index (CEI). In the early research, due to the lack of basic ecological environment information data and the systematic and comprehensive evaluation method, the practical application of CEI is difficult. At the end of the 20th century, with the increase of information demand in the comprehensive management of ecological environment, the development of various monitoring technologies and the improvement of analytical methods, CEI research has gradually become a hot spot, and there are related research at different scales. On a national scale, Hope et al. (1992), Butter and Eyden (1998), and Kang et al. (2002) respectively constructed CEIs for the United Kingdom, the Netherlands, and South Korea to evaluate the multi-year dynamics of the ecological environment quality of countries: at regional scales. Bergh and Veen-groot constructed CEI for 12 OECD countries to evaluate regional differences in the quality of ecological environment in 12 countries (Jeroen, 2001); on a global scale, 2005, Yale University Environmental Law and Policy The Research Center (YCELP) and Columbia University's International Earth Science Information Network Center (CIESIN) (Esty, 2005) built the Global Environmental Sustainability Index (ESI) and ranked the ecological sustainability of 146 countries; 2006 YCELP and CIESIN have improved ESI to make the evaluation more targeted. In China, Li Wei (2006), Wang Jun (2006), Wan Bentai (2004), Wu Kaiya (2003), Hao Yonghong (2002), and Liu Quanyou (1990) also constructed different regions from different perspectives. The indicator system and CEI have promoted the development of relevant research fields in China.

Although some studies have carried out different explorations, when evaluating regional ecological environments containing many different types of ecosystems, it is necessary to comprehensively consider the multidimensionality, complexity and uncertainty of the ecological environment, and the evaluation work is very difficult. China is not the same as the developed countries and the ecological environment problems that need to be solved first. Some CEIs established by developed countries are not in line with China's national conditions, and some domestic research tends to focus on the evaluation and evaluation of complex ecosystems. A large number of social and economic indicators have been introduced, which have weakened the ecological environment indicators and cannot provide clear and concise information for ecological environment management. The different climatic and geographical features of China have created the diversity of natural conditions in various regions. Under the combined effects of different natural conditions, history and culture, the socio-economic development stages and models of different regions are different, which are caused by natural ecosystems. There are differences in the types and sizes of stresses, and the emphasis of ecological environment management is different. The ecological environment effects and evolution laws have great spatial heterogeneity, and the degree of comprehensive ecological environment sustainability is different. Through comprehensive evaluation, it is helpful to distinguish the characteristics of various aspects of ecological environment in each region, which is conducive to the comprehensive and classified management of regional ecological environment in China.

1.1 the concept of evaluation

The so-called evaluation usually refers to a kind of judgment on the good and evil of things, the ugliness and the ugliness. In the past, evaluation was the meaning of bargaining. In the West, evaluation was first associated with economic activity. The evaluation in English is "Evaluate", "E" is emphasized, and "Value" is value. Value refers to the exchange value in the early stage. Later, under the influence and appeal of various schools and thinkers, the meaning of value is no longer limited to the economic scope, but is extended to a wider range of fields, such as social value, personal value, cultural value, aesthetics. Value, ecological value, political value and scientific value, etc. Therefore, the term "evaluation" that we use today has evolved from simply "commenting the price of goods" and "bargaining" to "generalizing the value of a person or thing", explaining the meaning of the existence of all people or things. judge. In other words, "evaluation" refers to all aspects of the evaluation object to the evaluation object, quantified and non-quantified according to the evaluation criteria, and finally a judgment of whether it has value, value and value. Bloom believes that "evaluation is the process of value judgment on certain ideas, methods and materials. It is a process of assessing the accuracy, effectiveness, economy and satisfaction of things using standards.

Evaluation is an understanding of things, and its process is very complicated. What it wants to point out is not the simple question of what it is, but what effect it has on things and what kind of effect it has. It is a cognitive activity that aims at grasping the meaning or value of integrity. In fact, all human activities are to discover value, realize value and enjoy value, and evaluation is a fundamental way for humans to discover value and reveal value. Evaluation is a means. Only through evaluation can we judge the value and effect of its behavior and effectively play a certain constraint. The establishment of the indoor environment design ecological evaluation system is to balance the indoor environmental design behavior.

1.2 The role and significance of the evaluation

As a kind of consciousness activity in which humans understand the world and transform the world, it is always in the whole process of human practice. Regardless of the individual's career choices or the country's policy guidelines, as long as the event is attended by people, there will be evaluations. Evaluation is a conceptual activity in which people grasp the meaning and value of objects to human beings. It is the value orientation and attitude of human subjects in evaluation activities, which directly affects the evaluation criteria. In addition, the evaluation is to determine the attribute of the object according to the clear target, and to turn it into a degree that satisfies the requirements of the subject, that is, to judge the value of the object under certain pre-set concepts, and to provide a practical process of decision-making basis. I like this dress; car exhaust pollutes the environment; inferior products endanger people and so on. Such expressions are cognitions formed by people's judgments on the value of objects through cognition and practice activities and may produce corresponding decision-making behaviors. I may buy them because I like this dress; car exhaust pollutes the environment, so the relevant government departments Various policies will be adopted to limit or reduce the emission of exhaust gas; due to the harm of inferior products to the lives of the people, the relevant departments will strengthen supervision and have laws to punish such behavior. It can be seen that evaluation plays a vital role in all aspects of human life. In human society, human beings not only maintain the survival and competitive instinct of living things, but also make full use of nature, can also change nature, create new things, new living environment and new social systems. The unity of purpose and regularity is the essential feature of all human creative activities. Therefore, with wisdom, human beings can actively and consciously evaluate their own behaviors and their relationship with the environment, and judge the purpose and regularity of their activities, thus summing up the lessons learned and the means of optimization. It can be said that "evaluation" has important guiding significance for the practical activities of human society, economy, life and other aspects: First, in practice, through the understanding of the relationship between goals and means, constantly adjust and correct the direction of advancement, and provide choices. The basis for the "satisfaction" scheme; the second is to test whether the method used is "suitable" and to make constant adjustments in order to improve the efficiency of the behavior.

Design evaluation is a measure and judgment of the value of "design". The design book is "human purposeful creative behavior", which is represented by a series of problem solving activities, namely, finding problems, analyzing problems and solving problems, is an uninterrupted design decision process. The design value is reflected in the "consensus" of the result and the "regularity" of the process; the design evaluation is both a judgment of the final "effect" and a measure of the "efficiency" of the process. Therefore, proper design decisions rely on continuous, effective design evaluation activities. In a broad sense, design evaluation is the value judgment of all human "creation" activities. The origins of the design can be traced back to the human ancestors purposefully tapping the stones to make stone tools, and at the same time, the simple "design evaluation" was born. Although this kind of evaluation consciousness is hidden in the intense and busy daily work, its role is direct and strong. From the selection of the type and shape of the stone, the angle and strength of the tapping, the speed of the throwing, and the "evaluation" of the lethality, all of this information is fed back to the designer in the most direct way in the survival competition. It continuously improves the method and gain effect. With the continuous accumulation of human experience, systematic knowledge has gradually formed. The ideas and methods of "design evaluation" have been continuously improved and developed, and relevant content has also appeared in the literature of various ancient creations. For example, the book "Tiangong Kaiwu", a famous science and technology book in the Ming Dynasty in China, provides a detailed review of the technology, crafts, materials and applications of the predecessors' "creation" activities, which provides valuable for the creative activities of future generations. Learn from. The more systematic design evaluation thoughts in the early Western period were about the design function, which can be traced back to William Hogarth's "Analysis of Beauty." Hershey believes that the "beauty" of design should meet the practical needs. The first chapter of the book begins with "About suitability." He writes: "Designing the purpose of each component allows the design to be formed, and is also an important factor in achieving overall beauty... for shipbuilding, each part is Designed to suit the purpose of navigation, when a boat is easy to drive, the sailor calls it beautiful, and beauty and purpose are closely connected." Since then, design theorists and thinkers have designed aesthetic standards and functions. Extensive design evaluation theory research on sexuality, manufacturability, usability, economy and social responsibility. Under the guidance of such evaluation theory, industrial equipment, daily necessities, art, public goods, and artificial environments have all become design evaluation targets. Until today, people continue to evaluate their various "creation" activities that adapt to nature and transform the world, in order to continuously improve their survival efficiency and increase their own interests.

In fact, no matter whether the human subject is aware or not, our daily life is always full of value judgments about ourselves, others, things, and the environment. Any of the premise of creative behavior under the concept of general design has the existence of design evaluation activities.

1.3 China's eco-environmental quality evaluation index system and method

Evaluation index system

Careful study of domestic and international literature on regional eco-environmental assessment (Esty, et al, 2006; Esty, et al, 2005; Clerici, et al, 2004; Wan Bentai, 2004; Kang, 2002; Hao Yonghong, 2002; Buttertal, 1998; Liu Quanyou , 1998; Hope, 1992) After seeking the opinions of many experts in ecology, environmental science and other fields, establish the ecological environment of China's provincial administrative regions according to the actual situation in China and the relevant indicators and the availability of relevant data. Evaluation System. The indicator system consists of four themes: natural conditions are the life support systems for human society and other living organisms, determining the ecological carrying capacity of a region and the size of ecological service functions; human stress refers to the production and living activities of human beings. Environmental disturbances and stress are one of the important driving factors for the degradation of ecological environment in various regions; ecological environmental effects are the most direct representation of regional ecological environment quality, and are the result of regional natural conditions, human stress, social response interaction and years of cumulative effects. External response; social response is the efforts of the whole society to protect the ecological environment, alleviate the pressure on the ecological environment, and repair damage and degraded ecosystems. This paper believes that when a region has good natural conditions, small human stress, small ecological environment effects and large social response, its ecological environment is sustainable.

The weight of each indicator relative to the target layer is obtained by the expert survey judgment matrix combined with the level analysis method. In the expert survey, 40 questionnaires were issued and 21 copies were returned, of which 17 were valid questionnaires (covering multi-disciplinary experts), using analytic hierarchy analysis. The law analyzes 17 questionnaires to obtain the weight of each index relative to each target layer. The average weight of the income of each expert questionnaire is taken as the weight of each index relative to the target layer (see Table 5-1: Ecology of provincial-level administrative regions in China) Environmental sustainability evaluation indicator system).

Table 5-1: Ecology of provincial-level administrative regions in China Environmental sustainability evaluation indicator system

Topic	contributing factors	indicators and relative weights
Natural situations	Climate suitability	I_1 annual rainfall /mm:0.2285; I_2 annual average temperature /°C: 0.1644
	Water supply	I_3 water network density / (km/km^2) :0.1742
	Vegetation cover	I_4 forest coverage rate /%:0.2000; I_5grassland coverage rate /%: 0.1310; cultivated land area as a percentage of national land area /%:0.1020
Human pressure	Human habitat stress	I_7population density / (person /km^2) :0.0709; I_8 construction land to land area ratio /%:0.0769
	Resource utilization stress	I_9 per capita energy consumption (standard coal)/(t/person): 0.1029; I_{10} per capita water consumption /(t/人 person): 0.1071
	Pollution stress	I_{11} Industrial wastewater discharge intensity /(t/km^2):0.1410;I_{12} industrial waste discharge intensity /(t/hm^2):0.1355;I_{15} fertilizer application intensity /(t/hm^2):0.1218
Eco-envi ronmental effects	Environmental pollution	I_{16} major river water quality is inferior to the proportion of 3 categories/%:0.2049; I_{17} air pollution index: 0.1733; I_{18} acid rain frequency /%:0.1212
	Ecological degradation	I_{19} proportion of endangered terrestrial spine species /%:0.1436; I_{20} soil erosion index: 0.1641; I_{21} desertified land area ratio /%:0.1929
Social response	Pollution control	I_{22} Environmental protection investment as a percentage of GDP /%:0.1684; I_{23}industrial wastewater discharge compliance rate /%:0.1663; I_{24} urban domestic waste harmless disposal rate /%:0.1143; I_{25} SO$_2$industrial production process produced SO2 removal rate /%: 0.1433
	Ecological protection	I_{26} nature reserves accounted for the proportion of national land area /%: 0.1684; I_{27} water-saving irrigation area arable land area ratio /%: 0.1146; I_{28} per capita biogas possession /%:0.1248

Data sources

The raw data of the indicators are mainly derived from the China Statistical Yearbook 2004, the China Environmental Yearbook 2004 and the 2003 State of the Environment Bulletin. Part of the indicator data is obtained from the original data by conversion or weighting.

Evaluation model

The comprehensive eco-environment sustainability index is constructed in two steps: the first step is to construct four sub-indexes by weighted average method for the four topic layers; the second step is to construct CEI by gray correlation method with four sub-index values.

Weighted average

The first formula is used to standardize the raw data values (P_{ij}) of the indicators in the table "Evaluation Index System of Ecological Environment Sustainability in China's Provincial Administrative Regions", and the relative weights of the various thematic indicators in the standardized numerical reuse table are obtained. W_j) and the second formula calculate the natural condition index (NSI), human stress index (HPI), eco-environmental effect index (EEI) and social response index (SRI).

$$E_{ij} = \frac{P_{ij} - P_{\min}}{P_{\max} - P_{\min}} \quad (i = 1,2,...,31; j = 1,2,...,28)$$

$$S_{ki} = \sum_{j=1}^{n} w_{kj} \cdot E_{kij} \quad (k = 1,2,3,4)$$

Grey correlation analysis

NSI, HPI, EEI and SRI are vectors in different directions in the multi-dimensional space of the integrated ecological environment. If they are linearly added and constructed CEI without vector projection, the contribution of some information will be exaggerated or reduced. In order to overcome this effect, this paper uses the four sub-indexes to construct CEI using the grey correlation method. The basic idea of grey correlation analysis is to judge whether the connection is tight according to the similarity between the sample vector and the optimization vector curve geometry. The closer the curve is, the greater the correlation between the corresponding sequences; the smaller the opposite.

Take the maximum of the natural condition index and the social response index, the minimum of human stress and the eco-environmental effect index as the optimal vector for the comprehensive ecological environment sustainability S ($S_{1,0}$, $S_{2,0}$, $S_{3,0}$, $S_{4,0}$), using the grey correlation method to calculate the degree of association between each sub-index and the optimization vector in each region (the first formula), and the average of the four correlation degrees as the comprehensive ecological environment sustainability Value CEI (second formula).

$$Ekj = \frac{\min_{k}\min_{i}\left|S_{k0} - S_{ki}\right| + P\max_{k}\max_{j}\left|S_{k0} - S_{ki}\right|}{\left|S_{k0} - S_{ki}\right| + P\max_{k}\max_{j}\left|S_{k0} - S_{ki}\right|}$$

(p is Resolution coefficient, it is 0.5 for the book)

$$CEI = \frac{1}{4}\sum_{k=1}^{4} E_{kj}$$

Multivariate statistical analysis

Pr n ipal component analysis is used to analyze each topic layer. The extracted principal components are used to analyze the leading and synergistic indicators in each topic layer, and the correlation analysis between each index or sub-index and GDP per capita is used to find out the cause. The dominant factor in the geographical differences of each sub-index.

Using the four sub-index values   obtained above as variables, the SPSS11.5 software package is used to perform rapid sample clustering in 31 regions of the country. The number of clusters depends mainly on whether each cluster has significant practical significance (each cluster) The characteristics of the ecological environment are distinct) and the significance of statistics (F test).

1.4 Characteristics of China's provincial ecological environment quality

Through evaluation models, the NSI, HPI, EEI, SRI and CEI values and rankings of various regions in 2003 were obtained, as shown in Table 5-2 below. The larger the NSI, SRI, and CEI values, the better, and the smaller the HPI and EEI values, the better.

Table 5-2 Results of sustainable assessment of ecological environment by region

Region	NSI		HPI		EEI		SRI		CEI	
	Index Value	Level	Index Value	Level	Index Value	Level	Index Value	Level	Index Value	Level
Beijing	0.4012	21	0.3698	2	0.2579	27	0.5092	1	0.6954	14
Tianjin	0.4395	20	0.3209	5	0.3223	20	0.4712	4	0.6692	21
Hebei	0.3705	23	0.1891	14	0.4125	7	0.3341	23	0.6176	26
Shanxi	0.334	26	0.134	23	0.448	5	0.3277	25	0.624	25

	7		5		0				6	
Inner Mongolia	0.2814	28	0.0623	27	0.6594	1	0.2938	28	0.6135	27
Liaoning	0.4576	19	0.1918	13	0.3667	14	0.4549	5	0.6878	17
Jilin	0.4703	18	0.0788	24	0.2485	29	0.3279	24	0.7255	8
Heilongjiang	0.3624	24	0.0655	26	0.2847	23	0.2975	27	0.6947	15
Shanghai	0.6742	9	0.8285	1	0.3942	11	0.3782	17	0.6042	29
Jiangsu	0.5296	15	0.3263	4	0.3304	18	0.4413	9	0.6682	22
Zhejiang	0.7705	3	0.2887	7	0.3728	13	0.4515	6	0.7526	5
Anhui	0.6136	10	0.1839	15	0.2652	26	0.3916	16	0.7276	7
Fujian	0.7770	2	0.3438	3	0.2398	30	0.3759	18	0.7524	6
Jiangxi	0.7582	5	0.2060	12	0.2663	25	0.4427	8	0.7958	4
Shandong	0.4957	17	0.2533	8	0.3235	19	0.4365	10	0.6787	20
Henan	0.5137	16	0.2112	11	0.3514	15	0.3381	22	0.6503	24
Hubei	0.6057	11	0.2508	9	0.2841	24	0.3738	19	0.6918	16
Hunan	0.7199	6	0.2192	10	0.3454	16	0.3561	21	0.7163	10
Guangdong	0.7683	4	0.2943	6	0.3153	21	0.2800	29	0.7049	11
Guangxi	0.7092	8	0.1718	17	0.2502	28	0.4899	2	0.8158	3
Hainan	0.8093	1	0.1583	19	0.1243	31	0.3999	12	0.8899	1
Chongqing	0.5337	13	0.1402	21	0.4061	9	0.3923	14	0.6861	18
Sichuan	0.5317	14	0.1352	22	0.3068	22	0.4195	11	0.7238	9

Guizhou	0.5826	12	0.0535	28	0.3853	12	0.2421	30	0.7024	12
Yunnan	0.7179	7	0.0512	30	0.3369	17	0.4815	3	0.8452	2
Tibet	0.3406	25	0.1432	20	0.4050	10	0.1684	31	0.5932	30
Shaanxi	0.4006	22	0.0770	25	0.4106	8	0.3056	26	0.6630	23
Gansu	0.2911	27	0.0468	31	0.5371	4	0.4486	7	0.6955	13
Qinghai	0.2586	30	0.0531	29	0.4173	6	0.3923	15	0.6852	19
Ningxia	0.2813	29	0.1606	18	0.5918	3	0.3977	13	0.6084	28
Xinjiang	0.1638	31	0.1823	16	0.6090	2	0.3652	20	0.5742	31

Natural Situation Index (NSI)

The natural conditions in each region have a clear transition from good to bad from southeast to northwest. Using the principal component analysis method to analyze the natural condition theme layer, the cumulative contribution rate of the first and second principal components is as high as 84.939%, which indicates that there is a strong synergy between the indicators. The contribution rate of the first principal component variance is as high as 60.42%. The rotating load vector has the dominant indicators of annual rainfall, annual average temperature, forest coverage and water network density. Their geographical differences dominate the natural conditions of China and the north and the south. Differences, and the expert survey also gave these four indicators a higher weight; with the increase of rainfall and water network density, the grassland gives way to the forest or is reclaimed as cultivated land, so the load is negative in both principal components. The area of cultivated land is less affected by rainfall, temperature and water network density, and the load is small in the first principal component and independent of the second principal component. If only from the objective information contained in the indicator data, grassland and cultivated land have little or no negative impact on the maintenance and contribution of natural conditions in a region. However, in some areas, grassland and cultivated land play a huge role in biodiversity conservation, CO_2 fixation and soil and water conservation. If the direct use of principal component empowerment is ignored, their effects will be ignored. Expert surveys have given these two indicators a certain weight, making them play a role in the geographical differentiation of natural condition indices in various regions.

Human pressure index (HPI)

In 2003, the stress caused by human activities in the coastal areas of the southeast was significantly higher than that in the central and western regions. Principal component analysis of the human stress theme layer obtained the first and second principal component variance contribution rate of 79.984%, there is a strong synergy between the indicators. The contribution rate of the first principal component variance is as high as 61.675%, and the population density, the area ratio of construction land, and the industrial "three wastes" emission intensity are synergistic, mainly reflecting the coercion brought by the city and industry to the natural ecosystem, which is the dominant in human stress. Factors; the second main component of per capita energy consumption, per capita water consumption, pesticide use intensity, fertilizer application intensity through synergy, mainly reflecting resource use and agricultural non-point source pollution caused by coercion. Per capita water consumption has a negative load in the first and second principal components, and there is a negative rank correlation with other stress indicators; however, due to the widespread shortage of water resources in China, the high per capita water consumption in some areas Ecological stress (such as ecological water shortage) cannot be ignored, so most experts give it a certain weight.

Correlation analysis found that there is a significant positive correlation between HPI and GDP per capita. Although there is no direct use of economic indicators in the indicator system, the corresponding high HPI is higher in areas with high economic development level, indicating that the current economic development in China is generally established. On the basis of increasing the stress on the ecological environment.

Eco-environmental effect index (EEI)

In 2003, the ecological environment effect in the northwestern region was significantly higher than that in the southeastern region. Principal component analysis of the eco-environmental effect theme layer obtained the first principal component variance contribution rate of only 36.187%, the synergy between the indicators is small, the dominant indicator is the desertification land area to the land area ratio and soil erosion index, reflecting the regional ecological degradation The main indicator in the second principal component is that the main river water quality is inferior to the class III ratio and the acid rain frequency, reflecting the regional environmental pollution effect: the third principal component leading indicator is the air pollution index, reflecting the urban environmental pollution effect. The river water quality is inferior to the class III ratio. The load is negative in the first and second principal components, and the low load in the third principal component. The proportion of the endangered species is relatively low in the three principal components. Principal component analysis, the regional ecological environment damage and degradation reflected by these two indicators will be weakened, resulting in evaluation errors; when the weighted average method is used to construct the eco-environmental effect index, consider their great impact on the regional ecological environment sustainability. Most experts have given them a higher weight, which is more in line with human value judgment and ecological basic principles.

Correlation analysis found that there was a significant negative correlation between EEI and NSI. Logistic regression was used, and the regression effect was significant, indicating that the ecological environment effect of a region is affected to some extent by the natural conditions in which it is located, and interferes with human activities. Under the circumstance, the ecological environment with poor natural conditions is sensitive, and it is more prone to ecological degradation and damage, showing more significant eco-environmental effects.

Social Response Index (SRI)

There is no obvious geographical differentiation in social response. In 2003, some areas with poor natural conditions and low economic development levels, such as Gansu and Ningxia, showed high social responses. Some areas with good natural conditions and developed economies such as Guangdong, Social response is low. Correlation analysis found that there were only 3 pairs of indicators in the social response topic layer with only 3 pairs of indicators (I23-I24, I23-I26, I23-I27) and only one pair of indicators (I23-I24). For the true correlation, it indicates that the synergy between the indicators is small, and the type of social response reflected by the indicator system is multi-dimensional, which is not suitable for analysis by principal component analysis. In view of the current ecological and environmental problems that China needs to solve first, experts generally believe that improving environmental protection investment, strengthening nature reserve construction and industrial water pollution control are the ecological environment management strategies that China needs to implement first. Therefore, I22 and I26 are The dominant indicator gives a higher weight.

Correlation analysis found that there is a significant positive correlation between SR1 and GDP per capita. After removing Shanghai, using linear regression, the regression equation is significant, indicating that economic development helps to improve the social response of a region. However, the regression coefficient of the regression equation is small, indicating that the level of economic development is not the only decisive factor for social response. The size of social response is also affected by regional macroeconomic policies, local development orientation and ecological environment awareness.

Eco-Environmental Sustainability Index (CEI)

Regional eco-environment sustainability is determined by the regional natural condition background, the interactive accumulation of human stress and social response, and the characterization of eco-environmental effects. In 2003, the ecological environment sustainability of each region in China was ranked from strong to weak, as shown in Table 5-2. Hainan, Yunnan, Guangxi, and Jiangxi were the four regions with the strongest ecological environment, and the natural conditions were superior. The level of development is low, human stress is small, the degree of ecological damage and degradation is small, and the degree of social response is high; Xinjiang, Tibet, Shanghai, Ningxia, and Inner Mongolia are the five regions with the least ecological sustainability, except for Shanghai humans. Excessive stress, human stress in other areas is small, but due to poor natural conditions, the ecological environment effect is very significant.

Analysis of the correlation between CEI and other sub-indices found that although there is no linear method in the CEI construction process, CEI still has a significant linear regression relationship with NSI and EEI (shown in Figure 5-2), indicating natural conditions and The eco-environment effect is the most direct influencing factor for the sustainability of a region's ecological environment; the effect of CEI with HPI and SRI is not significant, and human stress and social response have an impact on the ecological sustainability of a region through indirect effects, due to humans. There are many types of stress and social responses, and their impact on the sustainability of ecological environment is uncertain. Small human stress and large social response are beneficial to ecological environment sustainability, but there is no corresponding linearity in numerical value. relationship.

Cluster analysis

According to the NBI, HPI, EEI and SRI of each region, through the k-mean rapid sample clustering function of SPSS11.5, 31 regions in China are clustered into 6 categories with different ecological environment characteristics, and the suspension cluster center is shown in Table 5. As shown in -3, the difference test between categories is significant (a=0.01), and the table clustering effect is better.

Table 5-3 Rapid clustering of clusters of ecological environment in each region

Variable	Clustering					
	1	2	3	4	5	6
NSI (Natural Condition Index)	0.4647	0.3900	0.6742	0.7672	0.2544	0.6036
HPI (Human pressure index)	0.2924	0.0994	0.8285	0.2517	0.1130	0.1635
EEI (Eco-environ mental effect index)	0.3202	0.3765	0.3942	0.2773	0.5993	0.3144
SRI (Social Response Index)	0.4626	0.2994	0.3782	0.3844	0.3763	0.4124

According to the sub-index suspension cluster center (see Table 5-3), the main ecological characteristics of each cluster can be summarized. Each cluster has a significant geographical agglomeration, and similar geographical locations often have similar natural conditions, economic activities and social historical and cultural traditions, creating similar ecological environment characteristics. Cluster 1 is 5 regions in the eastern and northern coastal areas of China (Figure 5-3), accounting for 4.51% of the country's land area. It is a semi-humid and semi-arid region in China, with low forest coverage, few natural vegetation, and natural conditions, but the population. The density is large, the proportion of construction land is large, the level of economic development is high, human activities are stressful to the ecological environment, the pollution of the atmosphere and water is serious under human stress, and the ecosystem shows degradation to a certain extent, but the overall ecological environment. The effect is small, the government has invested heavily in responding to ecological degradation and environmental pollution, the degree of social response is high, and the overall ecological environment sustainability is at a medium level. Cluster 2 is distributed in China's plateau or mountainous areas, including the Qinghai-Tibet Plateau, Loess Plateau (Shaanxi, Shanxi) Plateau, Guizhou Plateau, and 8 regions of Hebei, Jilin, and Heilongjiang Mountainous areas, accounting for 34.42% of the country's land area, and the natural conditions are poor. The use of water resources is scarce, the ecological environment is fragile and sensitive, the population density is low, the level of economic development is not high, the proportion of construction land is low, the emission intensity of industrial pollutants is low, and humans have less stress on the ecological environment, which is affected by location distribution. The regions showed different eco-environment effects. The government's ecological protection investment was small, and the social response was small. In particular, the response to water-saving irrigation and biogas construction was lagging behind, and the comprehensive ecological environment sustainability was at a moderately weak level. Cluster 3 is Shanghai. Although its natural conditions are superior and its level of economic development is high, it is restricted by the development space. The area of natural conservation land is small, and the human stress on the unit area is too large. Although the social response is strong, the atmosphere The pollution of water bodies is still serious, the ecological and environmental effects are more significant, and the comprehensive ecological environment is weak. Cluster 4 includes 6 regions in the southeast of China, accounting for 8.48% of the country's land area. It is the best natural region in China, with abundant water resources, high forest coverage, and superior natural conditions. The ecological carrying capacity, population density is high, human habitat stress is high, per capita water consumption in resource utilization is large, industrial pollution stress is small, but agricultural non-point source pollution stress is large, due to high ecological carrying capacity, can withstand large The human disturbance is coercive, the ecological environment effect is small, and the response to industrial pollution control is large, but the response of agricultural water-saving irrigation and rural biogas construction is lagging behind, which is the most sustainable area of China's comprehensive ecological environment. Cluster 5 is distributed in 4 regions of northwest China, accounting for 34.96% of the country's land area. It is the worst natural environment in China. Water resources are seriously scarce, natural vegetation coverage is extremely poor, and poor natural conditions lead to low ecological carrying capacity in these areas. The ecological environment is very fragile and sensitive. The local population density and economic development level are low, and the stress on nature is also small. However, due to the lack of natural conservation, the ecological environment effect is extremely significant, and desertification, soil erosion and biodiversity loss are very serious. Despite the severe water shortage, the water-saving irrigation measures are not effective, and the rural biogas construction is also lagging behind other regions in China. The overall social response level is low, which is the worst area for China's comprehensive ecological environment. Cluster 6 contains some areas in central and southwestern China, accounting for 17.57% of the country's land area, good natural conditions, high water network density, low population density and economic development level, and less stress on human activities to the ecological environment. Smaller, mainly threatened by biodiversity loss, acid rain and water environment pollution, the overall social response is large, but the water-saving irrigation is not popular, and the comprehensive ecological environment is more sustainable.

Table 5-4 Characteristics of each cluster

	Cluster 1	Cluster 2	Cluster 3	Cluster 4	Cluster 5	Cluster 6
Number of districts	5	8	1	6	4	7

Average CEI	0.6799	0.6633	0.6042	0.7687	0.6229	0.7344
Total land area /10,000km^2	43.39	331.17	81.56	81.56	336.31	169.06
Population density /((person /km^2)	535	75.35	2716	341	22	255
Per capita GDP	16490	8370	13247	13247	7613	6973

Natural conditions-human stress-ecological environment-social response index system evaluates the characteristics of a region's ecological environment and comprehensive sustainability from the perspective of human-natural interaction, and can provide a region for eco-environmental management decision makers. The overall understanding of the geographical differentiation of the ecological environment promotes the digital management decision-making of the ecological environment.

The evaluation results show that in 2003, the natural conditions in each region have a clear transition from good to bad from southeast to northwest. The dominant factors causing regional differences are annual rainfall, annual average temperature, water network density and forest coverage. The human stress in developed areas is significantly higher than that in the western and central regions, and the economic development level of the same region is closely related. The northwest region is the region with the most significant ecological environment effect in China. The ecological environment effect is mainly affected by natural conditions, and the natural conditions are more likely to occur. Ecological damage and degradation, ecological and environmental effects are more significant; there is no obvious regional difference in social response, and economic development has a certain degree of promotion, but it is not a decisive factor. Based on the natural conditions, human stress, eco-environmental effects and social response status, the grey relational analysis method was used to obtain the sustainable ranking of ecological environment in various regions in China in 2003. The most sustainable areas were Hainan and Yunnan. Guangxi, Jiangxi and other places; the weakest areas are Xinjiang, Tibet, Shanghai, Ningxia, Inner Mongolia and other places.

With NBI, HPI, EEI and SRI as variables, through the rapid sample cluster analysis, 31 provincial administrative regions can be clustered into six categories with different ecological characteristics. The same clusters have similar ecological environment characteristics, and they are clustered in geographical location, and similar ecological environment management strategies can be adopted. Different cluster ecological environment characteristics have significant differences, and different management needs to be adopted according to their characteristics. Countermeasures.

1.5 Typical ecosystem service functions and their evaluation indicators

Many scholars at home and abroad have made in-depth research on ecosystem service functions, indicator systems and evaluation methods, and systematically studied the service functions of the five main ecosystems of forests, grasslands, wetlands, deserts and farmland, and achieved fruitful results.

Forest ecosystem

In the process of ecosystem service function research, the earliest and most studied type of ecosystem may be the forest ecosystem. The value of Costanza et al. in 1997 on global ecosystem services: in the evaluation, the service functions of forest ecosystems are attributed to gas regulation, climate regulation, disturbance regulation, water regulation, water supply, erosion control and sediment retention, soil 17 kinds of formation, nutrient recycling, waste treatment, pollination, biological control, shelter, food production, raw materials, genetic resources, leisure, culture, and then divide the forest ecosystem into tropical and temperate/northern forests and value them separately. Estimate. Among them, 13 service types (of the 17 service functions listed) were considered in the evaluation of tropical forest ecosystem service functions, while only 9 service types were considered in the evaluation of temperate/north forest ecosystem service functions. The value evaluation method adopted has been criticized by many economists (Ayres, 1998; Daly, 1998; Serafy, 1998; Heredeneen, 1998; Hueting, 1998; Rees, 1998; Templet, 1998; Toraan, 1998; Turner, 1998, etc.).

In evaluating the economic value of the public welfare function of the national forest, Japan's Forester Office considered six categories of water conservation, soil erosion prevention, prevention of soil erosion, landslides and mudslides, health recreation, wildlife protection, and atmospheric preservation in light of the actual situation in Japan. Features. The economic value of forest ecosystems in the protection of wildlife was also evaluated.

Xue Dayuan et al. used market value method, shadow engineering method, opportunity cost method and cost analysis method to evaluate the indirect economic value of forest ecosystem in Changbai Mountain Nature Reserve. The evaluation features are: considering the value of pest prevention in forest ecosystems; in the evaluation of water conservation services, annual runoff is used as a functional indicator to participate in the estimation; in reducing nutrient loss, only inorganic nutrients are considered, but organic matter is not considered; atmospheric regulation service The O2 release function is not considered. Ouyang Zhiyun et al. evaluated the service functions of Hainan Island and China's terrestrial ecosystems. The characteristics of forest evaluation were that the service functions considered were more comprehensive. Guo Zhongwei et al. evaluated the forest ecosystem services and their value in Xingshan County, Shennongjia District. In the evaluation process, they use the GIS to classify the evaluation area into 90 types according to the vegetation type, soil loam and slope. The measurement is divided into sections. The evaluation has the following characteristics: the travel cost method uses the tickets, travel expenses, and consumers. Residual and time cost; soil erosion rate and water conservation amount adopt the method of zoning estimation and recombination, which improves the measurement accuracy to some extent; the contribution rate of forest conservation water is used (compared with 3.7:1 of mixed grass and grass) for Determine the relative contribution of forests to runoff regulation and water accumulation; separate silt prevention and sediment deposition prevention, and evaluate them by cost analysis method (manpower dredging cost) and shadow engineering method (reservoir construction cost). Li Zhongkui and others evaluated the value of forest resources in Beijing. The ecosystem service functions involved include ten major service types, such as forest value and water source value. The characteristics are: consider the full range of service functions; consider environmental services The functions of sulfur dioxide, fluoride and nitrogen oxides absorption, dust retention, sterilization and noise reduction are considered; the value of biodiversity and the value of social benefits are considered. In addition, some domestic scholars have conducted in-depth research on the value evaluation of individual ecosystem service functions, such as: forest conservation soil value accounting theory research (Jin Yanping); forest conservation water source value accounting theory and method research (Jiang Wenlai); Study on the Value Accounting of Forest Carbon Sequestration and Oxygen-holding Function (Liu Wei); Research on Estimation Method of Benefits of Forest Purifying Atmospheric Toxic Gas (Huang Yi); Research on Index System of Forest Social Benefit Value Evaluation (Chen Yong); Forest Recreation Value Accounting (Hu Ming) and so on.

In summary, in the evaluation process of forest ecosystem service function value, the direct use value is mainly based on forest products such as wood and recreational value. Among them, timber and other forest products can be obtained based on regional GDP statistics and actual survey data. The value of recreation can be determined by the travel cost method based on actual conditions and evaluation purposes, comprehensive transportation costs, tickets and other expenses, and taking into account the opportunity cost of time. Attention should be paid to eliminating the influence of the human landscape. In the indirect use value evaluation, the more common service functions include soil conservation in forests (3 to 4 functional indicators), water conservation (1 to 2 functional indicators), carbon fixation and oxygen release, nutrient recycling and storage, and purification of the environment. SO2 absorption, etc.; other functions such as dust and noise reduction in the purification environment, wind and sand fixation, disaster prevention, etc. should be determined in conjunction with the actual situation of the evaluation area; some service functions such as shelter, pest control, biological pollination, diversity maintenance, social benefits The evaluation of et al. has yet to be further studied in basic theory.

Grassland ecosystem

The grassland ecosystem provides a range of products and services for humans, but only a few of them are known for their market value, such as meat, milk, wool, and leather. In fact, in addition to these important products of market value, the grassland ecosystem also gives humans many vital but often unrecognized services such as gas regulation, gene bank maintenance, climate regulation and soil conservation. It is much larger than the sum of the market value of the products that are currently known.

The service functions of the grassland ecosystem mainly include:
Mitigation of greenhouse gas emissions – Compared to ecosystems such as forests, grassland ecosystems absorb large amounts of carbon as soil organic matter and store it in the soil. When the grass is cultivated or converted into farmland, not only will carbon be rapidly transferred to the atmosphere, but greenhouse gas emissions such as N_2O will also increase. The rate of N_2O emissions from farmland is higher than that of

grassland and increases with the increase of fertilization intensity (Mosieretal, 1991). It is estimated that the economic losses caused by the conversion of grassland to farmland caused by the increase in CO^2 concentration have been: \$20.4/t (in terms of carbon) in 1991-2000; \$22.9 in 2001-2010 (in terms of carbon)); 25.4 \$/t (in terms of carbon) in 2011-2020; \$27.8/t (in carbon) in 2021-2030 (Fankhaugeretal, 1994). According to the above analysis, the value of stored carbon in grassland can be calculated as 160~400 \$/hm^2 [based on 0.02 \$/kg (in terms of carbon)], with an average of 200   \$/hm^2. In 1991-2030, the grassland reduces CH_4 relative to farmland. The economic benefit of emissions is 2.70 \$ / hm^2. In 1991-2030, the grassland reduced NO relative to farmland, and the economic benefit of emissions was 28.50 \$ / hm^2.

The impact of CH_4 and N_2O emissions from grassland destruction is minimal compared to CO_2. The most significant change after grassland destruction is the release of large amounts of carbon in the form of CO_2 in a relatively short period of time.

Genetic Gene Banks - An important service provided by the grassland ecosystem to humans is the maintenance of a gene pool that stores large amounts of genetic material; another important aspect of grassland is that it is the main source of origin for crops and livestock. The annual herb and legumes of the grassland ecosystem are very rich, and many domesticated animals such as goats, sheep, and cattle all originate from the grasslands of the Mediterranean region. Therefore, the genetic resources of the grassland ecosystem have important protective value for human beings.

Climate regulation—Changes in the structure, composition, and coverage of grassland vegetation caused by changes in grassland use patterns have led to changes in surface energy reflectivity, which have an impact on the climate.

Soil Conservation - Grassland destruction results in reduced subsurface seepage and increased runoff, resulting in enhanced soil erosion. Jones et al. conducted a comparative study on the soil erosion of wheat, sorghum, fallow land and native grassland in the Taxas areas of the United States. The results showed that the soil erosion of the native grassland was almost insignificant, while the soil erosion of the wheat field reached nearly 1200 kg/hm^2. (6-year average, the same below), the soil erosion of Sorghum land is about 2700 kg/hm^2, and the soil erosion of fallow land is more than 1700 kg/hm^2. Therefore, the soil conservation function of grassland ecosystem is very significant.

According to statistics, grassland resources are the largest ecosystem on land in China, with an available area of   3.10 x l08 hm^2. Due to the long-term natural and extensive management of grassland resources, heavy use, light construction, and light management, grassland resources generally have excessive grazing and chaos, and lack of unified management, low capital investment, and slow construction. For other reasons, the area of grassland degradation, desertification and salinization is growing, and the grassland ecosystem is seriously damaged. In this grim situation, it is of great significance to assess the value of grassland ecosystem services in China.

At present, research on the service functions of grassland ecosystems is not carried out very much, and it is only reflected in some regional ecosystem service functions. The selected service function types and evaluation methods are the same as those of forest ecosystems. Some areas, like Xie Gaodi, evaluated the value of Chinese natural grassland ecosystem services. They divided the national grassland into 18 ecosystem types (including swamps), and 7 of them were subdivided into 21 sub-categories. The service function type is the same as that of Costanza et al. Its outstanding feature is the use of the biomass index in the evaluation to correct the unit price of the ecosystem service function. Regarding the research on the service function of grassland ecosystem, we should pay attention to strengthening the research on the function mechanism of grassland ecosystem service in the future. Only on this basis can we select functional indicators and select appropriate value evaluation methods to obtain satisfactory results.

Wetland ecosystem

Although there are many studies on wetlands at home and abroad, it is difficult to give a recognized and precise definition at present, and different countries and researchers have different views on the classification of wetlands. It is generally believed that wetlands have over-wet soils (long-term water accumulation period each year), unique characteristics of animal and plant types that are different from terrestrial and aquatic ecosystems, and are transitional zones between terrestrial and aquatic environments. China has abundant wetland resources. There are 7 types of marsh wetlands, meadow wetlands, river wetlands, lake wetlands, coastal wetlands, estuary wetlands and constructed wetlands. If further divided, 26 natural species Wetlands and 9 types of constructed wetlands in the Ramsar wetland list are distributed in China.

The evaluation of the value of wetland ecosystem service functions is a recent phenomenon. In history, wetlands have always been regarded as abandoned land with certain value, and can only be enhanced by drainage and destruction. It is widely recognized today that wetlands provide valuable ecosystem services, but there is still ongoing debate on whether regional wetlands have the highest economic value and the extent to which wetlands should be protected and restored. Therefore, it is more and more important to carry out the evaluation of the value of wetland ecosystem services.

The service functions provided by the wetland ecosystem include a variety of service functions such as providing species habitats, reducing flood disasters, water purification, and recreation. Ewel lists three major categories of wetland ecosystems (biodiversity, water resources, global biogeochemical cycles) and 11 sub-category services; Woodward summarizes the 17 wetland ecosystem services proposed by Larson et al. It is 10 categories and gives its content and applicable value evaluation methods.

Desert ecosystem

Desert ecosystems are a widely distributed ecosystem type throughout the biosphere and an important subsystem in terrestrial ecosystems. Because of the harshness of its environment, desert ecosystems determine its vulnerability and instability. Because of this, from the special functions of desert ecosystems and the requirements of ecological environment construction, the study of desert ecology has more important practical significance.

There are few studies on desert ecosystems at home and abroad. Foreign studies mainly focus on semi-arid desert grasslands. Domestic research mainly focuses on desert ecological climate, vegetation, hydrology, soil, phenology and natural distribution characteristics, succession patterns and Research on wind-proof and sand-fixing benefits and ecological functions of artificial wind-fixing sand-fixing forests.

The service function research of desert ecosystem is quite special. It not only has unique animal and plant resources and ecological landscape characteristics, but also may be the only type of ecosystem that poses a threat to human survival as a whole. Research on the function of ecosystem services is still not available. It is very difficult to carry out this type of ecosystem service function alone. It can be considered in the regional evaluation depending on the specific situation.

Farmland ecosystem

Farmland ecosystems are also special, and they are the result of human transformation of natural ecosystems. Due to the increasing demand for food and cash crops by humans, the large-scale application of chemical fertilizers and pesticides in agricultural production, and the destruction of soil by irrigation and farming, farmland ecosystems have actually affected and destroyed the surrounding natural ecosystems. . In addition, because the farmland ecosystem is a complex system with a large amount of man-made material and energy input (such as manpower, mechanical energy consumption, farmland infrastructure, fertilizer, pesticides, etc.), its ecosystem service function mechanism and its value evaluation still need further the study. For humans, the largest service function of farmland ecosystems is the production of grain and crops. In addition, BjSrklund et al. summarize the predecessors' understanding of farmland ecosystem service functions, including: maintenance of fertile soil, biological management, nutrient cycling, Waste assimilation, CO_2 absorption and maintenance of genetic information, and research shows that the size of farmland ecosystem service functions is greatly affected by the intensity of agricultural production.

It can be seen that the evaluation of ecosystem service functions is mainly focused on the classification and value evaluation of ecosystem service functions, while the evaluation of the importance of ecosystem services is based on the evaluation of ecosystem service functions based on the capabilities and value assessment of typical ecosystem service functions. The comprehensive characteristics and spatial distribution characteristics. The results of the evaluation of the importance of ecosystem services will provide a direct basis for ecosystem science management, identification of key areas for ecological protection, and development of ecological protection and construction policies, but current comprehensive evaluation studies on the importance of ecosystem services are rarely carried out. As the scientific requirements for decision-making continue to increase, the importance of ecosystem service functions is increasingly important.

1.6 Ecosystem service function economic value evaluation method

Ecosystem service function evaluation can evaluate the quantity of substances and products supplied from ecosystems based on ecology, that is, material quality evaluation, and economic evaluation of these products and services, that is, value evaluation. Therefore, the evaluation of ecosystem service functions mainly includes material quality evaluation and value evaluation.

Material quality evaluation

The quality evaluation mainly refers to the quantitative evaluation of various services provided by the ecosystem from the perspective of material quality, that is, according to the structure, function and process of different regions and different ecosystems, based on the mechanism of ecosystem service function, using appropriate quantitative The method determines the amount of material produced by the service. The quality evaluation of the material is characterized by a more objective reflection of the ecological process of the ecosystem, which in turn reflects the sustainability of the ecosystem. The evaluation of ecosystem service functions is carried out by means of material quality assessment. The evaluation results are relatively intuitive and related only to the ecosystem's own health status and ability to provide service functions, and will not be affected by market price inconsistency and fluctuations. The quality evaluation is particularly suitable for the comparative study of the service capabilities of different ecosystems in different time periods and the comparative study of the same service functions provided by different ecosystems. This is an important means of ecosystem service function evaluation research.

The quality evaluation is based on the research of ecosystem service function mechanism. The research level of ecosystem service function mechanism determines the feasibility of material quality evaluation and the accuracy of results. The methods and methods used in the evaluation of material quality mainly include positioning experimental research, remote sensing, geographic information system, survey statistics, etc. Among them, positioning experimental research is the main means of service function mechanism and means of obtaining technical parameters. Remote sensing and survey statistics are the main methods. The data source, GIS provides a good technical platform for material quality evaluation, but the conversion and use of basic data at different scales needs further study. Research on quality assessment often requires a lot of manpower, material resources and capital. Material quality evaluation is the basis of value evaluation.

The method of simply using the material quality evaluation method also has limitations, mainly because the results are not intuitive and cannot attract enough attention, and because the individual ecosystem service functions are different in dimension, it cannot be aggregated, so that it is impossible to evaluate an ecosystem. Comprehensive service function.

In the evaluation process, the ecosystem types are different and the service functions are different. Therefore, there are great differences in the methods for evaluating the quality of the materials. The methods for evaluating the quality of the different service functions of each ecosystem type will be introduced in the subsequent research without the specific explanation.

Value evaluation

The value evaluation method is mainly the process of using some economic methods to value the service function. Many scholars have carried out exploratory research on the value evaluation method. However, due to the particularity and complexity of the ecosystem service, its evaluation and value measurement still It is a very difficult thing.

The value of ecosystem service functions can be divided into direct use value, indirect use value, choice value and existential value. The method of assessing the value of ecosystem services varies with the type of function.

1. Direct use value: mainly refers to the value generated by ecosystem products, including the direct value brought by food, medicine and other industrial and agricultural production materials, landscape entertainment and so on. The direct use value is estimated by the market price of the available product.

2. Indirect use value: mainly refers to the function of ecosystem services that cannot be commercialized, such as maintaining the biogeochemical cycle and hydrological cycle of living substances, maintaining biological species and genetic diversity, protecting soil fertility, purifying the environment, and maintaining atmospheric chemistry. The balance and stability support and maintain the function of the Earth's life support system. The assessment of indirect use value often needs to be determined according to the type of ecosystem function, usually the protection cost method, the recovery cost method, the alternative market method, and so on.

3. Choosing value: Choosing value is the willingness of people to pay for the direct or indirect use of certain ecosystem services in the future. For example, people will be willing to use the ecosystem to conserve water, purify the atmosphere, and enjoy recreation and other functions in the future. People often refer to the value of choice as insurance, that is, a kind of insurance money that people are willing to pay for ensuring that they can use certain resources or benefits in the future. The value of choice can be divided into three categories: self-use in the future; future generations of future generations, also known as heritage value: others will use it in the future, also called alternative consumption.

4. Existence value: Existence value, also known as intrinsic value, is the willingness of people to pay to ensure that ecosystem services continue to exist. The value of existence is the value of the ecosystem itself, and it is an economic value unrelated to human exploitation. In other words, even if humans do not exist, there are still existential values, such as the species diversity in ecosystems, the structure and ecological processes of ecosystems that conserve water. Existence value is a transitional value between economic value and ecological value, which provides common values   for economists and ecologists.

According to the existing ecosystem service function value evaluation technology and evaluation method, combined with the market development degree of ecosystem service and natural capital, the value evaluation method can be divided into the market value method (Direct market valuation) and the alternative market value method (Indirect market). Valuation and Surrogate market valuation, the specific evaluation techniques of ecosystem service functions include Direct market valuation, Opportunity cost approach, Shadow price method (Shadow) Price), Replacement engineering (Replacement cost), Factor income, Human capital, Hedonic pricing, Travel cost, Contingent valuation and Group valuation. Each method has its own advantages and disadvantages, and each service has a suitable evaluation method. Some service function evaluations may require some evaluation methods combined.

1.7 Evaluation criteria for the ecological design of indoor environment design

Now various values   and trends of thought continue to emerge, and the pursuit of material interests can easily confuse consumer values. In the field of design, whether it is a home space or a public space, modern people have intensified their plundering of natural resources in order to enjoy the extravagant life. The interior decoration environment is constantly being updated, and the demolished decorative materials are discarded because they cannot be recycled. The source of environmental pollution also causes serious waste of resources. As a designer, it should be responsible for evoking the return of people's social responsibility and ethics. Correspondingly, our design value judgment system and ethical judgment system should also add new content. The standard of ecological evaluation of indoor environment design is color, style, whether it is the form, fashion, ecology or ethics of beauty, which needs us to consider.

Indoor air quality

Traditionally, when people evaluate the advantages and disadvantages of an indoor environment, they often judge only from the perspective of whether the space form is beautiful or not, and ignore the indoor air quality is the standard. People's understanding of indoor air quality is only "Knowing it does not know why." The quality of indoor air quality should be the core position in indoor environmental assessment. It should be an important yardstick for evaluating design quality. In fact, from the designer to the consumer, from the construction enterprise to the society, this factor is basically not considered in the practice of indoor environment design. In the author's investigation visit, it was found that after the interior decoration was completed, the professional organization asked the air quality to be basically zero state, and most of the required tests were caused by the serious harm of indoor air, because people had to find out the cause of the disease. Whether it is going to be a lawsuit to detect indoor air is such a sad situation. Of course, this phenomenon is caused by many factors, the internal legal design system is not perfect, the market management is chaotic, the interior designer has no legal qualifications, and the bidding management system is imperfect, etc., which are the reasons for this result. We should actively explore feasible solutions and solutions. I will not discuss them here. I believe that under the joint efforts of all, this constraint will be resolved. The indoor air quality is directly related to people's health. When we evaluate the indoor environment, we should turn our attention to a deeper level of exploration. We should not judge from the aesthetic point of view. The connotation of the indoor space environment should be more extensive than before. The extension, it should develop into a suitable combination of environmental protection and health, indoor air cannot cause pollution to the human body and the outside world during use. If the indoor environment has a negative impact on oneself or on others, even if it is creative, we can't call it a good design. This design method is not worth promoting and promoting. American design theorist Victor Papanek (1927-1998) put forward his own views on the purpose of design in his book "Design for the Real World". He emphasized that design must consider the limited use of the Earth and must be protected. Earth Environment Service. In short, the indoor environment must not only meet the functional and aesthetic needs of consumers, but also meet the safety and health needs of consumers.

The details reflect energy saving

Energy conservation is one of the factors for evaluating the environmental design of indoor environment. Energy conservation is the rational and effective allocation of all types of decoration energy through scientific means, reducing waste, ensuring an efficient indoor environment and reducing energy consumption. Before proceeding with interior decoration, it is necessary to start from the details and carry out energy-saving renovation work to improve the comfort and safety in the indoor environment. Door and window seals, glass film, floor heating, energy-saving lighting, energy-saving sanitary ware, energy-saving lamps, solar water heaters, energy-saving refrigerators, energy-saving air conditioners, energy-saving sockets, sensor faucets and other smart devices are all means of energy-saving technology. At present, because energy-saving facilities are more expensive than ordinary facilities, and energy-saving renovations are not obvious in the short-term, these have become the main reasons restricting the application of energy-saving technologies.

Energy conservation and conservation are inseparable. In the construction process of indoor environment decoration, waste is particularly serious, and consumers generally have a tendency to pursue luxury and style. In some public building indoor environments, the owner excessively uses stainless steel, aluminum, copper, stone, glass and other materials. Even in the home space, the walls are decorated with marble and the columns are decorated with stainless steel. A large number of precious resources that are not renewable are used, and many available building materials are discarded. According to incomplete statistics, the household decoration of each family ranges from 30,000 to 40,000, and more than 100,000 and hundreds of thousands. These phenomena are contrary to the moderate consumption ideas and the conservation-oriented lifestyle advocated by the eco-design of indoor environment design.

Environmentally friendly materials and green technology
Materials and processes directly affect the ecological environment of the indoor environment. The ecological indoor environment is a complete process, including the design plan, the use of qualified decorative materials, and the green construction. In the purchase of decorative materials, environmentally-safe materials should be strictly selected. Eco-friendly decoration materials are gradually achieving clean production and product ecologicalization, and do not cause harm to the human body and the surrounding environment during production and use. At present, non-toxic paints, recycled wallpapers, etc. have been developed to achieve the above objectives to varying degrees; in the construction process, non-toxic or less toxic, non-polluting or less polluting construction techniques should be adopted as much as possible to reduce dust during construction. , pollution and damage to the environment caused by waste gas, waste water and noise. In the design of the scheme, for example, to make a frame or a wall, the designer can implement it in a simple way to avoid unnecessary waste. In terms of materials and processes, it should be considered more labor-saving and environmentally friendly. These factors are closely related to ecology. Another problem that needs to be pointed out is that in the materials, even if all the decoration materials that meet the limit standards for harmful substances in interior decoration materials are used, if large-scale paving is carried out, this will cause excessive standards, and the environmental protection standard is control. Within a certain range, this scale requires the designer to think about how much the board needs to be used without affecting the air quality, how much the ratio of paint and wood is controlled, etc., etc., which are considered by the designer in the early stage of design.

Simple Design

From the design stage, we must pay attention to environmental protection. In the evaluation system of whether the indoor environment is ecological, the design scheme plays an important guiding role. There are two reasons for the phenomenon that indoor air quality exceeds the standard. One is that the decoration materials used are non-environmental products themselves; the other is that various interior decoration materials are environmentally friendly products, but various materials and furniture. The released harmful substances are superimposed to cause the quality to exceed the standard. Therefore, for the designer, at the beginning of the decoration design, the amount of harmful substances that can be carried in the room should be calculated in advance, and the total amount of harmful substances should be controlled in an all-round way, not just the indicators of a single product. control. If the various functional spaces and shapes in the room are more, the amount of engineering will be larger. The more main materials and auxiliary materials are used, the higher the decoration cost will be, and the quality of the corresponding environment will be seriously suspected. Therefore, do not neglect the construction superposition effect of the decoration materials, the design should be reasonable, minimize the use of various types of plates, in addition, the decorative materials should be matched with appropriate proportions to reduce the total amount of pollutants.

The criteria for design evaluation have a very strong guiding role. After the Second World War, the American design only used sales as the only criterion for evaluating the design quality. It has a high commercialization tendency, resulting in a popular hedonistic attitude. People's material desires are stimulated by the so-called "beauty, taste, status symbol." For example, General Motors President Sloan and designer Earl, in order to continue to promote the sale of cars, consciously promote a system in their car design, called "planned abolition system", that is, when designing new car styles It must be taken into account that the local style of the car can be changed once every two years, once every three years, and the process of "psychological aging" caused by the constant change of design style, which is artificial in the design. The way to systematically cause the goods to fail in the short term, the new style is constantly introduced, causing the original products to be outdated and discarded by consumers. It can be seen that GM did not consider resource conservation, human-natural relationship in design evaluation. Their design philosophy is contrary to ecological ethics, which wastes a lot of natural resources and causes great harm. The main evaluation criteria recognized by the human social system will determine what our planet will eventually become. Interior design is very dangerous if it does not consider the ecological impact of design as an important evaluation criterion for design.

Design principles for indoor environment ecologicalization

The design principles of indoor environment ecologicalization have the following four aspects:

(1) the principle of health suitability. The indoor environment affects everyone's psychological feeling to a large extent. Therefore, the ecological indoor space should satisfy the comfort and health of the people, create an environment that is beneficial to the health of the human body, and produce no or less harmful pollution to the health of the human body. . It should be emphasized that health refers not only to the absence of disease in the body, but to an intact state of physical, mental and social. Health is defined as: "The body's various organ systems are well-developed, functioning properly, physically strong, energetic, and have a sound state of mind

and body and social adaptability. Usually measured by anthropometric, physical examination, various physiological and psychological indicators. The principle of indoor health requires attention to the concern of the indoor environment for the user's integrity, from the analysis of the influence of people's physical and psychological aspects in the living environment, and the study of the interaction between human-machine (building, facilities)-environmental systems. Optimization of various indicators (efficiency, health, safety, comfort, etc.). This requires comprehensive scheduling of indoor environment design and technical parameters, and meets various needs at multiple levels. In this sense, the healthy environment should be characterized by harmony with nature, making people physically and mentally healthy and full of life. Appropriate is a rational choice in the context of the deterioration of the energy environment. In the past, the goal of absolute comfort was highlighted, highlighting the principle of "moderate" and achieving relatively comfortable state through dynamic regulation of the comfort range.

(2) the principle of economic appropriateness. Indoor eco-design advocates moderate consumption thoughts and economical lifestyles, rather than extravagant luxury. At the same time of consumption, we should consciously consider the resource and environmental tolerance, and start from me to establish correct values and ethical order. Of course, some consumers are not very clear about the concept of environmental protection, which requires designers to take up this responsibility and guide consumption correctly.

(3) the principle of science. The rational design of the functional environment, natural ventilation, lighting, heat insulation, sound, light, color and other physical environments of the indoor environment are inseparable from the support of science and technology. The interior design relies on various decorative materials and various design methods. How to save energy, how to use renewable energy such as solar energy and wind energy, realize energy recycling, achieve energy saving and high efficiency, use new materials and new technologies, etc. All designers need to proceed from the scientific principle, through the scientific and technological means, to create artificial ecological beauty, so that the ecological environment of the indoor environment has achieved good results.

(4) the principle of "people-oriented". The human-oriented four-character has become the guiding ideology in various fields, but the phrase that reflects the Western humanistic spirit has been simply used or even misinterpreted by a large number of groups. We can't confuse the individual's "human" with the overall "human". People-oriented essentially means that all actions of the individual must serve the whole human being. Do not regard the "people-oriented" mistake as "my-oriented." We need to correct the connotation. In the field of design, we should not only be based on the people, but also based on the future development of our children and grandchildren and human beings, rather than on the confrontation and conflict between man and nature. The long-term interests of mankind come at the cost.

Chapter 2 Research on the Evaluation of Ecological Environment Efficiency Based on Circular Economy Mode

At present, China's economic growth is largely achieved by consuming large amounts of material resources. According to statistics, the energy consumption and material consumption per unit of output in China are significantly higher than the world average. Therefore, how to improve the efficiency of resource and energy use and reduce the environmental pollution load has become the core content of the development of circular economy. This section selects key industries based on indicators such as resources, energy consumption intensity and pollutant emission intensity. The IPAT model is used to analyze the energy, resource consumption and pollutant emission intensity of key industries, and identify the key industries to improve ecological efficiency. Obstacles, proposed a policy framework to improve the eco-efficiency of key industries, and selected case studies (cement, paper) for case studies.

2.1 Evaluation of ecological efficiency of key industries in China

Overview and problems of ecological efficiency in key industries

Eco-efficiency is the core standard of circular economy and the "node" indicator connecting resources, economy and environment. Ecological efficiency is the ratio of the value of economic and social development (ie, total GDP or industrial output) to the consumption of resources and the amount of pollutants discharged. It represents the decoupling indicators of economic growth and environmental pressure. Ecological efficiency can be further divided into resources. Productivity and environmental productivity (environmental efficiency), including: GDP per unit of energy consumption (energy productivity), GDP per unit of land (land productivity), GDP per unit of water consumption (water productivity), and GDP per unit of material consumption (substance) Productivity) Indicators related to environmental efficiency include GDP emissions from major pollutants. The reciprocal of eco-efficiency is actually what we usually say about unit GDP energy consumption, material consumption, water consumption and pollution emissions. The indicators of industrial eco-efficiency include three aspects: energy intensity indicators, raw material consumption intensity indicators and strong pollutant emission indicators. Based on the availability of data, this study uses resource energy consumption intensity as an indicator of industrial eco-efficiency, and pollutant emission intensity as an indicator of eco-efficiency input.

In order to analyze the current ecological efficiency of key industries in China, this study considers the energy contribution rate and pollution contribution rate of industry output value, from the three aspects of water environment pollution, atmospheric pollution and solid waste pollution, with typical pollutants as Evaluation indicators to identify key high energy consumption, material consumption and high pollution industries.

Water environment pollution key industries

The key industries of water environmental pollution are based on the COD emissions from industrial wastewater in this industry. According to comparison, key industries in the water environment are paper and paper products, food, tobacco processing and food and beverage manufacturing (including agricultural and sideline food processing, food manufacturing, beverage manufacturing, tobacco products), chemical manufacturing, textiles. industry.

In 2004, the COD emissions of these four industries accounted for 71.9% of the national key statistical enterprises' COD emissions. From the perspective of COD emission performance of industrial units' added value, the largest papermaking industry was 262.49kg/10,000 yuan, followed by Food processing industry, beverage manufacturing and chemical manufacturing.

Atmospheric environmental pollution key industries

The key industries for atmospheric environmental pollution are based on the emission of sulfur dioxide and dust from industrial waste gas. According to comparison, key industries in the atmospheric environment are electricity and heat production and supply, non-metallic mineral products, ferrous metal smelting and rolling processing, chemical raw materials and chemical products manufacturing, non-ferrous metal smelting and rolling processing.

In 2004, these five industries accounted for 83.4% of the national key statistical enterprises' dioxide emissions, of which electricity and heat production and supply accounted for 57.0%. From the perspective of SO_2 emission performance of industrial unit added value, the largest is the power industry. It is 256.30kg/million, followed by non-ferrous metal processing industry, non-metallic mineral products industry, chemical raw materials and chemical products manufacturing. In 2004, the non-metallic mineral products industry and ferrous metal smelting and processing industry dust emissions accounted for 85.6% of the industrial dust emissions of the statistical industry.

Solid waste pollution key industries
Considering that solid waste can reduce the impact on the environment through comprehensive utilization, the screening basis of key industries is determined as industrial solid waste discharge. According to comparison, key industries of solid waste include coal mining and washing, ferrous metal mining and mining, non-ferrous metal mining and mining, ferrous metal smelting and rolling processing, chemical raw materials and chemical products manufacturing.

In 2004, the total industrial solid waste discharge of the above industries reached 11.34 million tons, accounting for 72.1% of the total solid waste discharge in the statistical industry.

In summary, China currently has a large total amount of pollutants discharged into the environment, and the industrial industries with more serious environmental loads are:
(1) the key environmental pollution industries: paper and paper products, food and tobacco processing and food and beverage manufacturing (including agricultural and sideline food processing, food manufacturing, beverage manufacturing, tobacco products), chemical raw materials and chemicals Manufacturing, textile industry.
(2) the key pollution industries in the atmospheric environment: electricity and heat production and supply, non-metallic mineral products, ferrous metal smelting and rolling processing, chemical raw materials and chemical manufacturing, non-ferrous metal smelting and rolling processing.
(3) the key pollution industries of solid waste: extractive industries (including coal mining and washing industry, oil and gas mining, ferrous metal mining and mining, non-ferrous metal mining and mining, non-metallic mining and other mining industries)), ferrous metal smelting and rolling processing industry, chemical raw materials and chemical products manufacturing.

By comparison, the key industries defined in this study and the seven high-energy and high-pollution industries in the circular economy pilot program promulgated by the six ministries and commissions, as well as the key industries of the 10 major circular economy that China intends to determine.

Based on the definition of indicators, this study collects relevant statistical data and evaluates the ecological efficiency of these key industries. It can be seen that China's current energy-efficient industries are still these key industries. Through horizontal (inter-industry) and vertical (inter-annual) comparative analysis, we can see that these key industries have the following characteristics:

(1) the amount of pollutants discharged is large and the contribution rate of pollution is high. The key polluting industries are highly polluting industries, especially their main pollution factors, and their emissions account for an absolute proportion in the statistical industry.(2) the emission intensity of pollutants is basically declining. It can be seen that during the 10th Five-Year Plan period, the average pollutant emission intensity of these nine key polluting industries has declined to varying degrees. (3) the efficiency of resource utilization has increased, and the consumption of resources per unit of output has declined, but the total consumption of resources continues to climb. In 2004, the average industrial water reuse rate of the nine key polluting industries was 74.6%. The comprehensive utilization of industrial solid waste also increased significantly. However, resources and energy consumption are still on the rise. In 2004, the total industrial water consumption of key polluting industries increased by 8% compared with the previous year; in 2003, the total energy consumption of nine industries increased by 19% over the previous year.

It can be seen from the current situation that China's eco-efficiency growth has a large gap compared with GDP growth, which indicates that China's economic growth is too dependent on resource consumption. In order to further study the problems in improving the eco-efficiency of the industry, the paper industry, which has the greatest impact on the water environment, and the cement industry in the non-metallic mineral products industry, which has a great impact on the atmospheric environment, were selected as the case study.

2.2 The development trend of ecological efficiency in key industries

China's existing development model will undoubtedly bring great pressure on China's future resources and environment. In order to explore the environmental load brought about by the development of these key industries, the IPAT model will be used to make use of the national socio-economic and resource-environment statistics of the past years. A simple forecast.

In 1971, Ehrlich and Holdren proposed the classic equation IPAT for sustainability evaluation, which decomposed human environmental impact (I) into the combined effects of population (P), wealth (A) and technology (T). , where wealth is usually expressed in terms of total GDP or income produced:

$I = P \times A \times T$

Where: I - environmental load, including resources, energy consumption and waste discharge;

P - population;

A - per capita GDP;

T——The environmental load of the unit GDP.

In order to analyze the laws of China's industrial development and its environmental load growth, the World Bank-funded project "Policy Research on Promoting China's Circular Economy Development" (hereinafter referred to as the "Project") collected and observed industrial statistics from 1998 to 2005. Comparison and fitting, mainly including industrial added value, growth rate, total industrial water consumption, total industrial energy consumption, chemical oxygen demand emissions from industrial wastewater, sulfur dioxide emissions from industrial waste gas, and industrial solid waste production. According to data fitting, China's industrial added value is generally exponentially increasing. At the same time, the intensity of resource utilization and the intensity of pollution emissions have gradually eased, showing an exponential decline.

By selecting the appropriate parameters, the project predicts resource consumption and environmental load in the existing industrial development model. The forecast results show that in today's development model, industrial added value will continue to rise, reaching 11 trillion yuan in 2010, doubling on the basis of 2005; will reach 30 trillion yuan in 2020, in 2010 Doubled on the basis of the year.

However, in addition to economic growth, in addition to the reduction in industrial COD emissions, resource consumption and pollutant emissions will continue to increase. In 2010, industrial water consumption will increase to 135.3 billion m3, an increase of 8.9% over 2005; total industrial energy consumption will increase to 19,105,300 tons of standard coal, an increase of 44.4% over 2005; industrial SO2 emissions will increase to 27.3 million tons. This is an increase of 34.0% over 2005; industrial solid waste production will increase to 204.384 million tons, an increase of 56.4% over 2005.

At the same time, according to the development goal of the "Eleventh Five-Year Development Outline", the project sets the model parameters with 2005 as the base year, predicts the resource consumption and environmental pressure of the goal-oriented development model, and the inertial development model. The prediction results were compared. It can be seen from the results of inertia prediction that if the current development model is not changed, the development trend of China's heavy industrialization will be obvious in the future for a long time, the environmental load has not yet reached the peak, there is no sign of inflection point, and environmental pollutants are discharged. Will surpass the environmental carrying capacity of the ring. The goal-oriented development model shows that without affecting economic growth, taking corresponding measures will greatly improve China's industrial eco-efficiency, and the total pollutant discharge and resource consumption will decrease or grow slowly. This is also China's direction.

2.3 Policy recommendations to improve the eco-efficiency of key industries

1. Analysis of policy barriers to improve the eco-efficiency of key industries

China's key industries to develop circular economy and improve ecological efficiency mainly include industrial policies, technical policies, fiscal and financial policies (including investment, taxation and other policies) and environmental management policies. With the continuous improvement of the market economy, the basic role of market allocation resources is growing. However, the government's use of administrative management and economic means to regulate the market behavior of different entities still plays a considerable role in stimulating and guiding. Therefore, this study sorts out and analyzes China's current industrial, technical, and economic incentives, focusing on industrial restructuring policies, environmental standards and access systems, cleaner production policies, and resource development that are directly related to circular economy. We use the economic incentives such as policies and related taxes and fees to summarize the main policy obstacles in the implementation of the policy to improve ecological efficiency. International experience and previous experience in China have shown that industrial restructuring is the most important way to save energy and reduce emissions. However, China is still in the mid-industrial period. It is very difficult to achieve energy conservation, consumption reduction and emission reduction through industrial restructuring. Therefore, the key is to reduce resource consumption and pollution emissions.

The state has recently strengthened its requirements for environmental protection in the direction of industrial development. For example, in the past two years, the National Development and Reform Commission has successively announced the structural adjustment opinions of the nine industries of aluminum industry, cement industry, ferroalloy industry, coking industry, coal industry, calcium carbide industry, power industry, textile industry and steel industry, as well as "Stop the copper smelting". "Several Opinions on Blind Investment in the Industry", "Emergency Notice on the Orderly and Healthy Development of Refining and Ethylene Industry", etc., all of these opinions or notices will strengthen resources and environmental protection as important standards and basis. Especially in the "Outline of the Eleventh Five-Year Plan for National Economic and Social Development of the People's Republic of China", the environmental protection, resource conservation and development of circular economy have been raised to unprecedented heights and penetrated into all aspects of the planning outline. Premier Wen Jiabao specifically pointed out at the national teleconference on energy conservation and emission reduction work on April 27, 2007 that energy conservation and emission reduction should be regarded as the focus of strengthening macroeconomic regulation and control as a breakthrough point and an important starting point for adjusting economic structure and transforming growth mode. Carry out the scientific development concept and the important measures to build a harmonious society, and put forward the general requirements for energy conservation and emission reduction: unified understanding, clear tasks, strengthen leadership, and firmly implement, with greater determination, greater strength, and more effective measures To ensure the realization of the national "Eleventh Five-Year Plan" energy conservation and emission reduction targets, and promote the sound and rapid development of the national economy.

However, there are still some obstacles and problems in the relevant industrial policies, mainly in:
(1) the industrial guidance policy is not legally binding and lacks effective administrative means.
China's existing industrial guidance policies are less efficient, less restrictive, and difficult to regulate. The industrial structure adjustment policy is an important means for the state to strengthen the comprehensive utilization of resources and form a low-input, low-consumption, low-emission and high-efficiency and economical growth mode. In 2005, the National Development and Reform Commission successively issued the "Industrial Structure Adjustment Guidance Catalogue (2005 Edition).) and the Interim Provisions on Promoting Industrial Structure Adjustment. Recently, the state has strengthened its requirements for environmental protection in the direction of industrial development. However, from the perspective of legal orientation, the existing industrial guidance policy has low legal effect and is mainly guided. There are still no

specific implementation rules, lists and standards, and there are insufficient constraints on industries with serious pollution and waste of resources.

(2) economic policy is not motivating

Under the conditions of market mechanism, economic benefits are the biggest driving force for enterprises to develop circular economy and increase the utilization rate of resource recycling. However, some existing economic methods such as resource prices, taxes and fees to promote efficient use of resources have not played their due role. effect.

First of all, the existing tax collection method does not meet the current national conditions in China. In order to reflect the scarcity of resources, China has formulated a series of resource tax collection methods, including the "Provisional Regulations on the Resource Tax of the People's Republic of China" implemented on January 1, 1994 and the "Mineral Resources Compensation Fee" promulgated by the State Council in February 1994. Collection Management Regulations. However, due to the low proportion of resource taxes and fees, the low cost of resource development directly leads to the fact that resource prices cannot reflect their true value.

Secondly, the market price of resources has not been fully liberalized. On the one hand, resource prices cannot effectively and realistically reflect social needs, and it is impossible to regulate the production and consumption behavior of resources according to market rules through price mechanisms, which has led to the cheapness of resources to a certain extent. Even for free use; on the other hand, it has led to a large number of exports of resource-consumption products.

Third, the scope of various tax incentives is small, and it does not trigger the role of enterprises in comprehensive utilization of resources. According to the Notice of the Ministry of Finance and the State Administration of Taxation on Several Preferential Policies for Corporate Income Taxes issued in 1994 and the Notice on the Comprehensive Utilization of Some Resources and Other Product Value-added Tax Policies Issued in 2001, the VAT preferential treatment is only for the use of cities. The production of electricity from domestic garbage, the cement produced from waste residue, and the desulfurization by-products of power plants are rarely used for comprehensive utilization of resources; the income tax concession is also for the production of waste water, waste gas, waste residue and other wastes within the prescribed range. Products can be reduced or exempted from income tax within five years; the state tax authorities have not given certain tariff reduction and exemption support policies for enterprises to introduce key equipment for comprehensive utilization abroad, which is not conducive to encouraging enterprises to adopt advanced technology.

In addition, the sewage charging system formulated to encourage enterprises to improve resource utilization and reduce emissions has not achieved corresponding results. The state has not revised the pollutant discharge standards of certain key industries, and the sewage charges are low, which makes enterprises prefer to pay sewage charges, and is not willing to optimize technology and improve the comprehensive utilization of resources.

In 2003, China began to implement the "Clean Production Promotion Law". Although it has achieved certain results in practice, due to unfavorable supporting measures, the overall results have been limited. There are some institutional obstacles in the implementation of the Clean Production Promotion Law, including resource invaluable or low price, and environmental costs are not included in production costs, resulting in enterprises not saving resources, reducing the economic benefits of sewage discharge, engaging in cleaner production or environmental protection. Enterprises have faced unfair market competition because of increased costs; the government lacks supporting measures to encourage cleaner production, especially for SMEs. VAT and other fiscal and taxation policies not only do not encourage resource conservation, but also limit the resource recycling industry. Development; at the same time lack of relevant technological innovation, conceptualization of analytical methods, and clean production audits in the form of.

Third, the relevant standards for ecological efficiency in key industries are incomplete or low.
First of all, for environmental emission standards, since the 1980s, China has successively formulated emission standards for different pollutants in various industries, which has played a certain role in controlling pollutant emissions from the end, but from existing standards. In terms of system, there are two problems. First, the standards are not comprehensive enough. Some key industries have not been involved. Second, the standard update is not timely enough. From the perspective of standard implementation time, some standards are too old and it is difficult to promote technological progress. Industry structure adjustment and improvement of pollution control level.

Secondly, in order to promote the industrial structure upgrade and standardize the development of the industry, the National Development and Reform Commission formulated the "Qualification Requirements for Calcium Carbide Industry", "Access Conditions for Ferroalloy Industry" and "Entry Conditions for Coking Industry" in 2005. The requirements were made from five aspects: production enterprise layout, process and equipment, energy consumption and comprehensive utilization of resources, environmental protection, supervision and management. This can play a positive role in improving the eco-efficiency of these industries, but the existing access standards cannot reflect the environmentally friendly concept from the design, mainly based on safety and non-hazard, and it is recommended that the future industry standard setting process be more Integrate the concept of environmental protection and resource conservation, especially in product standards. In addition, environmental access standards are not high. Several industry environmental access standards have been introduced to simply meet the pollutant discharge standards.
Fourth, legal supervision is not in place and legal authorization is insufficient.From the perspective of the existing legal system, the corresponding law enforcement agencies have no corresponding legal authorization for compulsory punishment for enterprises with poor eco-efficiency. At present, the environmental protection department only has the power of administrative punishment, and does not have the compulsory means of seizure, freezing, seizure, compulsory allocation, etc., when it shuts down the enterprise, it lacks the legal authority to cut off water and power, revoke licenses, dismantle and destroy equipment, etc. The decision-making power is in the local government; in addition, due to the current illegal sewage companies, the maximum fine imposed by the law is only 200,000 yuan, which is not enough to deter environmental

violations. This has caused the corresponding departments to fail to exercise effective regulatory measures in the administrative control of heavily polluting enterprises.

2. Key policy framework for improving the eco-efficiency of key industries

To build key policy frameworks for key industries to improve eco-efficiency, it is necessary to comprehensively consider the role of policies and the types of policy instruments. The role of policy includes three links: reduction, resource and reuse, and harmlessness; policy instruments can be broadly divided into command-and-control direct control policies, market-based economic incentives, and voluntary agreements. There are three types of publicity education and public participation. Another type of policy, such as industry guidance policy, producer responsibility extension system, technology demonstration and support, is a whole process management or macro policy.

For different industries, due to the characteristics of the industry and their status in the national economy, the policy measures adopted are different, the policy focus is different, and the entry point of policy role is not the same. Therefore, according to the status of the industry in the national economy, resource utilization and environmental emissions, the industry is classified, and energy conservation and emission reduction policies suitable for industry characteristics are proposed. For industries with outstanding status, resource and energy consumption, and pollution contribution in the national economy (this book is called the first type of industry), such as steel, coal, electricity, and chemicals, it is the focus of China's development of circular economy. Comprehensive means such as law, administration, and economy promote industrial structure upgrading, improve resource efficiency, and make full use of resource prices and other mechanisms to promote key industries to develop circular economy, promote cleaner production, and reduce environmental load. Those industries with high pollution intensity but small status in the national economy (this book is called the second type of industry), such as the paper industry, the country should strictly adhere to the standards, limit exports, and encourage the lack of domestic demand through imports. Therefore, the roles and policy instruments of these two types of industrial policies are different. The key policy factors are analyzed for these two different industries, and the key policies and general policies are distinguished according to the policy factors of different links. According to the above analysis, in order to improve and formulate policies to improve the eco-efficiency of the industry, it is necessary to follow the principle of circular economy development, starting from the three links of reduction, reuse/resource and harmless.

(1) In the reduction link, key policies include vigorously promoting eco-design, key industry resource consumption and pollution emission quota management, and key resource tax price mechanism.

The eco-design policy refers to the units and individuals engaged in the design of processes, equipment and products and packaging materials. In the design process, it should be based on the requirements of energy saving, consumption reduction and pollutant reduction. It is preferred to adopt non-toxic, harmless, easy to degrade and easy to use. Materials and designs for recycling and recycling. For products that are closely related to human health and safety, such as electrical and electronic products, clothing, toys, interior decoration materials, etc., toxic and harmful raw materials listed in the list of toxic and hazardous substances shall not be used. The list shall be related to the comprehensive macroeconomic regulation and control department of the State Council and environmental protection. Department development.

Key industry resource consumption and pollution emission quota management system refers to the implementation of fixed-point management of energy consumption, water consumption, material consumption and major pollutant emissions per unit of output value of key industries. Relevant departments regularly release energy consumption per unit of output value and water consumption of key industries. Tariff indicators for material consumption and major pollutant emissions, as well as energy consumption, water consumption, material consumption and major pollutant discharge quota indicators for key industries. Relevant departments shall supervise and inspect the implementation of the quota indicators listed in the key industries. If the requirements are not met within the prescribed time limit, the relevant departments shall order them to suspend production for rectification within a specified time limit. If the inspection fails, the government department shall decide to close them within a time limit. The same system will be implemented for new projects in key industries, and the energy consumption, water consumption, material consumption and major pollutant discharge quotas will be reviewed. For projects that fail to meet the specified requirements, construction may not be approved or approved. For industries that have outstanding positions in the national economy but have large resources and energy consumption and large pollution, such as steel and electric power, this policy should be specifically adopted to promote the optimization and upgrading of industrial structure.

(2) In the recycling/recycling process, key policies include quota management of waste recycling in key industries, promotion of preferential policies for comprehensive utilization of resources, and promotion of construction of eco-industrial parks.

The key industry waste recycling quota management policy refers to the regular release of water reuse rate, waste recycling rate, waste resource utilization rate, waste heat and residual pressure utilization quotas in key industries. Relevant departments shall supervise and inspect the implementation of quotas listed in key industries or enterprises. It is the responsibility of the key enterprises listed in the list to report to the relevant local management departments the implementation of the previous year's waste recycling and resource quota indicators. Government departments should regularly announce the implementation of key enterprise waste recycling and resource quota indicators. For industries that have outstanding positions in the national economy but have large resources and energy consumption and large pollution, such as steel and electricity, special attention must be paid to making this policy work.

(3) In the harmless process, key policies include environmental access system, increase of pollution discharge fees, final disposal of industrial waste and environmental supervision.

The environmental access system mainly refers to the market access of industries, technological processes and products that severely waste resources and pollute the environment by setting thresholds and standards. Therefore, the system includes three aspects. First, industrial access, environmental access to production process management, environmental access system for key industries with high resource consumption and high environmental load, and establishment of environmental pollution intensity indicators and resources.

Constraining consumption indicators, restricting the development of these industries through environmental impact assessment and industrial guidance policies; second, access to technological processes, establishing access technology standards for key industries such as process technology, scale, and major pollutant emission intensity, and restricting the entry of backward technological processes The third is to implement environmental access management for products, implement product access systems with key energy consumption, water consumption and high pollution emissions, and prohibit products that do not meet the national minimum energy efficiency standards, water saving standards and environmental emission intensity standards. Production and sales on the market. To establish an environmental access system, the first thing to do is to establish a list of industries, products, and industries with high material consumption, energy consumption, and high pollution in key industries. All the processes and products listed in the list of the list need to adopt administrative, economic and technical means to strengthen management. This policy should be specifically adopted for industries that have limited contribution to the national economy, are small in size but have high resource consumption and strong emissions.

In addition to the above three key policies, the whole process management or macro management policies are also very important. These policies include producer extension system, industrial policy, technology demonstration and support, government green procurement, high energy consumption, and high Policies for the adjustment of pollution discharges and import and export tax rebates for resource products.

The above related policies should make the most of the implementation and effectiveness of the policy, and it is recommended to develop a supporting list and standard system as soon as possible.

Part 6　Research on the Status Quo and Causes of Ecological Environment Design Based on Circular Economy Mode

Chapter 1 Analysis of current situation of ecological environment design based on circular economy model

At present, China's circular economy practice activities are mainly concentrated in the three levels of enterprises, eco-industrial parks and society, and are in the pilot demonstration stage. This means that the practice of circular economy is still only the behavior of a few social economic entities, and is limited to certain aspects of social economic activities. On the basis of the pilot demonstration, China will face the problem of how to comprehensively promote the practice of circular economy, namely how to apply the principle of circular economy and comprehensively transform the social economic system. In essence, this is a technical model for the development of circular economy and a policy method for guiding the realization of the technical model. The technical model and implementation method are multi-level, with the enterprise micro level, the industrial park middle level, the regional and national macro level. China has accumulated relatively good experience at the level of enterprises and industrial parks, and has successful international experience to learn from. Its technical models and methods can be widely promoted. However, at the regional and national levels, although there are several pilot provinces and cities, there is no universally applicable technical model and policy approach. The region is a complex of social economy and resource environment. The regional model of circular economy development is qualitatively different from the model of circular economy activities in enterprises or industrial parks. At the same time, due to the differences in the connotation and practice of circular economy between developed countries such as China and Germany and Japan, there is no ready experience to draw on in this respect. From the nature of the components of the system and its structural relationship, the national model has a great similarity with the regional model. Therefore, the study of the regional model of circular economy development is the most urgent need for China from the state to the local government.

The regional development model of circular economy includes two aspects: the role, principles and tools of circular economy in coordinating the relationship between regional resource environment and economic and social development; and the establishment of production and consumption patterns in line with the principles and objectives of circular economy (referred to as circular type (sustainable) production and consumption patterns).

This section will systematically explain the regional development model of circular economy and related policy issues. At the same time, it proposes policy recommendations for the construction of eco-industrial parks.

1.1 The role of circular economy in regional coordinated development

The essential contradiction of regional coordinated development. The contradiction between regional resource environment and economic and social development is the contradiction between the infinite nature of economic activities with growth mechanism and the limited supply of resources and environment to ecosystems with stable mechanisms (Xu Dixin, 1987). Here, what is "demand" and "supply" is the ability of the economic resources and ecosystems in the natural ecosystem to purify the waste generated by social and economic activities, that is, the environmental capacity. Economic resources and environmental capacity are all useful resources for social and economic activities. The economic resources and wastes discharged into social economic activities are all substances, and they are the general term for the exchange of people and nature. The ability of natural ecosystems to supply economic resources and environmental capacity is limited, that is, it has "capacity". Therefore, the resource and environmental issues are essentially the imbalance of material exchange relationship between the socio-economic system and the natural ecosystem. The "flux" (resources and waste flows) exceeds the "capacity" (resource supply capacity and environmental purification capacity), and there is a shortage of resources. And environmental pollution.

Therefore, the fundamental way to coordinate the relationship between regional resource environment and socio-economic development must be to change the "flux" (efficiency) of material flow and the regulation of material exchange in the process of social economic activities, in order to adapt to the "capacity" of natural ecosystems. Develop a circular economy, transform traditional production and consumption patterns, and establish a cyclical production and consumption model.

1.2 Basic principles and policy tools for coordinating regional development

Within the regional ecological and socio-economic complex system, the goal and principle of developing a circular economy is to base on the resource supply of the regional ecosystem and the self-purification capacity of the environment (referred to as the resource environmental capacity), and the basic constraints on the socio-economic development of the regional resource environment. Under the regulation of the flow and efficiency of material flow, increase the resource and environmental space for development, and coordinate the contradiction between regional resource environment and social and economic development.

After studying the changing relationship between socio-economic systems and ecosystems for nearly 150 years, the World Bank proposed a growth hypothesis based on quantitative constraints and capacity. On the contrary, if the material use of the region is not changed, the demand for resources and energy for economic development will grow exponentially. However, through thorough management changes, the environmental and economic effects of (Factor 10) can be obtained, the demand for resources and energy can be reduced, and the decoupling between economic growth and resource consumption and pollution emissions can be achieved. This is the theoretical basis for the development of circular economy to increase the resource and environmental space for regional development. Therefore, identifying the basic types of regional ecosystem types and their resource and environmental capacity constraints on regional socio-economic development is a prerequisite for establishing a cyclical production and consumption model. The results of 'Shenyang city' study show that ecological function zoning and development main functional zoning are effective policy tools to identify the basic types of regional ecosystems and their resource and environmental capacity constraints on regional social and economic development.

Ecological function zoning

The purpose of ecological function zoning is to use ecological laws to provide a basis for determining regional social and economic development direction, structural layout and adjustment, resource development and protection, and to guide regional social economy to take a sustainable development path according to local conditions. The method of ecological function zoning is to systematically analyze the spatial distribution characteristics of regional ecosystems based on the evaluation of the current status of ecological environment, and to clarify the main ecological environment problems, the importance of ecosystem service functions and the spatial differentiation of ecological sensitivities. Different ecological function types identify key ecological functional areas and ecologically highly sensitive areas that play an important role. According to the "Shenyang Urban Ecological System Construction Plan", the city is divided into five ecological function types: central urban ecological function area; urban suburban ecological function area; central plain ecological function area; eastern hilly ecological function area; western and northern ecological functions Area.

Development of main function planning

The result of ecological function zoning is the division of different ecological function types. According to China's national economic and social development "Eleventh Five-Year Plan", it is also necessary to coordinate future population distribution, economic layout and land use based on existing development density and development potential. And the urbanization pattern, further provide clear guidance on the social and economic development direction, structural layout and adjustment, resource development and protection under different ecological function types, that is, the main function planning for development.

According to the results of ecological function zoning, the five types of ecological functional areas in Shenyang City were further divided into three types of functional main functional areas. Prohibited development zones: The forbidden development zone in Shenyang mainly consists of 13 various types of nature reserves with a total area of 1754.62km2, accounting for 13.5% of the city's total area. Restricted development zones: The restricted development zones in Shenyang are mainly desertification sensitive areas and areas that have important impacts on biodiversity conservation and water conservation, with an area of 2320.9km2, accounting for 17.9% of the total area. Optimization and key development zones: The optimization and key development zones mainly include agricultural resource development zones and urban construction development zones with an area of 8904.48km2, accounting for 68.6% of the total area.

Development and protection of the regulatory principles

Different main functional areas must correspond to the social and economic development content and structure that are compatible with them, implement different circular economy regulation principles, and ensure that resources and environment are coordinated with social and economic activities.

(1) Prohibition of development zones

From the perspective of ecological function, the forbidden development zone is a biodiversity conservation and water conservation zone that has a decisive significance for regional ecological and environmental security. At the same time, it is often a region with high ecological sensitivity, poor system stability and vulnerability to external disturbances. The regulation principle of prohibiting the development and protection of development zones is to strictly maintain the material exchange relationship of the balance of natural ecosystems, and it is not appropriate to develop industrial and agricultural. Therefore, the development zone is prohibited from being subjected to compulsory protection according to law, and the control of human activities interferes with the natural ecology. It is strictly forbidden to develop activities that do not conform to the main function of the main body.

Judging from the industrial layout of Shenyang City Kangping County's coal-aluminum electric production and processing industry is adjacent to the prohibited development zone, which is located in the restricted development zone. It is in serious conflict with the ecological function location of the zone, and it is best to implement the relocation. In the case of no relocation, it is necessary to achieve zero emissions in accordance with the circular economy concept to ensure that it does not affect the ecological environment. Its feasibility requires a strict environmental impact assessment to conduct in-depth demonstration. In addition, the ban on the development of animal husbandry in certain development zones in Shenyang should be strictly prohibited.

(2) Limit development zones

Restricted development zones refer to areas with strong ecological sensitivity and vulnerability, poor system stability, and weak resistance to external disturbances. At the same time, the area has important natural ecological service functions and plays an important role in maintaining the function of the prohibited development zones. It is closely related to the overall ecological function of the maintenance area. The regulation principle of restricting the development and protection of development zones is to develop moderately under the premise of maintaining the cyclical material exchange relationship of the balance of the natural ecosystems. It is generally not suitable to develop industries and moderately develop ecological industries such as ecological agriculture. Therefore, restricting the development zone should implement protection priority, moderate development, restrict the development of new towns, strictly control the development of urban construction land, control the population size of the population-populated residential areas that have been built, and strictly implement the discharge of domestic sewage standards. The ecological environment should be repaired in a planned manner; the industrial structure should be adjusted, the ecological industry should be focused on, and ecological industries such as economic forests, flower bases, and eco-tourism should be developed moderately.

(3) Optimization and key development zones

From the perspective of ecological functions, optimization and key development zones refer to areas with certain ecological service functions, good ecological environment stability, and ability to withstand certain human disturbances. The difference between optimization and key development zones is that the optimized development zone refers to the area where the land development density is already high and the resource environment carrying capacity begins to weaken; the key development zone refers to the resource and environment carrying capacity is strong, and the economic and population agglomeration conditions are the better region.

The principle of optimization and key development zone development and protection regulation is to comprehensively develop circular economy, transform or establish a cyclical material exchange relationship, improve ecological efficiency, and adapt the resource demand and waste discharge of social economic activities to the resource and environmental capacity of the region.

At present, the major industrial and agricultural development activities in Shenyang are basically optimized and key development zones. According to the existing industrial structure, Shenyang's key industries of circular economy are the development of ecological industries and ecological agriculture. The eco-industry consists of 8 ecological chains, which basically cover the main industrial sectors of Shenyang: chemical industry, pharmaceutical industry, environmental protection industry chain; pharmaceutical industry, chemical industry chain; light industry, chemical industry, pharmaceutical industry, tertiary industry and Livestock breeding chain: food and beverage industry, pharmaceutical industry, tertiary industry and poultry breeding chain; food and beverage industry, pharmaceutical industry, environmental protection industry chain; equipment manufacturing industry 'automotive manufacturing industry, pharmaceutical industrial chain; equipment manufacturing Industry, automobile manufacturing, metallurgical industry chain; electrical industry, metallurgical industry chain.

Eco-agriculture can promote 7 modes: "four-in-one" breeding and breeding mode; ecological farming mode; "planting, raising and adding" symbiosis mode; food waste recycling – feed processing mode; sewage recharge mode; "scale animal Poultry farm - anaerobic fermentation project - orchard - tourism and sightseeing mode; "cow manure - biogas - protein feed - waste - soilless cultivation - pond duckling, fish" ecological livestock model.

If the above-mentioned eco-industrial and eco-agriculture models can be implemented smoothly, the industrial eco-efficiency of Shenyang City will be greatly improved, maintaining a high level of resource and environmental carrying capacity.

Chapter 2 Research on the Influencing Factors of Ecological Environment Design Based on Circular Economy Mode

In the circular economy model, the design of the ecological environment is affected by more factors.

2.1 Impact of resource factors

The first goal of the design of the ecological environment is to recycle resources. The environment is also a natural resource. We cannot rely on a large amount of resources and waste of resources to achieve economic development. In the design of ecological environment, recycling resources is also one of the important requirements for the design of ecological environment. Through the circular economy, we can achieve sustainable use and development of resources, while not affecting the quality of economic development, conserving resources, protecting resources, and leaving more resources for sustainable use and development for future generations.

However, in recent years, because we only care about the development of the economy, we do not pay attention to the protection of ecological resources, resulting in the depletion of ecological resources. Therefore, under the circular economy model, we must implement the circular economy theory into the practice of ecological environment resource protection, and take corresponding measures to protect the ecological environment resources while developing the economy. In the process of designing the ecological environment, it is necessary to put the resource protection and the sustainable use of the ecological environment first, and change the previous models and concepts that only attach importance to economic development and neglect the protection of ecological resources.

2.2 National policy impact

After the 21st century, the contradiction between resources and environment and economic and social development has become a major bottleneck for Chinese comprehensive construction of a well-off society and the realization of sustainable development. As a result, Chinese economic and development relations have entered an important period of strategic transformation. Taking the scientific concept of development as the guide, building a harmonious society as the goal, building an ecological civilization and resource-saving and environment-friendly society as the path, transforming the economic growth mode, saving energy and reducing emissions into other major actions, for the environment and development Strategic transformation builds a clear roadmap. It is precisely in this new situation and new stage of Chinese economic and social development that Chinese circular economy development has basically completed the first leap from concept to national decision-making from the turn of the century to 2005. Since 2006, it has quickly entered the stage of comprehensive pilot demonstration; with the "Circular Economy Promotion Law" as a symbol, it began to enter the overall promotion stage in 2009. Comprehensive pilot demonstration and overall promotion mean the second leap in the development of Chinese circular economy. Chinese economic policy is paying more and more attention to the development of recycling and the protection of the ecological environment.

As the decision-making advisory body of the Ministry of Environmental Protection, the Environmental and Economic Policy Research Center of the Ministry of Environmental Protection has been concerned with and researched the issues related to the circular economy since 2001. It has completed the circular economy research project in the special fund project of the Ministry of Science and Technology in 2003. Key projects such as the Sino-German and Sino-Japanese circular economy cooperation projects and the UNEP circular economy Guiyang project provide support and attention to the development of circular economy and ecological environment protection in China.

Therefore, national policies are of great importance to the development of circular economy and the protection of the ecological environment, and are an important backing for the development of circular economy. Under the circular economy model, China's ecological environment design should be based on national policy guidance, and constantly update and improve the ecological environment design principles and methods to achieve the innovation and development of ecological environment design.

2.3 Conceptual factors of ecological environment designers

Regardless of the economic model, the most important subjective factors are the concept of eco-environment designers. Under the circular economy model, the concept of eco-environment designers should be changed in a timely manner, and the theory of circular economy should be deeply studied and recognized. The concept of circular economy should be applied to the design of ecological environment in order to better design the ecological environment. Ecological environmental protection is a long-term process. It must be constantly updated and improved. The theory of circular economy is constantly being updated and improved with the development of the times. Compared with the theory of circular economy, the theory of circular economy It has now been greatly improved. The protection of the ecological environment and the development of ecological civilization are closely related. China has been paying attention to the development of ecological civilization long ago, and ecologicalizion environmental design is the implementation and influence of the concept of ecological civilization. Therefore, eco-environment designers must constantly understand and learn the theory of circular economy, communicate and communicate with eco-civilization protectors in a timely manner, strive to update their design concepts, maximize environmental protection and resource conservation, and maximize the recycling of resources and protection.

2.4 Ecological civilization and environmental justice factors

1.Ecological civilization construction is a strategic choice for China's economic and social development in the new era

Building an ecological civilization is a major strategic choice made by the Communist Party of China from the basic national conditions and economic and social development of China. It is also the development goal set by the Communist Party of China for the economic and social development of China in the new era.

In 2007, the "Report of the 17th National Congress of the Communist Party of China" first proposed "constructing ecological civilization." The report pointed out: "Building an ecological civilization will basically form an industrial structure, a growth mode, and a consumption pattern that conserve energy resources and protect the ecological environment. The circular economy has formed a large scale, and the proportion of renewable energy has increased significantly. The discharge of major pollutants has been effectively controlled. The environmental quality has improved markedly. The concept of ecological civilization has been firmly established in the whole society."   In 2012, the "Report of the 18th National Congress of the Communist Party of China" introduced ecological civilization construction and emphasized: "Building ecological civilization is related to people's well-being and to the future of the nation. In the long run, in the face of the tight situation of tight resource constraints, serious environmental pollution, and degraded ecosystems, we must establish an ecological civilization concept that respects nature, conforms to nature, and protects nature, and puts ecological civilization construction in a prominent position, integrating economic construction and politics. In the whole process of construction, cultural construction, and social construction, we will strive to build a beautiful China and realize the sustainable development of the Chinese nation." In November 2013, the Third Plenary Session of the 18th CPC Central Committee made a decision on the major issues of the comprehensive deepening reform of the CPC Central Committee. "Providing clear requirements for the construction of ecological civilization : "The construction of ecological civilization, we must establish a systematic and comprehensive institutional system of ecological civilization, to achieve the most stringent source protection system, damage compensation system, accountability system, improve environmental management and ecological restoration system, using the system to protect the ecological environment."

Why did the political report of the Communist Party of China repeatedly put forward the issue of building ecological civilization? Why did the ruling party propose to put ecological civilization construction in a prominent position and integrate into all aspects and processes of economic construction, political construction, cultural construction and social construction? The answer is only one: The construction of ecological civilization is the only way to guarantee the sustained and healthy development of China's economy and society. It is a summary of the experience of the Communist Party of China in leading the long-term practice of China's economic and social development, and it is a strategic choice made after careful consideration of China's economic and social development prospects. Only by adhering to the construction of ecological civilization can we guarantee the great rejuvenation and sustainable development of the Chinese nation.

So far, the development of human civilization has gone through three stages: one is the original civilization, that is, the collection-hunting civilization. At this stage, human beings survive and develop entirely through the natural "gift". Humans have almost no ability to transform or control nature. Human beings fear nature; second, agricultural civilization. At this stage, the relationship between man and nature has changed a little. Because of the emergence of new labor tools, human beings no longer rely entirely on the "gift" of nature to survive, but through farming or animal husbandry, their material needs are basically met and their living conditions are improved. Humans begin to have the ability to transform or control nature. Human beings are no longer as awe-like as nature, and there is a rift between man and nature; the third is industrial civilization. At this stage, the industrial revolution has made human science and technology advance by leaps and bounds. The ability of man to conquer, control and transform nature has rapidly increased, and social productivity has developed rapidly. The great achievements of human development, utilization, and transformation have greatly exceeded the sum of all generations in the past. At the same time, human control and transformation of the natural world is also at its peak. People plundered natural resources unscrupulously and caused great harm to the natural world. The relationship between man and nature has undergone a fundamental change, and the two have become the relationship between conquest and conquest, plunder and plunder. The natural world began to retaliate against humanity, and an ecological crisis began to emerge. The development of human civilization is facing a turning point, and ecological civilization has emerged.

Ecological civilization refers to the fact that human beings follow the laws of economic and social development and respect the laws of nature in their own survival and development. They not only continue to use the objective material world to meet their growing material and cultural needs, but also strive to take measures to overcome them. Or avoid the adverse effects of their own activities on the natural world, protect the ecological environment, and guarantee the sum of various achievements in renewable conditions for renewable natural resources. Ecological civilization is the result of profound reflection on the development of industrial civilization by human beings. It is the correction and transcendence of industrial civilization. It aims to overcome the shortcomings of industrial civilization and inherit the positive energy of industrial civilization.

The most striking feature of ecological civilization over industrial civilization is the emphasis on harmony between man and nature. It requires human economic and social activities to conform to nature and protect nature; man and nature, human society and nature are interdependent and coexisting; human beings should follow natural laws when using nature, and make appropriate restrictions on their own development needs.

The core of ecological civilization is to require human beings to correctly understand and deal with the relationship between man and nature, human society and nature. Human beings must not use nature as their own object of conquest and the raw material pool or garbage dump of economic activities. Instead, they should regard nature as a friend of human symbiosis and coexistence, and reserve the necessary conditions for the existence and development of nature itself. The development of human economy and society should adhere to scientific development. Scientific development is the development of respecting the laws of nature, respecting economic laws and the laws governing social development. Strive to overcome the shortcomings of industrial civilization and correctly handle the relationship between economic and social development and the protection of the natural environment and the rational development and utilization of natural resources. Oppose the exploitation and exploitation of natural resources in a predatory manner, and refuse to use the natural world as a place to absorb pollutants produced by human activities, and to achieve coordination between human economic and social development and ecological environmental protection.

The construction of ecological civilization is a strategy to govern the country and govern the country with economic construction, political construction, cultural construction and social construction. The reason why the Communist Party of China made strategic choices for building ecological civilization is determined by China's basic national conditions and the status quo of economic and social development. China is a big country with a population of 1.3 billion. The great task of feeding a population of 1.3 billion has forced China to develop its economy at an extraordinary rate in recent decades, and at the same time has paid a heavy price for this development. Environmental pollution, depletion of resources, and the poor endowment of natural resources in China, the unsustainability of development is obvious. In the face of the development crisis, the Communist Party of China clearly proposed to completely change the way of economic development in the past and take the road of ecological civilization to ensure the sustainable development of the economy and society.

2. Environmental protection is the key to the construction of ecological civilization

As a national strategy for China's economic and social development, ecological civilization construction is a complex systematic project involving all aspects of economic and social development. However, the main front of ecological civilization construction is very clear, that is, environmental protection. Environmental protection as the main front of ecological civilization construction is determined by the basic purpose and requirements of ecological civilization construction.

The report of the 17th National Congress of the Communist Party of China and the 18th National Congress of the Communist Party of China clearly declared: "Building an ecological civilization will basically form an industrial structure, a growth mode, and a consumption mode that conserve energy resources and protect the ecological environment. The circular economy has formed a large scale, and the proportion of renewable energy has increased significantly. The discharge of major pollutants has been effectively controlled, and the quality of the ecological environment has been significantly improved. The concept of ecological civilization has been firmly established in the whole society." "Insist on the basic national policy of saving resources and protecting the environment, adhere to the policy of saving priority, protecting priority, and restoring nature, focusing on Promote green development, circular development, and low-carbon development, form a spatial pattern, industrial structure, production methods, and lifestyles that conserve resources and protect the environment, reverse the deterioration of the ecological environment from the source, and create a good production and living environment for the people. Eco-safety contributes. "Adhere to the development path of productive development, affluent life, and good ecological civilization, build a resource-conserving and environment-friendly society, realize the unity of speed and structural quality and efficiency, and coordinate economic development with population, resources and environment. Make the people in good life Produce life in an environment, and achieve sustainable development of the economy and society."

The essence of ecological civilization construction aims to awaken and enhance people's awareness of environmental protection, establish an ecological civilization concept, change the irrational understanding of nature or the natural environment, and establish the concept of respecting nature, adapting to nature, protecting nature, and coexisting with nature. Human beings cannot be above nature, and nature cannot be taken as an object of plundering. It cannot be obtained freely and wildly from nature. It should be established that "protecting the ecological environment means protecting the productive forces, improving the ecological environment is the development of productive forces", absorbing the modern concept of "the ecological prosperity is civilized, the ecological decay is civilized and decaying". Human beings should be kind to nature, get rid of the concept of anthropocentrism, and be clear-headed. The extreme importance and urgency of protecting nature, protecting the natural environment, preventing environmental pollution and ecological damage on economic and social development, and placing environmental protection at the priority and prominent position of ecological civilization construction.

The essence of ecological civilization construction lies in protecting the environment and solving environmental problems that affect the sustainable development of the economy and society. Through the construction of ecological civilization, the traditional way of economic growth has been completely changed, making the ecological economy and circular economy the basic way of economic development. Clean production has been fully realized, environmental problems have been basically solved, natural environmental quality has been significantly improved or improved, ecological security has been fundamentally guaranteed, and resource-saving and environment-friendly society has been basically completed.

The sustainable development of a country's economy and society usually depends on two basic supports: first, the support of a good natural environment, and second, the support of rich natural resources. Leaving these two basic supports, the sustainability of the development will be greatly affected. The construction of ecological civilization means solving two supporting problems, and the two supports constitute the whole of environmental protection work.

3. Environmental justice reform is the driving force for the construction of ecological civilization

The solution of environmental problems depends on three aspects of efforts: first, change the concept, that is, establish an ecological civilization concept; second, make full use of modern environmental protection science and technology means; third, implement environmental rule of law, use laws to regulate people's environmental behavior, and solve Environmental disputes and environmental justice.

The "Decision of the Central Committee of the Communist Party of China on Comprehensively Deepening the Reform of Some Major Issues" requires: "To build an ecological civilization, we must establish a systematic and complete ecological civilization system... and protect the ecological environment with the system." Xi Jinping, general secretary of the CPC Central Committee, pointed out that the construction of ecological civilization must Rely on the system and rely on the rule of law. Only by implementing the strictest system and the strictest rule of law can we provide reliable guarantee for the construction of ecological civilization.

Environmental law as an important means of solving environmental problems mainly includes three aspects: First, the establishment of a sound environmental legal system, so that environmental protection activities can be based on laws and regulations. This is the premise of environmental rule of law; the second is to strictly enforce the provisions of environmental laws. This is the key to the realization of the environmental rule of law; the third is to strictly investigate the legal responsibilities of environmental violations and criminal actors. This is the basic guarantee of environmental law.

The three aspects of the environmental rule of law can be attributed to two levels of problems. The establishment of a sound environmental legal system is a problem at the level of environmental legislation; while strictly implementing the provisions of environmental laws and strictly pursuing the responsibility of environmental violations and perpetrators is a matter of environmental law enforcement, including environmental administrative law enforcement. There are problems with environmental justice.

From the perspective of environmental legislation, since the enactment of the Environmental Protection Law of the People's Republic of China (Trial) in 1979, China has enacted more than 30 laws on environmental protection, pollution prevention and natural resource protection, and hundreds of other environments. Administrative regulations and departmental regulations, and more and more local environmental regulations.

The large number of legislation and the speed of legislation make it difficult to legislate in other fields. However, it is puzzling that China's environmental problems have not improved significantly with the increase in the number of environmental legislation. Environmental pollution and ecological damage are still growing, and the environmental situation is still very serious.

Generally speaking, the more legislation, the broader the scope of adjustment of the law to social relations, the clearer the legal relationship, the easier it is to solve the problem. However, there are no expected results in the field of environmental protection. The reasons are mainly in two aspects: First, the legislation itself is flawed, and the adjusted social relations have not yet been adjusted. Or the legislative adjustment has not yet found the crux of the problem-solving problem. The legal system and legal norms created are not appropriate, and it is difficult to adapt to the actual needs of the social relations being adjusted. No corresponding points were found between the legal norms and the adjusted social relations. Secondly, there are problems in the implementation of the law, usually manifested as administrative law enforcement or judicial issues.

As far as the field of environmental protection is concerned, the legal adjustments do not present promising results, and there are reasons for the legislation itself. After all, China's environmental legislation is only a short history of more than 30 years, and its experience is lacking. The problem is inevitable. But the more important reason is that there are problems in the implementation of the law, especially in the field of environmental justice. In other words, environmental justice does not affect the realization of environmental law in social life.

Carry out environmental justice reforms to change the situation in which the judiciary cannot do well in the field of environmental protection, and give full play to the indispensable role of environmental justice in the construction of environmental rule of law, and the promotion and protection of ecological civilization. Environmental justice reform is an important part of China's judicial reform. There are many aspects involved, such as environmental justice concept, environmental justice theory, environmental justice system, environmental justice system, environmental justice operation and environmental justice culture. Some of these problems belong to the common problems of the entire judicial reform and can be considered and resolved in the overall judicial reform. Some problems are the personality issues of environmental justice reform, and should be investigated and resolved as the special issue of judicial reform in China.

Generally Chinese environmental justice reform should focus on solving the following three aspects:

1. Establish a modern environmental justice concept

Any reform is always based on the word "idea" of ideas or concepts, from the source of the word, an old philosophical noun. The "concepts" in Plato's philosophy are often translated as "ideas." The "concepts" in Kant and Hegel's philosophy are also translated as "ideas." Therefore, many scholars in China have used concepts and concepts to mix and match.

The most basic meaning of a concept is the perception or thought of things. Speaking of the concept of environmental justice, that is, the perception, understanding or understanding of the nature, principles,

principles, internal laws, functions, functions, values, developments and changes of environmental judicial activities, used to guide or guide environmental justice activities, is environmental justice The basis of theory, environmental justice principles, environmental justice systems, environmental justice operations, and the formation and development of environmental justice culture. Certain environmental justice concepts determine certain environmental justice activities and environmental justice theories, principles, systems, operations and cultures that are closely related to environmental justice activities. The former is the dominant of the latter and the latter is the reflection or embodiment of the former. The concept is developing dynamically. A period has a concept of a period.

There are two important concepts in modern environmental justice:

First, the court may not refuse the acceptance of environmental cases. Judicature is the last line of defense to resolve disputes and resolve conflicts of interest. China is now in a period of high environmental problems, and environmental pollution and ecological damage cases have occurred from time to time, and most of the victims are residents and individual villagers. Compared with the victims of environmental pollution, victims are often in a weak position, and it is usually fruitless to negotiate pollution disputes with the injurers themselves. Seeking environmental administrative relief, it is difficult for both parties to reach an agreement. Therefore, the number of people seeking environmental justice relief is increasing. However, in practice, there are times when the court does not accept environmental cases. There are various reasons or reasons: some are subject to administrative intervention; some are afraid of offending enterprises and affect local economic development; others are shut out the case on the basis of no relevant case, resulting in nowhere for victims. The author has been exposed to the internal regulations of a local court on the acceptance of environmental cases. The core content of the "regulations" is that it is not easy to accept environmental cases, so as to avoid "trouble". Such a regulation is ridiculous.

The direct consequence of the court not accepting environmental cases is to force the victim to seek self-reliance. Self-reliance often causes the victim to violate the law due to improper methods, and often leads to mass environmental events. In this way, it not only increases the factors of social instability, but also increases the cost of the final solution.

The court may not refuse the acceptance of the case, which is an important part of the judicial concept of Western countries. According to this concept, the court or the judge may not refuse the case for any reason. This concept clearly embodies the spirit of justice for the people and the function of justice as the last line of defense. China's environmental justice should uphold this concept, give full play to the irreplaceable role of the judiciary in environmental protection, provide positive judicial relief to environmental pollution victims, effectively protect their interests, and reduce the occurrence of mass environmental incidents.

The court may not refuse the acceptance of environmental cases, but it is also a requirement of China's "judicial for the people" thinking. The law originated in disputes, and justice originated in resolving disputes. In modern society, the court is a specialized agency for dispute resolution. The basic duties are to resolve disputes and resolve conflicts. The court's refusal to accept environmental cases is contrary to the original intention of the judiciary and does not meet the basic requirements of our country's judiciary. The basic requirement of China's judiciary is that the judiciary serves economic and social development, the construction of "two-oriented society", the construction of ecological civilization and social stability. In short, justice serves the overall situation of national or social development. The overall situation of service is the basic requirement of the socialist judicial concept. The courts and judges should proceed from the overall situation and resolve the environmental disputes that are highly concerned by the society and strongly reflected by the people with a strong sense of social responsibility. If a party to an environmental dispute files a lawsuit, the court should carefully understand the case and accept the case in a timely and responsible manner to protect the legitimate environmental rights and interests of the victim. Especially for those environmental cases with large social impact and high social attention, they should be accepted in a timely manner and must not be turned away. Even if individual environmental cases consider the relevant provisions of the current law, it seems that "acceptance is unacceptable", but the court should also adhere to the concept of judicial pragmatism and actively fill the "loopholes" stipulated by the law. However, it is necessary to find a reasonable solution to the parties to the dispute by proposing judicial advice.

The courts must not refuse the acceptance of environmental cases. It is particularly important today that environmental problems are becoming more serious, because this directly affects the overall situation of ecological civilization construction.

Second, protect the public interest of the social environment. The public interest of the social environment, also known as environmental public welfare, refers to the public's interest in the natural environment or the natural environment, and belongs to the public interest. Pound believes that the public interest mainly includes the following contents: pursuing the interests of public security; pursuing the interests of institutional security; pursuing the social interests of social resource protection, that is, pursuing the legitimate use and sustainable use of social resources; pursuing social progress Social interests and the pursuit of social interests in personal life. Some scholars in our country advocate that the specific contents of social public interest are: social economic order, social and economic security, economic interests embodied in the name of the country, protection of the ecological environment and sustainable use of natural resources, economic growth and economic efficiency, and the disadvantaged groups. protection. Obviously, the public interest of the social environment is a social public interest.

The public interest of the social environment is embodied in a good natural environment suitable for people's production and living activities, such as clean air, clean and hygienic water, clean soil, and so on.

The public interest of the social environment occupies a special position in the public interest of society. Because it is related to the fundamental interests of human survival and development, it is the indispensable material foundation or basic condition for human survival and development. It is not only closely related to the fundamental interests of the contemporary people, but also to the fundamental interests of future generations. Its importance is significantly greater than other social public interests.

From the perspective of protection, the protection of the public interest of the social environment should take precedence over the protection of other social public interests.

In real life, pollution or damage to the natural environment itself, that is, damage to the public interest of the social environment, occurs from time to time, but often does not have the protection it deserves, especially the effective judicial relief, so that the public interest in the social environment Every issue on the issue is "the tragedy of the commons."

The natural environment itself is a public good. Like other public goods, such as public safety, national defense, and education, it is shared by all members of society and is not exclusive and competitive. Anyone can use or use it. However, due to the nature of public goods in the natural environment, the tragedy of the commons continues to occur. Because "the most people share the least care, everyone just wants to get their own interests, and almost does not consider the public interest." Both as "public land", in theory, every member of society may inadvertently or intentionally possess more Public resources, or excessive use of the natural purification capacity of the natural environment to discharge pollutants, or excessive exploitation and utilization of natural resources to meet their own needs, resulting in damage to the environmental public interests of other members of society.

China has long suffered from the damage to the public interest of the social environment and the lack of corresponding judicial relief. The protection of the public interest of the social environment has become the "dead corner" or "blind spot" of the judiciary. Investigating the reasons, the court usually boils down to the "loopholes" in the legislation, which ultimately renders the judiciary powerless. It is true that the "speaking" of the court is not unreasonable. 'In a country ruled by law with a more rational division of power, the function of the judiciary is to resolve disputes. Its legal procedures should ensure that every dispute has an appropriate channel to the court. "In fact, the arrangement of the current legal procedures does exist. However, is it because of the existence of the blasphemy that the judiciary can feel at ease and have a clear conscience? Obviously not. Because China is in a period of high environmental problems, environmental pollution or destruction is on the rise. Some environmental pollution or ecological environment destruction, once formed, is irreversible. Over time, it will inevitably pose a great threat to China's economic and social sustainable development capabilities. Environmental justice can not and should not stand idly by, sit idly by, or violate the "damage" There is a judicial principle of relief. In addition, the protection of social public interests should mainly be achieved by the administration of justice, and the protection of the public interest of the social environment should be the proper meaning of environmental justice and the important content of modern environmental justice.

2. Implementing environmental justice specialization
The so-called environmental justice specialization, its basic meaning refers to the establishment of a special judicial organ (environmental court) at the national or local level, or the existing court has set up a special judicial institution or organization (environmental court) to conduct special trials on environmental cases. In this sense, environmental justice specialization can be called specialization of environmental case trials.

China began to explore the specialization of environmental justice as early as the 1980s. In 1988, the People's Court of   Hongkou District of Wuhan City proposed to the Supreme People's Court a special environmental court based on the increasing number of environmental cases in the hospital and the complicated and special cases. However, the main reason for not receiving the support of the Supreme People's Court is that the research is not enough and the conditions are not yet mature. In the next 20 years, there are no such reform proposals in China. At the same time, foreign special environmental courts or environmental courts have sprung up.

According to statistics, from November 20, 2007, the establishment of the Environmental Court of the Qingzhen City People's Court to July 2013, China's 18 provinces and municipalities directly established the city have set up 134 environmental courts in the local third-level courts. In view of the rapid development of environmental justice specialization in local courts, in 2010, the Supreme People's Court clearly stated for the first time in the "Several Opinions on Providing Judicial Protection and Services for Accelerating the Transformation of Economic Development Mode". The court may set up an environmental court to implement specialized trials of environmental protection cases and improve the judicial level of environmental protection. At the same time, the "National Environmental Protection "Twelfth Five-Year Plan" (December 15, 2011, Guofa [[2011] No. 42) also "encourage the establishment of environmental protection courts."

The specialization of environmental justice has only six or seven years of history in China, but it has developed rapidly. From the birth of the first environmental court in Qingzhen City, Guizhou Province, to the establishment of more than 130 environmental courts in 2007, it fully demonstrates the vitality and rationality of this new thing. It is reasonable because it reflects the objective needs of society. It is reported that the Supreme People's Court of China is conducting a serious investigation and research on the specialization of environmental justice. It is planned to add an environmental resource protection court to the Supreme People's Court this year (2014). If this measure can be implemented smoothly, it will undoubtedly have the dual meaning of formal rule of law and substantive rule of law, and will vigorously promote environmental justice reform and promote environmental protection and ecological civilization construction. It can be described as the gospel of environmental justice reform in China, the cause of environmental protection and the gospel of ecological civilization construction.

In fact, environmental justice specialization is not a new judicial phenomenon. The phenomenon of judicial specialization has long existed. For example, dozens of years ago, there were specialized commercial courts, tax courts, labor courts, and insurance courts. China has also set up special water transport courts, forest courts, railway courts, etc., and now there are special railway courts and maritime courts. It is rumored that some places in our country are working on the establishment of specialized intellectual property courts. The establishment of these specialized courts is the product of judicial specialization. The specialization of environmental justice is just another new development of judicial specialization.

At present, China's environmental justice specialization presents six characteristics: first, local. China's existing more than 130 environmental courts are all located in local courts, and the Supreme People's Court has not yet been established; second, regional. The existing 130 environmental courts are only located in some provinces or municipalities; third, the existing environmental courts are mostly located in grassroots courts; fourth, the development is uneven, and the heads are big and small. The so-called "one big" means that the environmental courts are mostly located in the grassroots courts. The so-called "one head small" refers to the fact that there are fewer special environmental courts in local high-level people's courts. At present, only the Hainan Provincial Higher People's Court and the Fujian Provincial Higher People's Court have special environmental courts. Fifth, the names of environmental courts are inconsistent. Some are called "environmental protection courts" (Beijing, Guizhou, Hainan), and some It is called the "Eco-source Jurisdiction Court" (Fujian), some is called "Environmental Resource Protection Trial Court" (Yunnan), and some is called "Ecological Environmental Protection Court" (Henan); sixth, most environmental courts The trial of environmental cases adopts the "three-in-one" trial mode, that is, environmental civil cases, environmental administrative cases and environmental criminal cases are collectively and uniformly examined by environmental courts.

In recent decades, China has created a miracle of economic growth that has attracted worldwide attention, and it has also paid a heavy environmental cost. This price is actually the price of the public interest of the social environment. According to the current Constitution of China and relevant laws, all natural resources or environmental elements of our country are owned by the state. However, in real life, the natural resources and environmental factors belonging to the state have not been effectively protected. The "tragedy of the commons" has occurred from time to time, and the public interest in the social environment has been continuously damaged. Therefore, it is imperative to establish an environmental public interest litigation system in China and increase the judicial protection of the public interest in the social environment. The provisions of Article 55 of the new Civil Demolition Law and Article 58 of the new Environmental Protection Law Act objectively reflect the actual needs of the protection of the public interest of the social environment.

The environmental public interest litigation system built by the new environmental protection law has a certain distance from the environmental public interest litigation system that people expect or ideal. This distance is mainly reflected in the issue of the plaintiff qualification for environmental public interest litigation. According to the provisions of Article 58(1) of the new Environmental Protection Law, only environmental protection social organizations that meet the requirements of the law can file environmental public interest litigation. Other social organizations, state organs and individual citizens have no right to file. This is far from the foreign regulations on the qualification of environmental public interest litigation. Investigating foreign environmental public interest litigation systems, any individual, group, procurator general and government have the right to file a lawsuit against the environmental public interest damage. However, it is regrettable that China has the right to file a plaintiff qualification for environmental public interest litigation only to environmental organizations that meet the statutory conditions.

The protection of social public interests is, in theory, a matter of public authority. However, it is precisely because of the inadequacy of the public authority's ability to safeguard the public interest of the public that the issue of public interest litigation has arisen. Public interest litigation is relative to private equity litigation. Private interest litigation is a lawsuit that is harmed by private or personal interests and brought to the court by a direct interested party. It is characterized by litigation by a specific subject, that is, a subject that has a direct interest in the case. Public interest litigation is based on the public interest of the public, and the lawsuit against the public interest in the public is brought before the court. The biggest difference from private interest litigation is that anyone can file it except where the law has special provisions. And public interest litigation can be brought to the public interest in any field, such as the economic field, education, consumption, and environmental protection.

It is determined by the characteristics of public interest litigation. In theory, any person, including any individual, group, enterprise or government, can file a public interest litigation. The newly revised environmental protection law imposes stricter restrictions on the scope of plaintiffs who have the right to file environmental public interest litigation, which may be due to the consideration of China's specific national conditions. Although there are regrets, I can't hide it. After all, the environmental public interest litigation system has been established in China, and from any point of view, it is a matter of benefiting environmental justice and ecological civilization construction.

From this point of view, under the circular economy model, ecological civilization and environmental justice reform are of great significance to the design of ecological environment. Carrying out ecological civilization construction and environmental justice reform, providing legal system and legal means for ecological environment design, is conducive to the reform and development of ecological environment design under the circular economy model.

Part 7　Strategy and Thinking of Eco-environment Design Development Based on Circular Economy Mode

Chapter 1 Research on the development trend of ecological environment design based on circular economy model

In the process of promoting circular economy from concept to practice, it is necessary to formulate micro-policies for specific waste recycling, and to develop a number of comprehensive economic policies with overall resources and recycling. From the link and effect of the policy role. At present, under the market economy mechanism, the most important policies to promote the development of circular economy have two types.

The first category is the administrative management method based on laws and regulations and direct control. Such policies mainly regulate and regulate the economic activities and behaviors (production, consumption, etc.) of the relevant subjects of the circular economy (units and individuals within the territory of the People's Republic of China) through administrative coercive measures.

The second category is economic incentives. This kind of policy mainly adjusts the economic interests of all relevant subjects of the circular economy through economic means such as price, taxes and fees, changes the economic profitability of circular economy projects, and provides economic incentives for resource conservation and environmentally friendly behaviors.

By creating an environmentally friendly cultural system, strengthening environmental culture and ethical construction, and adopting information disclosure to encourage the public to participate in waste recycling voluntarily, and supervising producers, it also plays a vital role in the development of circular economy. .

This section first analyzes and identifies key economic policies that promote the development of China's circular economy through the construction of a policy matrix. By studying the interest relationship of the main body of the circular economy, this paper analyzes the cost-price system of reconstructing relevant economic activities, proposes a proposal to improve the comparative advantage of the circular economy, and conducts key economic policies through the Computable General Equilibrium Model (CGE). Quantitative analysis, on this basis, put forward key economic policy recommendations to promote the development of circular economy.

It should be noted that the direct control policy measures have been clearly defined in the Circular Economy Promotion Law reviewed and approved in August 2008, and the World Bank has also supported this project. Therefore, administrative management tools will not be the focus of this chapter. This chapter will focus on the key comprehensive economic policies that promote the development of circular economy in order to improve the economic viability and market drivers of circular economy. These policies are aimed at constructing the interest mechanism of circular economy development through economic means such as price and taxation, providing economic power based on market mechanism for the relevant subjects of circular economy, and avoiding the "circulation" and "economic" existing in the practice of circular economy. And the "economic" is not a "circulation" problem.

1.1 Identification of the Key Economic Policies for Promoting China's Circular Economy Development

According to the analysis of the connotation characteristics of Chinese circular economy in the first chapter, the development of circular economy has two goals: one is to improve resource utilization efficiency and build a resource-saving society; the second is to protect the ecological environment and build an environment-friendly society. From an economic point of view, the development of circular economy must follow the laws of the market and ultimately contribute to sustainable economic development. Otherwise, it can only stay at the pilot level. The circular economy is not only a simple recycling of waste, it involves all areas of production and consumption, involving all aspects of resource extraction, production and utilization, circulation, consumption and waste disposal. Therefore, the role of circular economy policy should start from the two major areas of production and consumption. From the perspective of policy means, Chinese circular economy development policy has the characteristics of combining policy and instrumental policies.

The policy is a programmatic and targeted policy of the central government, providing an ideological basis and a goal for the development of a circular economy. Such policies include guiding policy documents, such as the 11th Five-Year Plan for National Social and Economic Development and the State Council's opinions on promoting the development of circular economy.

The instrumental policy is a mandatory or guiding policy for all relevant subjects of the circular economy. It is a combination of direct regulatory policies, economic incentives and voluntary policies.

Policy policies need to rely on instrumental policies to influence the behavior of market players. From the perspective of administrative behavior, the policy reflects the government's intentions and expectations. Instrumental policies are a series of specific, actionable policy provisions that directly affect the behavior of market economy entities.

Since the policy is a strategic, advocacy and declarative policy, the purpose is to enhance the strategic position of the circular economy and raise awareness of the circular economy at all levels of government, as well as enterprises and the public. The current policy has basically reached the stage in China. Sexual policy goals. However, as the circular economy develops to a large-scale practical stage, whether the ultimate goal of the policy can be realized and whether the circular economy can be implemented as a universal economic development model, the key lies in whether it can formulate and implement appropriate instrumental policies. .

For instrumental policies, the World Bank's recommended policy matrix divides policy instruments into direct control or command laws, market-based economic incentives, and public participation, information disclosure, and other voluntary policies. The main body of practice of the ring economy is the government, enterprises and the public. The circular economy activities mainly involve three links: the entrance, the intermediate process and the output. Therefore, some studies choose the main body of the policy and the policy means to choose the J circular economy. The main links are combined to propose a policy system for the development of circular economy. It is proposed that there are three sets of mechanisms and three kinds of policy tools for the development of circular economy, namely, modern government-state administrative system, enterprise-market mechanism, non-governmental organization and Public-social mechanisms, corresponding policy instruments include regulatory policies, market policies, and participatory policies. The administrative mechanism embodies the top-down efforts of the government. The social mechanism can promote the bottom-up efforts of non-governmental organizations, and the market mechanism can stimulate the horizontal efforts of for-profit organizations.

In the instrumental policy, they can be divided into traditional "command-control" policy tools and market-based policy tools according to their mode of action. The "command-control" type of policy tool is characterized by a series of prohibitive regulations, including various administrative regulations, environmental standards, technical standards, and so on. They are important policy tools for environmental protection and resource conservation, and are basic policies for the development of circular economy. Only by strictly "blocking" those activities that are not conducive to environmental protection and resource conservation will it be more beneficial to channel them to the direction of the circular economy development goals. In this sense, the traditional "command-control" policy tool can be said to be the basis of the development of circular economy, or the premise of the development of circular economy, and the market-based policy tools are equally important. This is also a basic experience in the development of circular economy in developed countries.

The circular economy policy that utilizes the market mechanism is actually a policy mix of "carrots" plus "big sticks".

The goal is to achieve environmental protection and resource conservation goals through a combination of unblocking and blocking. As far as the development of the circular economy itself is concerned, the most crucial is the market-based policy tools, because they need to rely on them to establish a market mechanism that meets the needs of the circular economy. Only in this way can the circular economy function properly under the market economy system. Because the development of circular economy must focus on both production and consumption, the policy matrix promoted by European countries to promote sustainable production and consumption is also worthy of reference. The policy matrix divides policy instruments into "hard policies" and "soft policies" with the effect of policy. From the types of policy tools, they can be divided into reward/penalty policies, incentive policies, and voluntary support policies. Policy instruments mainly include legal constraints and legal responsibilities, market-based economic incentives, voluntary and cooperative means, research and publicity and education. Based on the classification of this policy approach, the policy of developing a circular economy can form the following policy toolkit.

Whether it is drawing on the World Bank's policy matrix or the European countries' sustainable production and consumption policy toolkit, the main policy types and instruments are basically the same. The key point is that to build China's circular economy development policy system, we need to comprehensively consider China's current development stage, policy status, policy objectives, etc., sort out and improve existing policies, supplement the lack of policies, and form an institutional environment conducive to the development of circular economy.

From the point of entry of the circular economy and the entry point of the policy role, the existing circular economy policy can be roughly based on the source management policy, process management policy and end (product) management policy. The source management policies include: comprehensive industrial policies for circular economy and technology development policies for circular economy; process management policies include: cleaner production policies, promotion of waste resource utilization and reuse preferential policies; end (product) management policies include: resource taxes and resources Price policy, circular economy related resources import and export policy, circular economy green product and ecological construction policy, etc. (Appendix summarizes the current list of existing circular economy policies to promote the development of circular economy, need to start from all aspects of circular economy development, find The entry point for policy intervention. There are six main links in the development of circular economy, from resource extraction, transportation, production, distribution and distribution, to waste disposal and disposal. According to the UNEP Sustainable Production and Consumption Center for sustainable production and consumption. The assessment of policies, the current policy interventions, is mainly concentrated in the production process, and the resources mining stage, consumption stage and waste disposal and disposal stage are limited. According to its evaluation, only 80% of the current policy efforts are only 20% of the society. And environmental risks, leading to policies Dislocation of the action link. Therefore, there are many policy implementation spaces and opportunities in the exploitation, consumption and disposal of natural resources. In China, similar situations exist. Therefore, while continuing to pay attention to the production process, the future is particularly It is necessary to strengthen policy interventions in the exploitation, consumption and disposal of natural resources, adopt policies of life cycle management to formulate relevant policies, and accurately define policy entry points. According to the objectives, priority areas and mechanism of action and existence of China's development of circular economy The problem should be to implement circular economy development policies for all links in the value chain, that is, to promote the development of circular economy in all aspects of natural resource extraction, transportation, production and utilization, consumption (product end) and reasonable disposal and disposal of waste. The key policy should be The comprehensive economic policies for constructing economic incentive policies under the market economic mechanism and promoting the development of circular economy can be summarized into three categories: one is to formulate a reasonable resource tax policy in the natural resource exploitation, and the other is to deal with consumption and terminal waste. ,system The reasonable waste emissions tax (fee) policy: Third, large resource consumption and pollution emissions intensity of industry, subsidies for the basic content of the various forms of support incentives.

1.2 Design of Benefit Mechanism for Promoting China's Circular Economy Development

The role of the policy is to regulate the interests of all relevant entities in the development of circular economy, and through policy intervention, establish an interest-driven mechanism conducive to the development of circular economy.

In a market economy, prices link the contributions of dispersed market players to their interests, thereby addressing the issues of what to produce, how much to produce, how to produce it, and for whom. The core mechanism here is to establish a correspondence between the contribution of economic activities and the interests of the main players. Then, under the guidance of interests, people will adjust their economic activities in a dispersed and spontaneous manner, so that the output of economic activities is in line with people's needs. This kind of adjustment of interest is manifested by price fluctuations. Generally from the perspective of supply, the price of a product is high, which means a larger interest, and people will produce more of them: on the contrary, it means less interest, and people will produce less. From the demand side, the price of a product is increased, which means that the price will be reduced, and the demand for it will be reduced; on the contrary, it means less cost, and people's demand for it will increase. Modern economics has been proved by rigorous mathematical forms that can achieve optimal results in economic activities. As a rational economic man - the characteristic is that when the price of a factor of production rises, in order not to lower the profit, the producer will innovate, save this element, or find a low-priced alternative. Therefore, the key to promoting the development of circular economy is how to adopt a reasonable price formation mechanism, including resource depletion cost and environmental damage cost, which will make the consumption of raw resources and wastes expensive, and make recycling waste. The circular economy model has become profitable, turning the circular economy model into the first choice for producers and other related economic entities. This should be a basic feature of the key policies of the circular economy.

Here we can combine the various links between the circular economy material flow and the value flow, and the mutual relations between the various subjects of the circular economy to analyze how to adopt reasonable policy means and establish a price formation mechanism and interest-driven mechanism that is conducive to the development of circular economy. First, according to the market economic mechanism, the material and value flow from the exploitation of natural resources to the producers and consumers. However, due to the externality, the waste is discharged to the environment through the end treatment and disposal of producers, sellers, consumers and waste. There is still a certain hidden value stream in the waste, but if there is no proper policy intervention, because the value in the waste is high or low, the high-value available waste resources can still be recycled back to the production-consumption system, but low. It is difficult for value-based waste resources to flow back to the production-consumption system through market mechanisms because of the uneconomical nature. This requires relevant economic policies to directly or indirectly increase their implicit value, so that the subjects engaged in circular activities are profitable and achieve economic feasibility and technology. A viable goal, this is an important point of policy adjustment and intervention. Improving the benefits of recycling and recycling of waste resources is conducive to the formation of a profit mechanism for the development of circular economy.

Second, the reasonable choice of consumers also needs to adopt the government's policy guidance, through the collection of consumption tax on resource products, government green procurement, etc., so that consumers can choose sustainable consumption methods that are conducive to resource recycling.

Third, the final waste that is difficult to recycle needs to be disposed of in an environmentally safe manner to avoid environmental pollution. Due to the existence of externalities, the final disposal and disposal of waste requires the government to adopt environmental pollution discharge tax (or sewage charges) to conduct policy interventions, to promote enterprises to actively recycle waste, and to properly and safely dispose of the final waste. The economic drive of the development of circular economy.

1.3 Analysis of Key Economic Policy Simulation Results for Promoting China's Circular Economy Development

Simulation method of key economic policies for circular economy development

According to the above analysis, this study selects three types of key economic policies, uses static CGE model, and carries out quantitative simulation and analysis: resource price policy simulation, mainly analyzes the impact of shortage of basic resource price increase on resource consumption and macroeconomic growth rate; The tax policy simulation mainly analyzes the resource saving effect caused by the tax increase of resources and the impact on the growth rate of macroeconomics; the simulation of environmental tax policy mainly analyzes the taxation of environmental use, such as increasing sulfur dioxide emission tax and carbon dioxide. Environmental impacts such as emission taxes, sewage discharge taxes, and solid waste discharge taxes, and the impact on the macro economy.

This study mainly uses the CGE model to simulate the effect of policy effects. The study refers to the monograph of Davis et al. on CGE model and Zhang Zhongxiang's China economic-energy-environment policy analysis CGE model. Combined with the characteristics of China's dual economy, a CGE model for China's environmental policy analysis was established. This model establishes a macroeconomic model based on microeconomic theory by setting the behavioral equations of economic entities in a period and linking them through various equilibrium mechanisms. The model consists of the following eight aspects:

The first is the production function. We set out that there is an alternative between capital, labor, and integrated intermediate inputs in the production of various products: there is generally no substitution between the various intermediate inputs; however, there is an alternative between coal inputs and petroleum processed inputs. We use a multi-level nested CES function and a Leontief function to describe the relationship between output and input for each production department that contains these content.

The second is the elemental demand. The labor demand and intermediate input demand of each production department are derived from profit maximization. With regard to capital demand, we assume that in any year, the existing capital stock of each sector cannot flow between sectors. Therefore, in the base year (2002), the capital stock of each production sector is both quantitative.

The third is the price. In the basic version of the CGE model, the price of all products is determined by the competitive market: in the revised version, the price of some products (coal, oil, petroleum processing, gas, electricity) is determined by the government. Whether it is a basic or modified version, the producer price of each item is unique and does not vary from user to user.

The fourth is income. Residents' income consists of wages, capital gains, and government transfers. Government revenues are mainly derived from income taxes on residents and businesses, production taxes on domestic products, and tariffs on imports.

The fifth is consumption. The model assumes that urban and rural residents' consumption expenditures each account for a fixed proportion of their disposable income; the structure of consumer demand is determined by the maximization of utility under budget constraints; the utility function uses the Cobb-Douglas utility function. The total consumption demand of the government is treated as an exogenous variable; the government consumption structure is different from the consumption structure of the residents, but the two are determined in the same way.

The sixth is savings and investment. The disposable income of each economic entity minus consumption is their net savings. The model assumes that the total investment (fixed asset investment plus inventory changes) is equal to the total savings (net savings plus depreciation). The ratio of fixed assets investment to total fixed assets investment in each department is equal to the ratio of the profit of each department to the total profit. The total amount and structure of inventory changes are treated as exogenous variables, taking the actual value in 2002.

The seventh is international trade. Describe the import and export of various tradable goods. The CGE model accepts the ARMINGTON hypothesis: there is a difference between the national product and the imported product, which cannot be completely replaced. At the same time, the model assumes that the world average price of imports and exports is set externally, and China is in the position of price acceptor. The eighth is market settlement and macro balance. The general equilibrium requires the commodity market to be settled and the factor market to be settled. It is important to point out that the settlement of the labor market does not mean that the model is necessarily a full employment model; our model treats the total labor as an exogenous variable, and the difference between the import and export in the model is related to the exchange rate: we use the exchange rate as Endogenous variables, the difference between the import and export as an exogenous variable (or vice versa, the exchange rate as an exogenous variable, the import and export difference as an endogenous variable).

It should be pointed out that this CGE model is a large economic model, but it is still a basic model. According to different policy mechanisms, it is necessary to expand and improve this basic CGE model.

This chapter mainly simulates the effect of policy operation by comparing static analysis. With the support of existing data, it focuses on simulating the macroeconomic impacts of resource prices, taxation policies and sewage charging policies for developing circular economy, and the direction of simulation results on such policies. Reasonable inference with the final effect provides quantitative analysis and support.

Key economic policy simulation results of circular economy

Resource tax simulation results

The resource tax design of this study considers two kinds of resource taxes: comprehensive energy resource tax (including coal resource tax and petroleum resource tax) and comprehensive mineral resource tax. The method of collection is to tax the resource exploitation department and the amount of resources extracted (yield). . The model analyzes the impact of 10% and 20% of the energy and mineral resources tax on the macro economy and the production and consumption of coal, petroleum, metal minerals and non-metallic mineral resources. The analysis results show that the resource tax can greatly reduce resource consumption and domestic resource consumption through the role of the market price mechanism, and has only a small negative impact on GDP. The comprehensive tax on coal and petroleum resources, which is 20% of the value of coal and oil, will reduce coal consumption by 6.4%; reduce domestic coal resource consumption by 8.9%; reduce domestic oil resource consumption by 10.2%, and reduce GDP by less than 0.1%. . A 20% comprehensive mineral resource tax will reduce the consumption of domestic metal resources by 11.75%; reduce the consumption of domestic non-metallic mineral resources by 8.13%; reduce the production of metal minerals by 11.75%, and reduce the output of non-metallic minerals by 8.13%. Therefore, resource tax is a good policy tool to achieve resource conservation.

Improve resource price policy simulation results

In order to compare with the previous resource tax, this study proposed a resource price increase program: coal price increased by 18.5%, oil and natural gas price increased by 6.6%, gas price increased by 5.8%, petroleum processed product price increased by 5.0%, and electricity price increased by 3.2%. This program is close to the impact of 20% of the coal and petroleum resources tax on the prices of these five products.

The analysis shows that the resource-saving effect produced by the appropriately designed price increase plan for coal and petroleum products is substantially the same as the resource-saving effect generated by the corresponding resource tax. However, the impact of the two on social distribution is very different. The resource tax increases the government's income (125 billion yuan) and the income of other economic entities decreases. The price increase plan reduces the income of residents and increases the income of other economic entities. The price burden is generally on the residents. Although there are differences in the impact of the two on social distribution, it is important that both will effectively save resources and achieve the goal of improving resource efficiency. At the same time, raising resource prices will also result in high service costs (including transportation, labor, etc.), which will also promote resource efficiency. Therefore, raising resource prices is a more effective economic tool.

Sewage charges simulation results

In this study, the CGE model was used to study the impact of sulfur dioxide emission charges, wastewater discharge fees, and solid waste discharge fees on the economy.

The economic impact of sulfur fees is mainly to change the pattern of income distribution: government revenues rise, and incomes of other economic entities decline. The sulfur price has little effect on sulfur emissions (the sulfur rate of 2,000 yuan per ton makes the sulfur dioxide reduction in the industrial sector less than 0.4%). If the government uses the sulfur fee income to purchase and build sulfur dioxide treatment equipment, it can significantly improve the sulfur treatment capacity (the sulfur fee income obtained by the sulfur rate of 2,000 yuan per ton, if it is used for the purchase of sulfur dioxide treatment equipment, it can increase 35.5%. The sulfur treatment capacity can reduce 18.3% of sulfur dioxide emissions).

The economic impact of wastewater discharge fees is mainly to change the income distribution pattern: government revenues rise and other economic entities' incomes decline. Wastewater discharge fees have little effect on wastewater discharge through price. If the government uses the wastewater discharge fee income to purchase and construct wastewater treatment equipment, it can greatly improve the wastewater treatment capacity (the emission fee income obtained from the wastewater discharge rate of 3 yuan per ton. If it is used for the purchase and construction of wastewater treatment equipment, it can be increased. 50.3% of wastewater treatment capacity).

The main impacts of solid waste discharge fees on the macro economy are: a slight decline in GDP; a rise in government revenues; a decline in income from other economic entities; an increase in investment and a decline in consumption. The impact of solid waste discharge fees on the solid waste discharge of the entire industrial sector is not very large, and the impact on the solid waste discharge of the metal mining and dressing industry is large (the solid waste discharge rate of 50 yuan per ton, making the entire industrial sector Solid waste reduced by 2.2%, which reduced the solid waste of metal mining and mining industry by 4.2%.

The economic impact of sewage charges is mainly to change the income distribution pattern: government revenues rise, other economic entities' incomes decline, and the impact on GDP is small. Sewage charges have little effect on waste emissions through price. Sewage charges only have a large or small impact on the output and prices of a few sectors, and have little impact on the output and prices of other (most) sectors. If the government uses the sewage fee income to purchase and build pollution control equipment, it can significantly improve the pollution control capacity.

Chapter 2 Development Strategy and Thinking of Ecological Environment Design Based on Circular Economy Mode

2.1 Key economic policy recommendations to promote the development of China's circular economy

Establishing a cost and price mechanism that balances fairness and efficiency

According to the above analysis, it is necessary to rebuild the cost and price formation mechanism of the Chinese economy through the collection of resource taxes, waste discharge taxes (fees), financial subsidies for circular economy projects, or tax incentives, and establish benefits that are conducive to the development of circular economy. Drive the mechanism to adjust and balance the interests of all relevant entities.

1. Increase the initial resource price and increase the comparative advantage of circular economy

The reduction of resource consumption is the basis of circular economy. However, the current price of China's initial resource use rights is relatively low, and there is not enough cost pressure on resource consumption. The power of enterprises to save resources and recycle resources and waste is relatively insufficient.

There are five main reasons why the initial resource market price is too low.

(1) The property rights of the basic mineral resources are unclear and the management is chaotic. A large number of mineral resources are mined in the absence of detailed exploration of resources, resulting in disordered resource exploitation and low resource extraction costs and recovery rates.

(2) The cost of resource exploration has not been reasonably compensated. The resources that the country spends a lot of money on exploration have been arbitrarily digging in various ways, resulting in the mining cost of mineral resources being too low and the recovery rate is not high.

(3) The state has not levied sufficient resource taxes and resource usage fees on state-owned mineral resources, resulting in a small number of people using state-owned mineral resources at low cost or even without compensation, artificially reducing the cost of resource use. For example, resource usage fees are not levied on reserves, but are based on very low usage fees (the coal resource tax is only 3 to 5 yuan per ton, accounting for less than 3% of the market price), resulting in a large number of miners only mining The mining area of easy mining, some coal mines have a recovery rate of only 10% to 20%, and a large amount of resources have been abandoned.

(4) The water fee for groundwater and river water is too low. For example, some tributaries in the upper reaches of the Yellow River have a water fee of less than one horn. Even some units in the suburbs of Beijing that are seriously deficient in water have a water fee of less than one yuan.

(5) Resource mining enterprises exchange low-cost and sales profits of resource products at the expense of the poor working conditions of miners and extremely low wages.

Too low initial resource prices make the resource-saving input and output efficiency not high, so that recycling resources and waste do not have the comparative advantage of technology and economy, forming the phenomenon of "circulation and non-economic", which seriously hinders the development of circular economy. Market efficiency. For example, the cost of recycling wastewater is 2 to 3 yuan per ton, and the area where the price of fresh water is lower than this price has no economic benefit of recycling wastewater. Therefore, the state should make up its mind to improve the cost of initial resource use and mining by clarifying the property rights of mineral resources, strictly and rationally regulating the use of resources, and formulating strict laws and regulations for maintaining the safety of life and property of miners and reasonable wages and benefits. , so that the price of the initial resource truly reflects its value.

2. Increase waste disposal costs and increase the cost advantage of recycling waste

An important reason for China's environmental pollution is that it has not used the environment as an economic factor for reasonable pricing and paid use in the past. Therefore, in our market price formation mechanism, environmental cost factors are not fully considered, at least the environmental cost of waste discharge is too low. This makes the low price of Chinese products above the cost of increasing environmental pollution. Recycling waste with the goal of protecting the environment does not have an economic advantage. For the purpose of protecting the environment, waste control is controlled from the end, waste discharge costs are increased, and external costs of pollution are internalized. Waste discharge becomes an integral part of the cost of the enterprise and becomes an element of price formation, thereby recycling The transformation of waste into an economic way for enterprises to reduce the cost of environmental use can improve the comparative economic benefits of recycling waste and encourage enterprises to develop circular economy. For example, the implementation of the producer environmental responsibility extension system for bulk products, the products produced by the producers responsible for recycling and recycling after consumption retirement, will force enterprises to increase ecological design and environmental protection investment, the most easy recycling and recycling The way to design and produce products that prevent pollution from the source.

Therefore, it is recommended to further strengthen the waste discharge charging system during the "Ten-Five" period, and gradually increase the waste discharge fee in China to the cost of treating waste, so that waste recycling and harmless treatment enterprises become profitable enterprises. Each waste discharge cost standard is dynamically verified based on the cost of recycling and safe disposal, and is imposed.

3. Reduce waste recycling costs and increase the comparative benefits of renewable resources

Turning waste into renewable resources often requires complex technical processes and requires high cost inputs. Many companies process and recycle waste because waste emissions can pollute the environment. For these enterprises, recycling wastes reduces waste emissions, brings environmental benefits to society, and has high positive externalities, but it is likely to have only low returns, or even Negative economic benefits. From this perspective, recycling waste is a public resource (ecological and environmental capacity) protection behavior, the government should provide some compensation and support for the development of circular economy through the internalization of external benefits. For example, tax relief for activities that recycle waste recycling; financial support for research and development of resource conservation and waste recycling technologies; provision of preferential financing conditions and preferential land use, etc., to reduce the cost of recycling waste resources increases the comparative advantage of the price of renewable resources.

In order to ensure the investment of circular economy, the state finance should establish a special account for circular economy and environmental protection, and include waste discharge fees and resource use fees into special accounts. If there is necessary, it can also raise funds through the issuance of environmental bonds for the use of circular economy infrastructure. Construction, research and development of circular economy technology, recycling and harmless treatment of toxic and hazardous waste, and subsidies for the recovery and treatment of important pollutants.

4. Reduce transaction costs and market development costs of the circular economy and improve the efficiency of circular economy

In order to maximize this external benefit, it is internationally accepted that the government internalizes this external benefit because of the positive environmental externalities of recycling resources and waste. There are five main aspects of its measures.

(1) The government adopts policies such as green procurement and market access priority under the same conditions to prioritize the selection of circular economy products in government procurement, reduce the market entry threshold for circular economy products, make it easier to enter the market, and ensure stable Market share, reducing the market transaction costs of recycling resources and waste.

(2) The government adopts free certification and labeling methods to publicize publicity products for circular economy products, improve the social credibility of circular economy products, reduce the market development costs of enterprises, and save consumers' market search costs.

(3) The government provides free information support, technical training, management consulting, and service guidance for recycling resources and waste, and reduces the cost of technology and market information search for enterprises to develop circular economy.

(4) The government provides free guidance to enterprises for international cooperation and guides enterprises to make extensive use of international sources of technology and economy.

(5) The government invests in the construction of a circular economy infrastructure and network system to provide basic conditions for the development of circular economy.

In summary, increasing the initial resource price by increasing the original mineral resource usage fee, resource tax and maintaining the interests of miners, increasing the waste disposal price by increasing the environmental use cost, and extending the producer's environmental responsibility system will make China The initial resources and market prices of products with more serious environmental pollution have increased. Reducing the circular economy tax burden and operating costs through preferential policies for recycling resources and waste, reducing the market entry cost and transaction cost of the circular economy through the government's unpaid service and management guidance, will reduce the price of circular economy products. . Restructuring China's market price formation mechanism from both directions will make products that use the initial resources and production processes with more serious pollution emissions become relatively expensive, and circular economy products become relatively cheap. Such a price system will actively promote resource conservation, waste recycling and environmental protection.

Establish a scientific tax adjustment policy

Establish a scientific tax adjustment policy in accordance with the organic and unified approach of promoting environmental, economic and social benefits.

1. Establish a scientific tax adjustment policy for different aspects of the circular economy

(1) In the production process, tax incentives should be conducive to reducing waste generation from sources, improving resource utilization efficiency, and reducing environmental pollution. New equipment for reducing raw materials and energy consumption, and heat recovery equipment using clean energy such as solar energy, heat energy, wind energy, etc., allow accelerated depreciation and deductible input tax before value-added tax; use waste materials in the development and smelting process of enterprises Products recovered and produced are exempt from VAT (first retreat).

(2) In the circulation link, tax incentives should mobilize and encourage enterprises to mobilize and distribute waste materials. In addition to tax incentives for corporate income tax reduction and exemption, regular exemption from VAT (first retreat) can be implemented. policy.

(3) In the distribution process, the taxation policy can implement the policy of exempting income tax on the income from the use of waste water, waste gas, waste residue and other wastes as the main raw material production, and the enterprise will use energy-saving technology to transform domestically produced equipment to a certain proportion of investment. The policy of adding income tax in the year to de support the enterprise's energy-saving technological transformation.

(4) In the consumption chain, adjust the taxation scope of consumption tax and rationally design tax burden level, encourage consumers to use clean energy, and constrain consumers' unhealthy consumption behavior. Consumer goods and luxury goods that are detrimental to the environment and excessively resource-intensive are included in the scope of consumption tax; high-tax rates are imposed on consumer goods that pollute the environment and destroy resources.

(5) Intensify the development and support of high-tech, environmental protection technology, energy-saving technology, material-saving technology and human resources, highlight the scientific and technological guiding role of tax preferential policies, and establish a set of support for science and technology investment, product development and promotion. Science and technology tax preferential policy system for the transformation of scientific and technological achievements.

2. Establish a coordination mechanism between tax policy and other fiscal and financial policies to play a synergistic role

(1) Coordination with fiscal policy. By optimizing the financial investment structure, flexibly using financial subsidies and scientifically using fiscal transfer payments, it provides financial security for the development of circular economy.

(2) Cooperate with monetary policy. First, the state policy banks, commercial banks and other financial institutions may provide certain tax reductions and exemptions for interest losses incurred in support of the circular economy; second, they shall use the loans of banks and other financial institutions to carry out "three wastes" treatment. Interest expenses incurred in the development of energy-saving technological transformation and other resource comprehensive utilization projects are allowed to be paid before tax.

(3) Cooperate with the price policy. First, improve the adjustment level of environmental and resource taxation, incorporate resource and environmental taxation factors into the enterprise's financial cost

accounting and national economic accounting system, and establish a price adjustment system that protects the environment and conserves resources; second, it is based on the scarcity of environment and resources. Sexuality and demand trends, improve the paid use system and price system of resources, and promote the sustainable use of resources.

3. Reform and improve the current tax and fee system

It is necessary to gradually establish environmental capacity as a policy concept of resources, reform the environmental resource pricing system, establish a system of paid use of environmental resources, change the existing high law-abiding costs, and low illegal costs, and internalize environmental costs by raising sewage charges. At present, the level of sewage charges for major pollutants (sulphur dioxide, COD, solid waste) should be gradually increased to bring it closer to environmental governance and damage costs.

At present, China has the conditions to implement the emissions trading market. It is recommended to establish emission rights and carbon emissions exchanges as soon as possible.

Resources, environmental taxes and fees, and related fiscal and taxation policies need to be coordinated with the country's overall tax reform. Through the balance of the overall tax burden, the impact on the macro-economy caused by rising resource and environmental costs should be minimized. The impact and negative impact on socially disadvantaged groups.

Establishing the objectives, principles and reform directions of key economic policies

In China, low-cost resources, high product prices, waste-free or low-cost emissions are fundamental issues that constrain resource efficiency and reduce pollution emissions. Therefore, the economic policy goal of establishing a circular economy is to build a new cost-price system based on resources, products and wastes. The principle is to form a profit-driven mechanism, and the direction is to reform and adjust key economic policies.

There are three types of key economic policies: resource taxation and price policy for natural resource exploitation; environmental tax (fee) policy for end treatment and disposal; and support incentive policies for consumption and other links.

The direction of key economic policy reforms is: increase initial resource prices, increase the comparative benefits of circular economy; increase waste discharge costs, enhance the cost advantage of recycling waste; reduce waste recycling costs, increase the comparative benefits of renewable resources; Economic transaction costs and market development costs increase the efficiency of circular economy.

Improve resource tax and environmental charging standards

(1) China can increase the energy tax of all resources by a large margin, for example, 10% to 20%, and can implement differential taxation according to factors such as the natural attributes of resources, the degree of

scarcity, and the damage to environmental costs. For non-renewable, non-replaceable resources, the unit tax should be higher than renewable, alternative resources.

CGE model analysis shows that if the coal and oil tax is increased by 20%, it can reduce coal consumption by 6.4% and oil consumption by 10.2%, and the impact on GDP is only 0.1%; increase the comprehensive mineral resource tax by 20%, which can reduce metal minerals. The resource consumption is 11.75%, which reduces the consumption of non-metallic mineral resources by 8.31%.

Although raising resource prices and raising resource taxes have similar effects on resource conservation, the burden of price increases has fallen from the overall population. Therefore, from the perspective of promoting social equity, raising the level of resource tax collection should become the main reform direction.

(2) The CGE simulation results show that the emission reduction standard for major pollutants has little impact on the macro economy. If all the sewage charges collected are used for the construction of key pollution control facilities, the level and capacity of pollution prevention and control will be significantly improved and improved. Therefore, in the near future, China should gradually increase the level of sewage charges for major pollutants (sulphur dioxide, COD, solid waste), so that it will gradually approach environmental management and damage costs.

Cancel the export tax rebate policy for high energy consumption and high pollution products

The data show that China's current energy consumption of some high-energy and high-pollution export products accounts for about 15% of domestic energy consumption. Therefore, it is recommended that China develop a list of high-energy and high-pollution products, and export the listed products for many years. The tax rebate policy and even the export tax will reduce the production of high-energy and high-pollution products, and encourage enterprises to improve energy efficiency and reduce the pollution emission intensity of unit products.

Establish and improve the tax preferential policy system

Establish scientific tax incentives in accordance with the organic and unified approach of promoting environmental, economic and social benefits.

(1) In the production process, tax incentives should be conducive to improving resource utilization efficiency and reducing pollution emissions. New equipment for reducing raw materials and energy consumption, and heat recovery equipment using clean energy such as solar energy, heat energy, wind energy, etc., allow accelerated depreciation and deductible input tax before value-added tax; use waste in the development and smelting process of enterprises Products recovered and produced are exempt from VAT.

(2) In the circulation link, the tax preferential policies should mobilize and encourage the enthusiasm of enterprises to recycle and distribute wastes. In addition to the preferential income tax reduction and exemption, regular preferential VAT exemption policies can also be implemented.

(3) In the distribution process, the taxation policy can implement the policy of exempting income tax on the income of enterprises using waste water, waste gas, waste residue and other wastes as the main raw material

production; for enterprises to use energy-saving technology to transform domestically produced equipment, a certain proportion according to investment Deduct the policy of adding income tax in the year to support the energy-saving technological transformation of enterprises.

(4) In the consumption chain, adjust the taxation scope of consumption tax and rationally design tax burden level, encourage consumers to use clean energy, and constrain consumers' unhealthy consumption behavior. Consumer goods and luxury goods that are detrimental to the environment and excessively resource-intensive are included in the scope of consumption tax; high-tax rates are imposed on high-end consumer goods and consumer behavior as well as consumer products that pollute the environment and destroy resources.

(5) Intensify the development and support of high-tech, environmental protection technology, energy-saving technology, material-saving technology and human resources, highlight the scientific and technological guiding role of tax preferential policies, and establish a set of support for science and technology investment, product development and promotion. Science and technology tax preferential policy system for the transformation of scientific and technological achievements.

Promoting sustainable production and consumption requires a complete set of economic policies, but the sound tax incentives are complicated to operate, and it is easy to cause confusion in policy content and reduce taxes. Therefore, relative tax taxes and export tax rebates are relatively high, and tax incentives may be less effective.

2.2 Policy recommendations to improve the eco-efficiency of key industries

The seven industrial sectors of iron and steel, non-ferrous metals, coal, electric power, chemicals, building materials and light industry are China's high-resource energy consumption and high-polluting industries. (The energy consumption per unit of main products is 40% higher than the world's advanced level. Above), accounting for more than 70% of all industrial energy consumption, is the main emitter of industrial waste water, waste gas and solid waste in China. The total amount of pollutants discharged accounts for 70%~80% of the total pollutant discharge of all industrial sectors. Moreover, the predictions show that the pressure on the environment has not come to the forefront of these industries without changing the development model. Therefore, these 7 major industries should become the key industrial industries for the development of China's circular economy, promote their ecological transformation and improve ecological efficiency.

Establish and improve a policy system to improve the ecological efficiency of key industries

China can establish and improve the policy system to improve the eco-efficiency of key industries along two technical routes.

1. Key policies with direct objectives of reduction, reuse/resources and harmlessness. In the reduction process, key policies include ecological design systems, resource consumption and pollution emission quota management systems, and raising taxes and prices for key resources. In the process of recycling and resource utilization, key policies include the quota management system for waste recycling, tax preferential policies and the development of industrial park policies for waste recycling. In the harmless process, key policies include environmental access systems for industries, technologies and products, raising pollution emission standards, and final disposal of industrial wastes and environmental supervision.

2. Management policies for the whole process of production and consumption activities, including producer responsibility extension system, industrial policy, technology demonstration and support, government green procurement, high resource energy consumption and import and export tax rebate policies for high-pollution products.

Policies to improve the eco-efficiency of the paper industry

China needs to take comprehensive measures to address factors such as raw material structure, enterprise size, technology and cost that constrain the ecological efficiency of the paper industry.

1. Relying on the international and domestic markets, replacing the grass fiber raw materials in the papermaking industry, solving the problem of heavy paper pollution and recycling of waste materials.

2. Shandong and Henan are the concentrated areas of China's paper industry, facing the double challenge of grass fiber raw materials and SMEs. Small and medium-sized papermaking enterprises in the region should be listed as national key pollution control targets, and mergers, reorganizations and joints should be implemented to increase structural adjustment and improve the technological and economic foundation of circular economy development and pollution control.

3. Strictly implement the environmental impact assessment system of the construction project and the "three simultaneous" environmental management system, and no longer approve new papermaking projects with non-wood fiber, especially wheat straw or straw as fiber chemical pulping. For the new papermaking enterprises that use the wood fiber raw material caustic soda chemical pulping, it is necessary to support advanced alkali recovery equipment to improve the alkali recovery rate.

4. Revise the current pollutant emission (COD) emission standards of papermaking enterprises and improve the access conditions for papermaking enterprises.

5. Case studies in Shandong and other places show that if the waste water discharge fee of the papermaking enterprise is raised to 1.5 yuan/t and the fresh water water fee is raised to 1 yuan/t according to the principle of slightly higher than the depth of wastewater treatment cost, the local Many paper companies can achieve zero discharge of wastewater.

Policies to improve the eco-efficiency of the cement industry

There are two types of policies that play an important role in promoting China's improvement of the eco-efficiency of the cement industry.

1. Start with the cement use link, improve the cement clinker, cement and concrete markings, improve the durability of the building, reduce the absolute amount of cement; increase the bulk rate of cement, and save packaging materials.

2. The focus of recycling in the cement industry is the coordinated disposal of various types of waste in the cement production process. China should attach great importance to it and vigorously promote it.

To the end, China should formulate the "Guidelines for Collaborative Disposal of Waste in the Cement Industry", "Standards for Collaborative Disposal of Cement Production" and "Standards for the Use of Waste Cement" as soon as possible to guide the cement industry to scientifically, rationally, safely and effectively use various types of waste. Avoid secondary pollution caused by disposal of waste and ensure safe use of cement. Establish and improve the economic incentive policy for the cement industry to co-dispose waste. Financial subsidies for cement enterprises that use and dispose of domestic garbage and hazardous waste, and more preferential tax reduction and exemption policies for existing wastes; funds and taxation for the pretreatment of wastes that can be used by cement companies support. Establish a national-level technology research and development center, specializing in the technical research and development of the utilization and disposal of waste in the cement industry; and carry out pilot projects for the coordinated disposal of domestic waste and hazardous waste in cement production.

Policy recommendations to promote waste recycling and harmless disposal

In the field of production, especially consumer waste, China is faced with two problems of increasing recycling and preventing secondary pollution. In areas such as electronic waste, the private self-organized recycling industry based on pure market mechanism is more developed, but The secondary pollution problem is very serious. Therefore, improving the degree of recycling and preventing secondary pollution are the basic objectives of China's formulation of relevant policies.

Establish and improve the waste recycling and harmless policy system

Chinese waste recycling and harmless policy system should mainly include four aspects:

(1) Waste recycling industrial system and management system. Strengthen government regulation and control, restructure existing state-owned recycling enterprises with existing private professional enterprises as the main body, organize the "picking army", establish market operation mains for professional recycling and safe disposal, and develop waste recycling and safe disposal industries. . The Development and Reform Commission is responsible for industrial management, and the environmental protection department is responsible for environmental pollution prevention and control.

(2) Special laws and industry standards for waste recycling, recycling and harmless disposal. On the basis of the solid waste law and the Circular Economy Promotion Law, a number of recycling and recycling of wastes such as electronic waste, waste rubber, used ships, scrap cars, scrap steel, waste non-ferrous metals, waste plastics, and waste paper will be formulated. Utilize and harmless disposal of special laws and industry standards.

(3) Responsibility mechanism and economic incentives. In the three important aspects of waste recycling, recycling and safe disposal, it is necessary to clarify the responsibilities of the government, producers, importers, sellers, consumers, etc., and establish corresponding economic incentives such as deposits, taxes, fees, subsidies, etc. policy.

(4) Environmental management of imported waste. China has become a major importer of wastes in the world. It must implement strict environmental supervision in three stages to prevent the import of waste that does not meet the environmental protection control standards. The enterprises with pollution prevention and control capabilities recycle imported waste to prevent the sale of imported waste. Implement supervision and inspection from approval and utilization to final safety disposal.

Promote the treatment and disposal of domestic waste and leapfrog development

Drawing on the lessons of Germany and Japan, in terms of domestic garbage disposal and disposal, China does not have to go from landfill, incineration to recycling. It can be in the form prescribed by law (such as EU Waste Disposal Directive), requiring first garbage. The materials (renewable resources) and energy (heat) are recycled, and finally the parts that cannot be recycled are landfilled. At least, China can now carry out pilot work in this area in developed cities along the eastern coast.

Establish an electronic waste recycling and harmless disposal policy system
China can establish and improve the electronic waste recycling and harmless policy system from the following eight aspects.

(1) Establish laws and regulations on recycling and harmless disposal of electronic waste. China should enact the "Electronic Waste Recycling and Harmless Disposal Law" in a timely manner, under which the relevant implementation regulations, management methods, technical policies and standards are formulated and improved.

(2) Establish an efficient management system. In order to solve the outstanding environmental pollution problems in China's electronic waste recycling, we have established a management system that is closely coordinated by the Ministry of Environmental Protection and the National Development and Reform Commission, and the Ministry of Information Industry and the Ministry of Commerce.

(3) Establish an extension system for the responsibility of producers of electronic products according to national conditions. China's electronic product producer responsibility extension system can include four aspects: general environmental responsibility from product production to consumption; responsibility for collecting and disposing of low-market value e-waste; payment or collection of e-waste disposal costs Responsibility: Information disclosure responsibility.

(4) Collection of electronic waste disposal fees or electronic product consumption tax. The CGE simulation results show that the e-waste disposal fee or the electronic product consumption tax is levied on producers or consumers, and its policy effect is close, which has little impact on the macro economy, but has serious impact on the export of communication equipment, computers and other electronic equipment manufacturing industries.

According to the tax and fee reform process, China may levy a disposal fee or consumption tax in a timely manner, and the relevant export-oriented enterprises may adopt an export tax rebate method to eliminate the impact of levy or taxation. The disposal fee or consumption tax income can be managed uniformly through the establishment of special funds for the harmless disposal and research and development of electronic waste.

(5) Financial subsidies and technical support for enterprises engaged in the safe disposal of electronic waste. The harmless disposal of electronic waste has the property of public goods. The government should bear certain responsibilities and should provide necessary subsidies and technical support to enterprises engaged in the harmless disposal of electronic waste.

(6) Formulate policies to promote eco-design and green consumption of electronic products. China should introduce an electronic product eco-design system. On the one hand, the electronic products are modularized, the components are easily disassembled to improve the reuse rate, and on the other hand, the production of the products avoids or reduces the use of toxic and hazardous substances, reducing the pressure of end treatment.

In addition, the establishment of an environmental labeling system for electronic products and the government's green procurement system encourages the production and consumption of environmentally friendly electronic products.

(7) Renovate existing recycling systems to achieve the dual goals of efficiency and environmental safety. Through economic incentives such as subsidies and tax incentives, specialized recycling and recycling companies are more competitive in the market when they recycle electronic waste than individual purchasers; and guide the recycling and recycling industries to scale through economic incentives and regulations. Development and intensification.

(8) Establish an electronic waste recycling industrial park, and implement management of the circle area and qualification management. In view of the diversified industrial distribution of e-waste recycling and the status quo of small enterprises, China can establish an electronic waste recycling industrial park in areas where electronic waste recycling activities are concentrated, implement circle management, and implement recycling enterprises. Qualification management, elimination of family workshop-style enterprises, and backward recycling technologies and technologies to promote industrial upgrading.

Regional model and policy recommendations for the development of circular economy

1. Based on the ecological function and development main function zoning, formulate the regional circular economy development plan by means of material flow management.

In order to comprehensively develop a circular economy in provinces and cities, China needs to scientifically plan and construct a recycling-oriented production and consumption system based on ecological functions and developmental functional zoning, and control regional social and economic activities in regional resource and environment. Within the carrying capacity, the relationship between regional resource environment and social economic development is fundamentally coordinated.

According to the ecological law, the ecological function zoning divides the area into different types of areas with different ecological service functions, and provides the basis for resource and environmental carrying capacity for the development of functional zoning. The main functional zoning of the development further defines the social and economic development direction of different ecological functional areas. Structure layout and adjustment, resource development and protection tasks. The development of circular economy can continue to maintain a high regional resource and environmental carrying capacity and expand the development space.

According to domestic and international experience, material flow management methods can be used as a basic method for developing circular economy development plans for regional and industrial parks.

2. Implement the principles of classification development and protection regulation and management strategies.

The development and protection principles of different development subject functional areas are different. It is forbidden to implement compulsory protection in the development zone, strictly maintain the cyclical material exchange relationship of the balance of natural ecosystems, and it is not suitable to develop industrial and agricultural. Restrict development zones to implement protection priority, and moderately develop ecological industries such as ecological agriculture on the premise of maintaining a cyclical material exchange relationship with a balanced natural ecosystem. Optimization and key development zones should comprehensively develop circular economy, transform or establish a cyclical material exchange relationship, improve ecological efficiency, and adapt the resource demand and waste discharge of social economic activities to the resource and environmental capacity of the region.

To ensure the scientific development of functional areas of different developmental subjects, five key policies must be in place first. The state legislates on ecological function and development of functional zoning, establishes legal basis and enhances the seriousness of implementation; establishes fiscal transfer payment and ecological compensation system for prohibiting and restricting development zones, and ensuring that local residents enjoy similarities with other regions. The public service and living standards; the state implements a green national economic accounting system, reforms the local government performance evaluation system with GDP as the core, eliminates the motives of the local governments for improperly developing and prohibiting the development of the region; and invests in strengthening the ecological environment protection At the same time of the measures, the strict implementation of the environmental impact assessment system for construction projects and development plans is an important access system to prevent the development and destruction of development zones; for the optimization and key development zones, the implementation of the current state-changing economic growth mode is strictly implemented. Policy and circular economy policy.

2.3 Establish a scientific and complete regional recycling production and consumption model.

At the heart of the regional model for circular economy development is the construction of circular (sustainable) production and consumption patterns. The circular production and consumption model is an ecological industry and an environment-friendly consumption mode supported by an efficient shared public resource energy infrastructure system. The ecological industry includes ecological industry, ecological agriculture, waste recycling, resource and harmless disposal industry, and green service industry. The eco-industry can be realized through clean production of enterprises, construction of ecological industrial parks and ecological industrial networks. At present, China's ways to cultivate environmentally friendly consumption methods include: resource and energy conservation, environmentally friendly product certification, green community creation, government green procurement and advocating public reasonable consumption, and green consumption.

Vigorously develop ecological industrial parks.

The construction of eco-industrial parks is an important form of constructing an eco-industrial system. China should attach great importance to it and vigorously promote it. It is of great significance to the construction of eco-industrial parks to improve the eco-efficiency policies of key industries, promote waste recycling, resource utilization and harmless policies, and promote key economic policies for the development of circular economy. In addition, China's development of eco-industrial parks should pay attention to four aspects of policies and methods.

The focus of the construction of China's eco-industrial parks is to transform a large number of various economic development zones and industrial parks at various levels according to the principles of eco-industrial science. Accurately grasp the three key links in the construction of eco-industrial parks to avoid simplification and unilateralization. The first is to build a relationship between the by-products and wastes in the park enterprises and the energy cascade utilization, that is, the industrial ecological chain; the second is to build an efficient sharing system for the infrastructure resources (water, electricity, gas, etc.) infrastructure; Harmless disposal system. The information platform is also an important part of the construction of eco-industrial parks. Improve the quality of eco-industrial park planning, especially in the planning process, invite enterprises from the park to participate, enhance the technical and economic feasibility of planning, and improve the consciousness of implementing planning. 4 Establish a long-term mechanism for the construction of eco-industrial parks based on government guidance and services and enterprises based on market interest mechanisms.

2.4 Research on the Evaluation Index System of Circular Economy Innovation

The circular economy is a green, low-carbon sustainable development model, in line with the inherent requirements of the scientific development concept. Practice has fully proved that the development of circular economy must be driven by innovation. Regarding the innovation of circular economy, we should carry out all-round innovation and macro-level innovation from the macro, meso and micro levels, mainly conceptual innovation and institutional innovation; meso-level innovation, mainly policy innovation; micro-level innovation, mainly management Innovation and technological innovation The concept innovation of circular economy, institutional innovation, policy innovation guarantee the implementation of circular economy model, management innovation and technological innovation provide management methods and technical support for the development of circular economy. These five aspects of innovation are the organic whole that are interconnected and promote each other, and constitute a realistic force for promoting the in-depth and healthy development of the circular economy. The degree of innovation in the circular economy and its quality and efficiency, it is necessary to have a scientific evaluation system in line with the principle of circular economy. Only in this way can we systematically quantitatively evaluate the innovation of circular economy, in order to truly understand the effects of various innovative measures of circular economy at the macro, meso and micro levels, so as to adjust the direction in time and explore the basis and way out for deepening innovation.

The circular economy innovation evaluation system, as a measurement system reflecting the degree of innovation in the circular economy, has the following functions: First, describe the function: describe and reflect the level and status of circular economy innovation in a period, and understand the circular economy for the public, the government and relevant decision-making departments. The state of innovation provides reliable information. Second, the evaluation function:. Comprehensively measure the degree of innovation in circular economy and its index, and evaluate the innovation of circular economy as a whole. As an important parameter for the evaluation of local economic and social development performance, it is the guiding function: using indicators system to guide the government, enterprises and the public to accelerate Circular Economy Innovation Fourth, early warning function: evaluate and monitor the trend and speed of circular economy innovation in a certain period, predict the structure and function of future systems, and provide practical and feasible decision-making programs for the practice of circular economy development model.

The Construction Principles of the Evaluation Index System of Circular Economy Innovation

The principle of integrity and hierarchy

The evaluation index system should comprehensively reflect the characteristics of circular economy innovation. It must have indicators that reflect the main characteristics and status, as well as indicators that reflect the dynamic changes and development trends of subsystems within the system. At the same time, the selection of indicators should also be hierarchical, that is, high-level indicators are the synthesis of low-level indicators, low-level indicators are the decomposition of high-level indicators, and also the basis for the establishment of high-level indicators.

Principles of principal component and independence

The most important component variables that are small enough to characterize the essential behavior of the system should be screened out from the numerous variables according to their importance and the order of contribution to the system behavior. Considering that the indicators describing the innovation status of circular economy often have the reality of overlapping information, the indicators with relative independence should be selected as much as possible, thus increasing the accuracy and scientific of the evaluation.

Dynamic and static principles

Circular economy innovation is both a goal and a process. Therefore, the indicator system should fully consider the characteristics of dynamic changes, and can comprehensively reflect the current status and future trends of the development of circular economy systems, so as to facilitate forecasting and decision-making. However, in a certain period of time, the indicator system should not be changed frequently, and its relative stability should be maintained.

The principle of combining economic, social and resource and environmental indicators

The design of evaluation indicators must fully and profoundly reflect the ''3 R' requirements, promote the efficient use of resources and reduce the level of investment, reduce the burden on the environment and resources, and continuously improve the citizens while the economy achieves stable and rapid development. Production and living environment.

Scientific and practical principles

The determination of the weight coefficient of the evaluation index system and the selection, calculation and synthesis of data should be based on recognized scientific theories and methods, fully considering the operability and practicality, and strive to be complete, scientific and accurate.

The concrete construction of the evaluation index system of circular economy innovation

According to the above construction principles, draw on the circular economy evaluation index system, fully consider the unique characteristics of the circular economy innovation evaluation object, combined with the stage characteristics of economic and social development, this paper determines the whole index system into the circular economy innovation situation evaluation indicators and cycle Two major indicators of economic innovation effectiveness evaluation indicators. The evaluation indicators of circular economy innovation cover the innovative behaviors and situations of circular economy in terms of concept, system, policy, management and technology. In order to avoid too many indicators, this paper condenses it into the following three indicators: green development concept indicators, technology support indicators, systems and organizational guarantee indicators. The evaluation index of innovation effect of circular economy selected six indicators including resource output index, resource consumption index, comprehensive resource utilization index, waste discharge index, ecological environment index and social economic development index. Under the above nine primary indicators, there are 52 secondary indicators as indicators in the circular economy innovation evaluation system.

Determination of the weight of the evaluation index of circular economy innovation

Weight is an important factor in the comprehensive evaluation of multiple indicators. Weights and variable values   are the two major factors affecting the evaluation results. In the case where a single indicator has been determined, changes in weight will inevitably lead to changes in the evaluation conclusion. To express the impact of these indicators on the innovation of circular economy, it needs to be solved by mathematical tools.

Method for determining index weights

There are two main methods for determining the weight of indicators: one is to determine the weight based on the experience and subjective judgment of the researchers, such as the Delphi method (Delphi method), the empirical weight method, etc.; the other is based on various mathematics. The method mainly determines the index weights, such as AHP method (AHP) and principal component analysis. The former method concentrates on the experience of researchers and the accumulation of knowledge of experts, but it is inevitably mixed with subjective randomness. The latter type of method focuses on objectivity, but it is also difficult due to the difficulty in collecting, collating and analyzing the original data, and the subjectivity of the data provider. Therefore, a better method is to combine the two methods organically to determine the index weight. In this paper, the Delphi method (Delphi method) is used to determine each indicator, and then the AHP method (AHP) is used to determine the weight of each indicator, thus improving the accuracy of the indicator weight.

Basic steps for weight calculation

The first step is to construct the hierarchical structure of the indicator system. The hierarchical structure is in a system with an H-layer structure. The first layer has only one element. Each level of the element belongs to only one level, and each element in the structure is at least with the upper layer of the element or There is a certain relationship between a certain element in the lower layer, and there is no direct relationship between the elements in the same layer and between the elements in the adjacent layer. In any comprehensive indicator system, due to the different types of indicators carried by the indicators, each indicator subsystem and specific indicator items play different roles in describing a social phenomenon or social situation. Therefore, the comprehensive indicator value is It is not equal to the simple addition of the sub-indicators, but a relationship of weighted summation.

The second step is to construct a judgment matrix. After the establishment of the comprehensive hierarchy system of the hierarchical structure, the degree of relative importance obtained by comparing the indicators of the previous level with the sub-indicators associated with the next level is constructed, and the judgment matrix is constructed.

The third step is the determination of the weight of the hierarchy and the consistency test. According to the judgment matrix, the relative weights of the index subsystems or index items are calculated, that is, the maximum eigenvalues of the judgment matrix and their corresponding feature vectors are calculated.

The fourth step is the calculation of the combined weights of each level. The weight value obtained by each judgment matrix is the separation weight value of each level indicator subsystem or indicator item relative to a certain factor of the upper layer. Therefore, it is necessary to combine these separation weight values into the combined weight values of the specific indicator items with respect to the highest level. The formula for calculating the combined weight is:
Where: W_i is the weight value of the j-th layer of the i-th indicator; k is the total number of layers.

$$W_i = \prod_{j=2}^{k} w_i^j$$

Each judgment matrix consistency test has an overall satisfactory consistency through judgments that are not equal to the entire hierarchical structure. Therefore, an overall consistency check is also required.

Determination of the weight of indicators at all levels
According to the above steps, the weights of the indicators at all levels in the circular economy innovation evaluation index system are calculated. In order to increase the accuracy, this paper multiplies the weights of each indicator by 10 in the score assignment. The total score of the index system is 1 000 points, and the weights of each indicator for the total target are obtained.

The scoring method and scoring standard of the circular economy innovation evaluation index system
To give the index scores of circular economy innovation evaluation in different regions, it is also necessary to set a scoring standard for each index, that is, the value of the corresponding index when the rated index is set to the full score, and the corresponding index when the score is 0. Value; for qualitative indicators, the scores corresponding to the different situations are set closely around the content of the analysis.

When the scoring standard is determined, for the quantitative indicator, the sub-item specific scores of the index value between the full score and the zero score must be designed. In combination with the conventional index evaluation method, according to the comprehensive consideration of China's circular economy development and national economic policies, this paper sets the index score standard of circular economy innovation evaluation index system that reflects China's national conditions. The specific assignment of each indicator is only a scale method, and the degree of importance of different indicators in the score sequence is only relative.

Circular economy innovation is a systematic project involving a wide range of comprehensive and comprehensive. In order to scientifically evaluate the innovation status of circular economy, it is necessary to use a corresponding data and information to establish a circular economy innovation evaluation index system with reasonable design and strong operation, which provides data support for circular economy management and innovation. The evaluation index of circular economy innovation is not only one of the basic work of the state to establish a statistical system for circular economy, but also an important basis for the government, parks and enterprises to formulate circular economy development plans and strengthen management. Therefore, the establishment of circular economy innovation evaluation index system is of great significance for the development of circular economy. According to the current development of circular economy and the innovation of circular economy in China, this paper mainly constructs the evaluation index system of circular economy innovation from the macro level, which is mainly used for the overall quantitative judgment of the whole society and the innovation of circular economy, providing a basis for the development of circular economy. And guidance.

References

1. Lin Chunzheng. Smart City and Ecological Design [M]. Beijing: China Building Industry Press, 2013.

2. Zheng Hua, Gao Jixi et al. Regional ecological environment quality assessment and ecological function zoning [M]. Beijing: China Environmental Science Press, 2009.

3. Wen Juan et al. Eco-environment design of small towns [M]. Beijing: Chemical Industry Press, 2012.

4. Zhang Lixin, Zhang Lixia. Design and Openness of Ecological Virtual Environment [M]. Beijing: Science Press, 2011.

5.Sun Jingliang. Ecological Management and Environmental Design of Urban Rivers and Lakes [M]. Beijing: China Water Resources and Hydropower Press, 2016.

6. Chen Gen. Ecological design and classic case review [M]. Beijing: Chemical Industry Press, 2015.

7. Zheng Yuqing, Qiu Ni. Research on Urban Ecological Habitat Environment Greening: Taking Guangzhou as an Example [M]. Beijing: Science Press, 2012.

8. Ren Yong, Zhou Guomei et al. Models and policies for the development of China's circular economy [M]. Beijing: China Environmental Science Press, 2009.2.

9. France is also Western culture, Xu Ying translation. New ecological landscapeism: French filter garden environmental technology design works album [M]. Liaoning: Liaoning Science and Technology Press, 2015.

www.ingramcontent.com/pod-product-compliance
Lightning Source LLC
Chambersburg PA
CBHW080757030726
47598CB00007B/2613